Beginning Security with Microsoft Technologies

Protecting Office 365, Devices, and Data

Vasantha Lakshmi

Apress®

Beginning Security with Microsoft Technologies: Protecting Office 365, Devices, and Data

Vasantha Lakshmi
Bangalore, India

ISBN-13 (pbk): 978-1-4842-4852-2   ISBN-13 (electronic): 978-1-4842-4853-9
https://doi.org/10.1007/978-1-4842-4853-9

Managing Director, Apress Media LLC: Welmoed Spahr
Acquisitions Editor: Smriti Srivastava
Development Editor: Matthew Moodie
Coordinating Editor: Shrikant Vishwakarma

Cover designed by eStudioCalamar

Cover image designed by Freepik (www.freepik.com)

Distributed to the book trade worldwide by Springer Science+Business Media New York, 233 Spring Street, 6th Floor, New York, NY 10013. Phone 1-800-SPRINGER, fax (201) 348-4505, e-mail orders-ny@springer-sbm.com, or visit www.springeronline.com. Apress Media, LLC is a California LLC and the sole member (owner) is Springer Science + Business Media Finance Inc (SSBM Finance Inc). SSBM Finance Inc is a **Delaware** corporation.

For information on translations, please e-mail rights@apress.com, or visit http://www.apress.com/rights-permissions.

Apress titles may be purchased in bulk for academic, corporate, or promotional use. eBook versions and licenses are also available for most titles. For more information, reference our Print and eBook Bulk Sales web page at http://www.apress.com/bulk-sales.

Any source code or other supplementary material referenced by the author in this book is available to readers on GitHub via the book's product page, located at www.apress.com/978-1-4842-4852-2. For more detailed information, please visit http://www.apress.com/source-code.

Printed on acid-free paper

*I would like to dedicate my first-ever book to my mother,
Geetha Sabhahit, for being my world.*

Table of Contents

About the Author ix

About the Technical Reviewer xi

Acknowledgments xiii

Introduction xv

Chapter 1: Current State of Security 1

    Intelligent Security Graph 3

    Email Protection 3

    Device Protection 5

    Identity Protection 6

    Data Protection 9

Chapter 2: Securing Emails and Office 365 11

    Exchange Online Protection 11

    EOP Setup 13

        Antispam Protection 14

        Antimalware Protection 14

        Thwarting Spam 14

        Connection Filter 18

        Spam Filter 20

        Outbound Filter 23

    Quarantine and Action Center/Restricted Users 24

    "Security & Compliance" Window for ATP Policies 26

    Office 365 ATP 28

        Features and Capabilities 28

        Office ATP Quarantine 38

Chapter 3: Device-Level Security **43**

   Prebreach 44

      Advanced Security Mode: Device Guard 45

      Windows Defender Application Control 45

      Windows Defender Exploit Guard 62

      Windows Defender Application Guard 84

      Windows Defender System Guard 89

      Windows Defender Antivirus 91

   Postbreach 98

      Windows Defender ATP 99

      Microsoft Threat Protection 118

Chapter 4: Identity Protection **121**

   Windows Defender Credential Guard 123

      Enabling Windows Defender Credential Guard 125

      Advanced Threat Analytics 128

   Azure Advanced Threat Protection 139

      Architecture 139

      Setup 141

      Azure ATP Timeline 146

   Azure Active Directory Identity Protection 150

      Risky User Accounts and Vulnerabilities 157

      Privileged Identity Management 162

      Access Reviews 171

Chapter 5: Data Protection **173**

   Azure Information Protection 173

   AIP Policies 176

      Checking the Protection 184

      Document Tracking for Document Authors 185

      Applying Settings in the SharePoint Document Library and Exchange Online 189

Labels and Data Loss Prevention in Office 365...193

Windows Information Protection...197

    Deploying Through Intune..198

    Intune Policies for Device and Data Protection 204

    Protecting Data at the Front Gate Using Intune/Azure AD Conditional Access 207

Microsoft Cloud App Security...208

    Framework 209

    Architecture..209

    Dashboard 210

    Risk Score 214

    App Connector Flow 216

    Blocking Download Policy for Unmanaged Devices 220

    Compliance Manager...227

Microsoft Secure Score..229

Final Thoughts...230

Index...231

About the Author

Vasantha Lakshmi works at Microsoft India as a technology solutions professional and was previously a partner technical consultant. She has been working on various security products within Microsoft for the last four years. She has more than nine years of experience working as an architect of end-to-end solutions for Microsoft 365 and Azure's infrastructure as a service. She has created many integrated security solutions for the modern workplace that seamlessly integrate Advanced Threat Analytics, Windows and Microsoft Defender Advanced Threat Protection, Microsoft Cloud App Security, Intune, and Office ATP. She is also certified on Microsoft 365 Identity and Services; MS-100, Microsoft 365 Mobility and Security; MS-101, Microsoft 365 Modern Desktop, Windows 10; MD-100, Microsoft 365 Managing Modern Desktops; MD-101, and Microsoft 365 Security Administration; MS-500.

About the Technical Reviewer

 **Steef-Jan Wiggers** is an Azure technology consultant at Codit, and is all in on Microsoft Azure, the Internet of Things, integration, and data science. He has almost 20 years' experience handling a wide variety of scenarios, such as custom .NET solution development, overseeing large enterprise integrations, designing and building APIs and cloud solutions, managing projects, experimenting with data, SQL server database administration, teaching, and consulting. Steef-Jan loves combining challenges he comes across in the Microsoft playing field with his domain knowledge in energy, utility, banking, insurance, health care, agriculture, (local) government, biosciences, retail, travel, and logistics. He is very active in his community as a blogger, book author, InfoQ editor, and global public speaker. For these efforts, Microsoft has recognized him as a Microsoft MVP for the past nine years. Steef-Jan can be found on Twitter at **@SteefJan.**

Acknowledgments

I would like to express gratitude to my lovely mother, Geetha Sabhahit, for being a constant in my life and for being a guiding beacon at every step of the way! I give a big thank you to her for all the selfless acts she's performed throughout our lives.

I could not be who I am today without my grandmother, Nagaveni Sabhahit, and her go-getter attitude that has successfully inspired me!

Muralidhar Kshipathi, my husband, has been very supportive and understanding and has helped me prioritize the writing of this book. I also give a big shout-out to him for becoming my support system in life.

I cannot forget Dolly, my pet, who is in my thoughts every day teaching me about friendship and having an outgoing nature.

You are what your ecosystem is! All my extended family—my aunts, uncles, cousins, mom-in-law, friends, mentors, managers, and peers at work—are that ecosystem. My interactions with them have shaped me into what I am today.

Introduction

Beginning Security with Microsoft Technologies is intended to give readers a holistic picture of establishing enterprise security using Microsoft technologies. In the book, I take a step-by-step approach to understanding an attacker's path into an organization's network. We will be learning about securing email, devices, identity, and cloud apps.

We will be looking at the email security available with Office 365 Exchange. As far as device security, we will be focusing on Windows 10 Security (Windows Defender and Windows Defender Advanced Threat Protection are applicable to other operating systems as well). With identity protection, we will be considering Windows servers domain controllers/on-premise active directories; in specific Azure AD. When it comes to data protection, we will see how Microsoft's CASB (Cloud Access Security Broker) solution, Azure Information Protection, Microsoft Information Protection, and other tools come together to provide data loss prevention.

This is not a be-all-and-end-all guide for security options from Microsoft technologies. It will for sure help you get started by introducing you to several security services. However, there is still a lot more that Microsoft can provide, especially when it comes to security from Azure (e.g., Azure Security Center, Azure secure score [Microsoft secure score], Azure SQL, and Azure Advanced Threat Protection). I hope this book becomes a starting point to your security journey with Microsoft security technologies or services.

CHAPTER 1

Current State of Security

In today's world, it would be hard to find an organization that hasn't been in the radius of a hacker or a user account that was never in the range of an attack. We have all seen reports of high-profile attacks and substantial financial losses for companies that were attacked. Bots have taken significant control of the Internet since their advent. These tireless bits of code can sift through the trillions of available Internet addresses, mark targets and execute penetration attempts and remote code and exploits, and compromise systems and add them to the bot fleets used to launch major denial-of-service attacks on high-profile targets.

We have also seen, heard, and read about all the high-profile attacks in the news. Attacks have brought down an entire country's power grid, and the WannaCry/WannaCrypt and NotPetya ransomware have created havoc by encrypting files on users' PCs and charging a ransom over them. Internet of Things, or IoT, botnets have caused distributed denial-of-service (DDOS) attacks. User accounts stolen from credit card, taxi and media service companies have been sold. We also have zero-day attacks, vulnerabilities, and Minecraft apps and exploits contributing to our security woes.

We have come a long way from the first detection of viruses and worms in the late 1970s and early '80s to the botnets, DDOS attacks, and ransomware we have today. We have gone from simple self-replicating programs affecting various operating systems, routes, and switches to routers sending numerous spam emails; stealing personally identifiable information, known as PII, and credit card details; and performing cyberespionage and mass surveillance that records all activities (conversations, screenshots, etc.).

These attacks can cause a lot of damage for any organization suffering them. The most frequent reason for the attacks is not having enough tools and technology in place to identify them before they happen. This gap allows the attacker to stay in the system/network for a very long time before the attacker gets detected and by that time,

© Vasantha Lakshmi 2019
V. Lakshmi, *Beginning Security with Microsoft Technologies*, https://doi.org/10.1007/978-1-4842-4853-9_1

the damage is inflicted by the attacker. So, it becomes essential to upgrade our tools to match the protection to modern-day attacks. These attacks now use multiple domains, intelligence taken from multiple data sets (to help in social-engineering attempts), and phishing/vishing (voice phishing) emails.

With the advent of such sophisticated attacks, how far are organizations prepared to go today to protect themselves? To what extent is your email secured against the phishing attacks today? Does your email provider scan the attachments received for any threats or attacks? If a phishing email gets past your provider's software, does your organization have the multilayer security in place to cover the device-level security and security for detecting attacks, such as pass the hash, pass the ticket, and golden ticket, against lateral movement? How about the protection for data stored in cloud/SaaS (software as a service)–based applications?

Each customer needs to comply with data protection, privacy laws, and cybersecurity frameworks, such as NIST (National Institute of Standards and Technology) 800-53 and 800-171; GDPR (General Data Protection Regulation) ISO 27001 and 27018 in the EU; and HIPAA, the type depending on their sector or affiliation, such as health care, the European Union (EU), the International Organization for Standardization (ISO), and so on. To comply with these regulations, Microsoft has technology available to help you perform ongoing risk assessments and provide you with a compliance score. We will learn more about this in Chapter 5, "Data Protection."

In its ability to help us address all these questions and scenarios, Microsoft can be considered a strong security provider. Microsoft has been providing security since the beginning of the millennium or in the early 2000's and the result is clearly seen in the full range of security products that are offered by Microsoft today. Some of them are Office Advanced Threat Protection, Windows Defender Advanced Threat Protection, Advanced Threat Analytics/Azure Advanced Threat Protection, Microsoft Cloud App Security, Azure Active Directory identity protection, Azure Security Center, and privileged identity management. There are a lot of other monitoring tools and technologies offered as well, most of which leverage security intelligence derived from the cloud, which in turn uses machine learning to better adapt and provide context for every organization.

Intelligent Security Graph

In today's agile world, where the attackers are always on their toes looking out for new malware or vulnerabilities and creating new variants of an existing attack, we need to combat the attacks with data and intelligence. In came Intelligent Security Graph, a layer of data provided by Microsoft that uses advanced analytics to link a massive amount of threat intelligence and security data to thwart cyberthreats.

Unique threat indicators are regularly generated by Microsoft and its partners by the millions and shared across many Microsoft products and platforms. Every day we see 400 billion emails analyzed to detect malware and phishing scams, 450 billion authentications, 1.2 billion devices scanned for threats, 2.6 billion unique file scanned, and many more measures taken. All this monitoring contributes to the production of a massive breadth and depth of intelligence and the strict maintenance of data privacy and compliance.

Machine-learning models and artificial intelligence are also leveraged to identify vulnerabilities and threats, promoting fast threat detection and automated responses. On the topic of machine learning, we see the importance of the massive breadth and depth of data collected by Microsoft products for threat intelligence. Intelligent Security Graph is able to efficiently detect and remediate phishing attacks, identify and block malicious content on the web, and perform many other applications. It is also able to aid in integrating and co-relating (understanding the context of) alerts from various products and to automate the remediation process. Due to this thorough process, we will have many less false positives and a well-informed investigation will take place.

Email Protection

Most targeted attacks start with compromising users' emails and the attempts to do so are always evolving. Attackers do a preexploitation reconnaisance by gathering information about the victim's PC or the selected targets (performing malware delivery through such methods as spear-phishing attacks and vishing attacks).

To protect against such attacks, email messages that are received should go through a set of filters to identify the sender or domain from which they were sent and to check the URLs in the emails to see if they are clickbait leading to malicious web sites that will further compromise the user credentials or secretly install executable functions (see Figure 1-1). The email protection platform should enable you to create policies to do such things as quarantine or delete emails and help identify spam, phishing emails, and the like. You can also step up your security a notch by leveraging a sandbox environment to test any unsafe attachments.

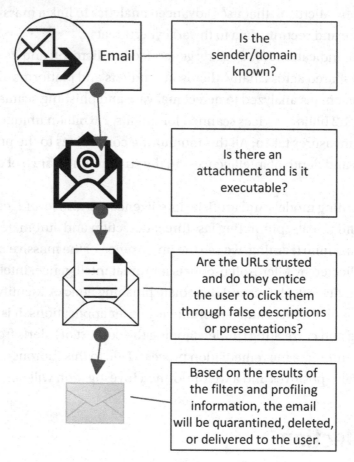

Email — Is the sender/domain known?

Is there an attachment and is it executable?

Are the URLs trusted and do they entice the user to click them through false descriptions or presentations?

Based on the results of the filters and profiling information, the email will be quarantined, deleted, or delivered to the user.

Figure 1-1. *Email protection process for filters*

Microsoft offers Exchange Online Protection with Office Advanced Threat Protection to fight against email threats. We will look into the details of this in the next chapter.

Device Protection

After a successful phishing attack, the next logical step of any attacker will be to compromise the device. They might try to do so by executing a remote script that connects to the command and control server, giving them innate access to the device and user information.

It has now been more than 20 years since the first advent of viruses. Keeping up protection against the significantly changed current threats has become ever so important. The current malicious codes, written mostly to compromise users' devices, include a wide range of trojans, exploits, rootkits, and spyware, as well as classic viruses and worms. These attacks can be sourced from a variety of platforms such as a malicious web site or a phishing email executing a hidden script. A hidden script that is part of any application can also harm a device. We have seen times when all being equipped with security meant was to have antivirus software installed on your devices. But taking just that step to protect a device is not sufficient anymore. With advanced persistent attacks and data theft now the norm, we must up the ante to better protect our devices.

We have EPP (endpoint protection) and EDR (endpoint detection and response) systems to help with keeping devices secure now (I'll refer to these devices as "endpoints" throughout this book).

EPP focuses on file-based malware attacks, malicious activities, and helping with investigation and further analysis. And today, as most of solutions do, it leverages multiple detection techniques as well as cloud-powered protection.

It also works on the device itself to enable drive encryption and create policies around data loss prevention.

On the other hand, EDR solutions must detect security incidents, isolate the compromised endpoint, investigate security incidents (in such ways as forensic investigation and submitting files for malware analysis), and provide remediation steps.

Along with these components, a system can be hosted to protect the device or the enterprise-level services by locking the device at the front gate. Using policies defined by the MDM (mobile device management) provider can also aid in data loss prevention and the abuse of company resources. In short, the devices that fail a health check or are compromised will not be able to gain access to company resources, data, and other such features.

In the following chapters, we will look at various components that keep the device protected, such as Windows Defender Antivirus, or WDAV (an EPP solution), Windows Defender Advanced Threat Protection, or Windows Defender ATP (an EDR Solution), and Microsoft Intune, as shown in Figure 1-2. These components enable configuration and conditional policies that determine if the device meets the security conditions before accessing the company resources (Exchange, Skype, and other SaaS-based apps configured on Azure Active Directory).

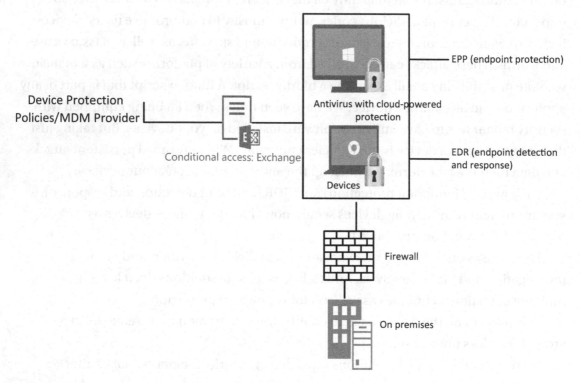

Figure 1-2. *Device protection*

Identity Protection

If the attacker manages to compromise a device and it goes undetected, they can move laterally into the victim's organization. They can then use the victim's credentials (local admin creds) to authenticate many more of the organization's services by stealing Kerberos tickets.

Identity is the primary and most important piece of any organization, as the compromise of identity could lead to corporate espionage, blatant theft, and so on. It could also end up costing companies a large amount of money. And in the threat landscape that we see today, techniques that involve threat prevention only will not suffice to take on advanced persistent threats.

When protecting identies, we need to know for sure that the user credentials for accessing corporate systems are only being used by legitimate employees. As with most cyberthreats, the damage is already done by the time the attacker is detected and any corrective actions can take place. Credential theft techniques are used and leveraged after the attacker has managed to secure their initial place in the victim's environment. Some of the tactics used in a credential theft attack include keylogging, passing tickets, token impersonation, and capturing plain-text passwords.

A challenge that arises is that there are very limited security technologies to help us detect an adversary once the breach has already occurred. We might add multiple barricades before the credential is stolen such as having multifactor authentication, smart cards, and so forth. However, using these would not solve the issue of credential theft itself.

The attacker's goal is to achieve domain dominance, and once that happens it could lead to a lot of further activities including theft of assets. But while they are trying to achieve the domain dominance, it is likely they are being very noisy with all the actions and scripts they are running. So, it will be beneficial to take an "assume breach" mindset. This mindset will help you detect when the bad guy has breached your initial line of defense in the form of firewalls/antivirus engines, intrusion detection systems, and so on.

Microsoft's Advanced Threat Analytics and Azure Advanced Threat Protection leverage the active directory into a powerful postbreach detection tool. To their advantage, Azure ATP & ATA use both signature analysis and UEBA (user and entity behavior analytics) techniques. Furthermore, you can protect cloud identities with Azure Active Directory Identity Protection. It also helps to keep a lookout for compromised identities using adaptive machine-learning algorithms and heuristics to detect anomolies and threats.

We have looked at the importance of protecting identities. It is also a good idea to keep a tight grip on your identities by minimizing the number of users with access to secure information. You can do this by assigning interim approvers for certain roles and providing just-in-time access for a certain period.

Regarding Azure, some organizations might have an entire or partial infrastruture hosted on the service and it is possible to have credential theft attacks on these virtual machines (VMs) as well. We could see a brute force attack, a bitcoin mining attack, DDOS attacks, and more. Credential stealing is also seen, and Azure Security Center comes in handy in helping identify these attacks. Microsoft's threat intel aids in recognizing these indications and providing alerts. By enabling just-in-time access and network-level authentication for Azure VMs among other steps, you can definitely aid in thwarting the attackers.

Figure 1-3 shows that users access application/data using such tools as on-premise servers/domains, SaaS-based apps, and cloud-hosted emails. For each action, the user needs to be authenticated and have access to the relevant tokens to seamlessly access and work on corporate apps and data. Scenarios such as these require identity protection to safeguard the credentials from any perpetrators trying to get access to the corporate data.

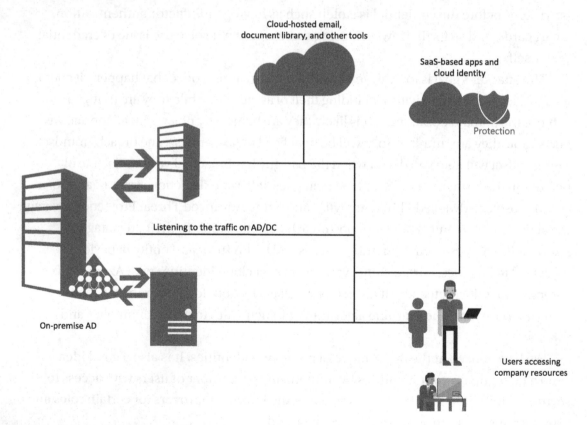

Figure 1-3. Identity protection

Data Protection

With the advent of GDPR, the importance of protecting company data has only increased. We no longer just want to protect the data at rest or on our mobiles or wherever it may be (see Figure 1-4) but also to classify and label the data for ease of use and to protect and monitor sensitive data.

Corporate data travels across the whole globe through emails, SharePoint, and other SaaS-based applications such as Box, Dropbox Business, and SalesForce. We might have the need to trace, label, and categorize a document along with protecting it. To have complete control of the data means having the capability of revoking access to the documents at any point in time.

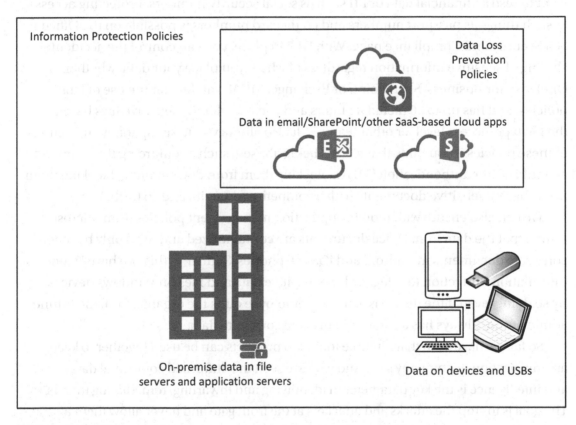

Figure 1-4. *Data protection*

Microsoft 365 provides various tools to get started with data protection. Azure Information Protection (AIP) embeds the encryption at the document level and helps with classifying and labeling it. This protection can be used for documents, email templates, a SharePoint library, and with on-premise sharepath that uses an AIP scanner. Microsoft Cloud App Security (MCAS) along with Azure Active Directory enables conditional access to corporate data, allowing you to apply access and session controls where you can protect data with Conditional Access App Control. We can now monitor user sessions and have control in real time based on access and session policies. In doing so, we can have control of downloading sensitive files or choose to encrypt the files upon download.

Policies for data loss prevention (as required by business standards and industry regulations) can also be applied for Office 365 applications or from MCAS. You might want to restrict financial data or PII such as social security numbers. Protecting access to such things as passport numbers and credit card numbers is possible on the Office 365 Security and Compliance page. With DLP in place, you can control the accidental sharing of sensitive information regardless of where you place your data, whether in OneDrive for Business, SharePoint, or Exchange. MCAS can further the use of DLP policies, as it has up to 20 metadata filters and you can identify sensitive files based on the file type, access level, or other features. It also allows you to set up follow-up actions to these policies if you think that a file is being abused, such as enforcing that users get an multi-factor authentication (MFA), blocking them from downloading, blocking them from sharing sensitive documents with a competitor domain, and so forth.

We can also ensure with mobile application management policies from Microsoft Intune that the data from Office documents are containerized and used only by other corporate documents in Android and iOS cell phones. Similar to this, we have Windows Information Protection to safeguard the sensitive data and files on Windows devices. By so doing, even if the device is lost or an employee quits the organization, the Intune administrator always has a choice to erase the corporate data.

So far, we have seen that multiple tools and products can be used together to keep an organization or company safe. And we have seen that informed contextual data and intelligence is the key parameter in identifying and thwarting/remediating threats. The goal is to stop the attacks and attackers at the front gate and never allow them a passageway to the domain dominance, being that the consequence for a company of having this compromised might be in the millions. We will look at the effects of attacks and the options for remediating them in detail as we get into further chapters. Stay tuned!

CHAPTER 2

Securing Emails and Office 365

The most common form of an attack starts with compromising an email. Receiving an email with abusive attachments and URLs can be part of the first round of reconnaissance or be precise preexploitation reconnaissance, which, if successful, will continue to execute backdoors and make way for the attacker to enter the corporate device and network until reaching domain dominance. Our goal is to ensure that we have security products in place to help mitigate threats coming an organization's way.

For organizations to stay secure from malware, compromised URLs, and compromised content, Microsoft offers cloud-based Exchange Online Protection (EOP), which provides an email filtering service that serves organizations of all sizes. A messaging policy customized for an organization will also help protect it from human errors and violations. In this chapter, we will be focusing on Exchange Online and Office 365 products, though EOP is also capable of protecting your on-premise Exchange server.

Exchange Online Protection

Figure 2-1 shows a simple workflow of EOP.

© Vasantha Lakshmi 2019
V. Lakshmi, *Beginning Security with Microsoft Technologies*, https://doi.org/10.1007/978-1-4842-4853-9_2

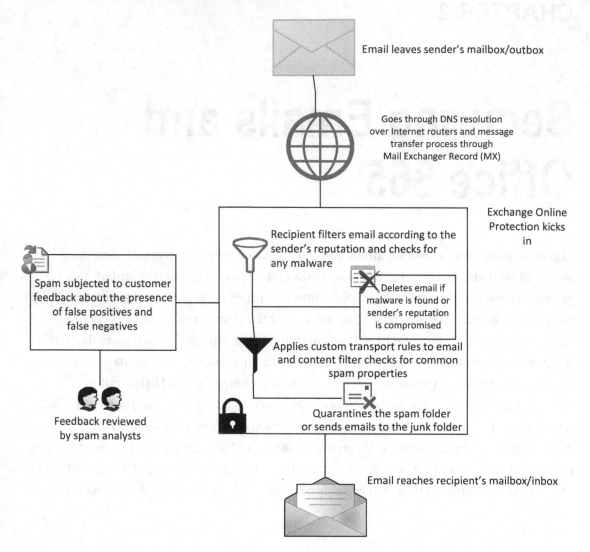

Figure 2-1. *Exchange Online Protection process for guaranteeing secure emails*

With EOP turned on, your email takes multiple steps before reaching its destination. First, Exchange's mail servers verify the email (through their registrar) and send it to the Exchange online server of the company or domain. When it is received, a filter kicks in that checks the sender's reputation and if there is malware. If malware is detected or the reputation of the sender (the domain in our case) is tainted, the email gets automatically deleted.

If the email passes both of the filters, it will then be subjected to custom transport rules, which consist of additional rules every organization creates to ascertain security.

The content filter keeps a tab on spam by checking the content of the mail. The spam check is continuously improved based on the input of customers (false positive or false negative). The input is investigated by spam analysts and then added to the service-wide filters if it meets classification criteria.

Note

False positive   An email incorrectly identified as spam that is actually legitimate.

False negative   A message that should have been identified as spam but was missed by the spam filter.

EOP Setup

In the process of going through the steps of setting up EOP in the Exchange admin center, we will learn about some of the salient features of its protection.

Figure 2-2 shows all the filter options that are available in the admin center.

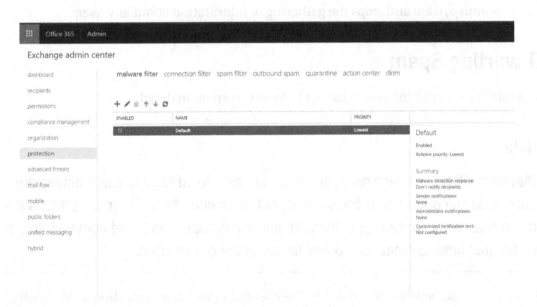

Figure 2-2. *EOP protection filters*

Antispam Protection

The inbound and outbound spam detection is always enabled in EOP. The connection and content filter together contribute to custom policies to send spam mail to the junk folder. You can choose to receive notifications for outbound spam email, too.

Hackers can send email messages to suspicious destinations and nonexistent recipients. To address this scenario, NDR backscatter can be configured, and upon such incidents, EOP will deliver an NDR (non-delivery report) back to the sender.

You can also choose to have a bulk message marked as a spam message by a setting up a policy to check for a bulk header stamp.

EOP already recognizes several URLs as spam and about 750,000 of known spammers aid in identifying a spam/phishing attack.

Antimalware Protection

Antimalware scanning for all email messages is automatically enabled in EOP and cannot be turned off. To protect customers at all times, multiple antimalware engines are provided. The system scans the entire email and its attachments for malware and also provides antispyware and stops the gathering of information about any user.

Thwarting Spam

Let's take a look at all the practices that help thwart spam in detail.

Note

Malware filter   As we already know, we are able to edit and tweak antimalware policies to suit our organization's needs, but we cannot delete these policies. As we customize them, we can apply them to different groups, users, and domains, so we do not just have to create one policy for the entire organization.

Figure 2-3 is a screenshot of a malware filter setting in which we can choose what will happen if malware is found in an email attachment we receive.

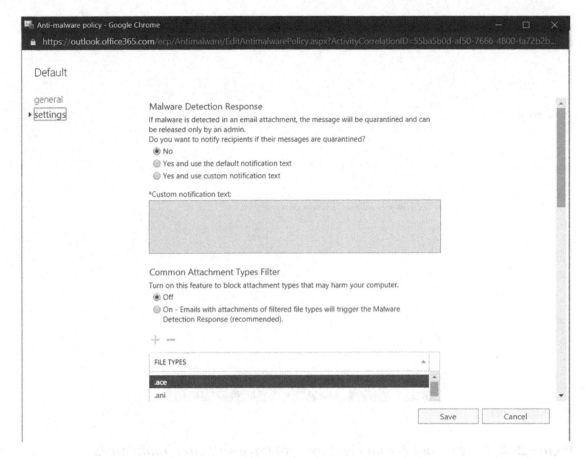

Figure 2-3. *Filter allowing us to choose what happens if malware is detected*

In Figure 2-4, I have selected a custom notification text specific to my organization that will be sent out if malware is detected in an attachment. In the event that your organization would like to block email attachments with certain types of file extensions, you can choose to block those under the "Common Attachment Types Filter." This is an important requirement if you would like to stop a hacker from sending phishing emails with executables that connect to their computer's command and control center. If such emails do get through, they might download additional malware and also upload collected data such as login credentials, banking information, and so on.

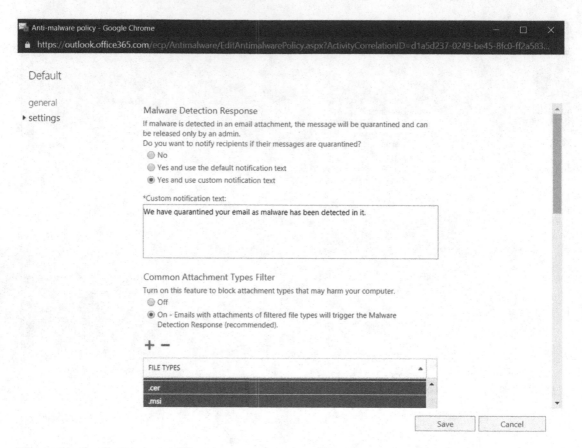

Figure 2-4. *Custom notification text you can have sent out if malware is detected*

After activating the "Common Attachment Types Filter," the next step is to block the file extensions that might harm your computer. Figure 2-5 shows how you can block Word documents with embedded macros, executables, and the like by restricting certain file types. I am choosing to block these file extensions because they might cause harm to the device and user by collecting data, performing reconnaissance activities, and other such processes.

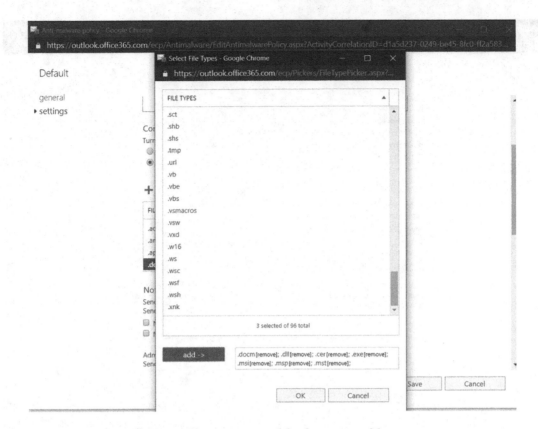

Figure 2-5. *Malware filter allowing us to block certain file types*

We also have the option to inform the email's sender, whether internal or external to the organization, that the message hasn't been delivered.

As shown in Figure 2-6, if you would like the administrator to be informed about every undelivered email to help with further forensics, you can choose to add the admin email address to be notified.

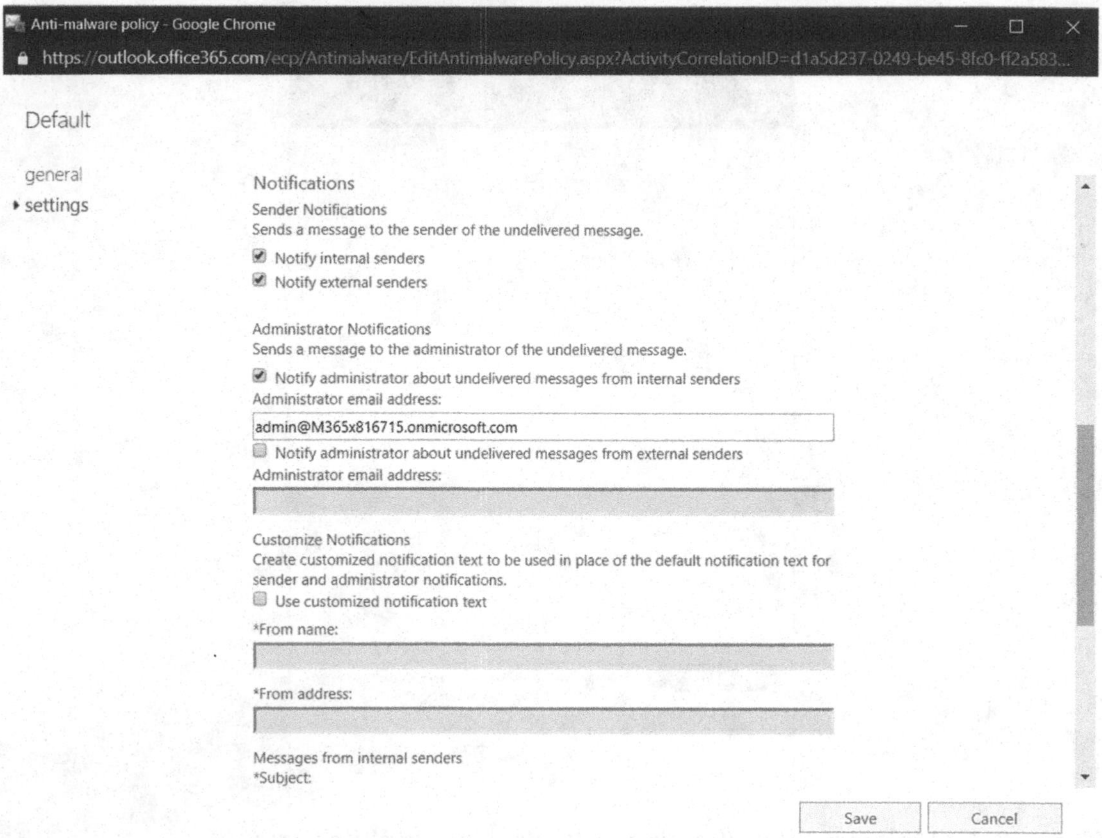

Figure 2-6. *Malware filter allowing you to notify your administrator about undelivered emails*

Connection Filter

It becomes very important to check the reputation of the sender and with connection filtering, we can do just that. Doing so will help keep spam email at bay. On the other hand, creating a safe sender list ensures that every email from a whitelisted IP address range of safe senders will be received.

We can also create a list of known spammer IP addresses and add them to the blocked senders list to keep spam away. We also have some spoof intelligence features (to prevent domain spoof emails) that further aid in blocking spam. As we will see, this as a part of Office 365 Advanced Threat Protection (ATP).

Figure 2-7 shows a screen on which you can add a list of IP addresses for incoming emails that you would like to allow and a blocked list in which you can block IP addresses from known spammers.

Microsoft gets information about trusted sender lists from subscribing to various third-party sources. By enabling a safe list, emails sent from safe senders do not undergo connection filtering and are never marked as spam.

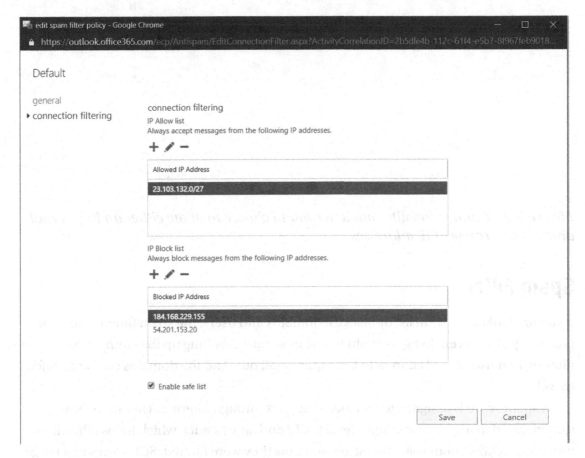

Figure 2-7. *Connection filter allowing you to create safe and blocked senders lists*

Figure 2-8 shows that you can either specify individual IP addresses or a range of individual addresses with CIDR (classless inter domain routing).

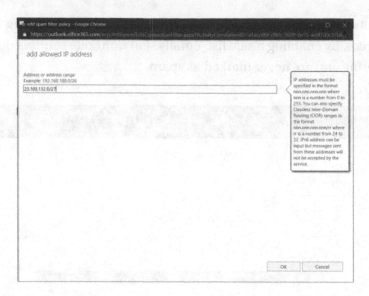

Figure 2-8. *Connection filter allowing you to choose to allow either an individual address or a range of IP addresses*

Spam Filter

If you are looking to whitelist or blacklist domains and users, the spam filter is the right place to go. However, doing so might not be as secure as setting up the connection filtering that uses the IP address to filter spam mail out. And the domains can be spoofed as well.

A spam score is assigned to an email that goes through filtering. That score is in turn mapped to a spam confidence level (SCL) and an x-header, which helps admins by providing details about spam messages and how they were filtered. SCL scores can range from –1 to 9, where scores of –1, 0, and 1 indicate that the email is clean and nonspam and scores of 5, 6, 7, 8, and 9 are considered high-confidence or definite spam.

Figure 2-9 shows the "spam and bulk actions screen" screen that allows you to choose the action you want associated with any spam mail you receive. By default, it is set at "Move message to Junk Email folder," but you can also opt for any other action. For each choice, there are additional settings that need to be configured as well. If I opt to "Quarantine message," for instance, I will then have to choose additional settings such AS (required?) the period to retain these spam emails.

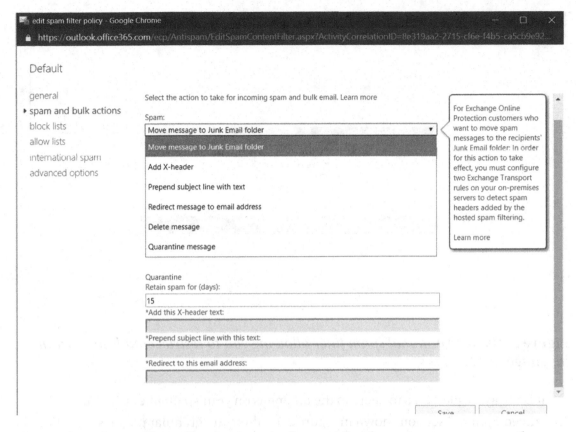

Figure 2-9. *Spam filter allowing you to choose what happens to spam email*

Under "block lists," you can block the list of user email IDs you know to be spammers and you can also block the domains that you usually get spam from. This is the section where you will decide the course of action for the email if it is recognized as spam. Upon detection, the email can be quarantined or sent to the junk folder or we can input an x-header (email header) to warn the user about the suspected spam email.

Similar to blocked lists, we also have allowed lists. Allowed users' email IDs can be added to allowed sender lists so that any emails received from these email IDs will never be marked as spam. We can also choose to allow all emails from certain domains.

Figure 2-10 shows that under "international spam" we can choose a list of foreign languages and regions from which we would like to keep emails at bay.

Note   In Figure 2-10, I've randomly selected the first and last options available for the languages and regions from which I would like to restrict e-mails. You will have to make these selections according to your organization's specific requirements.

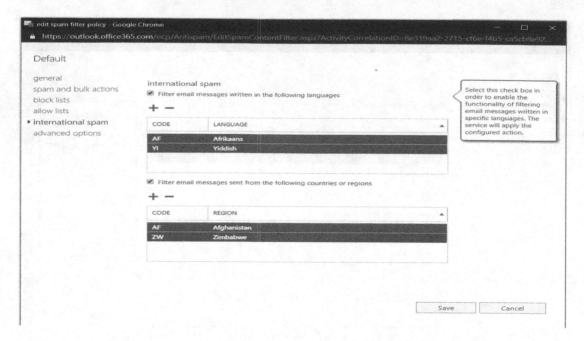

Figure 2-10. *International spam filter allowing you to restrict emails for certain languages and regions*

It is always a good idea to keep up the antennas on your spam filters. In the "advanced options" section shown in Figure 2-11, there are granular policies that allow you to choose to increase a spam score if certain conditions are met, such as images that link to remote sites or have numeric IP address in the URL. You can also choose to directly mark certain emails as spam if they, for instance, have no contents or have java script or VBScript (Visual Basic script) in HTML.

Along with the "On" and "Off" drop-down options, there is also an option that allows you to test if the selected option should be sent with an X-header or if it should be BCCed to an admin's email ID if it does not meet the spam criteria defined (e.g., it is not part of the blocked list of user IDs or domains).

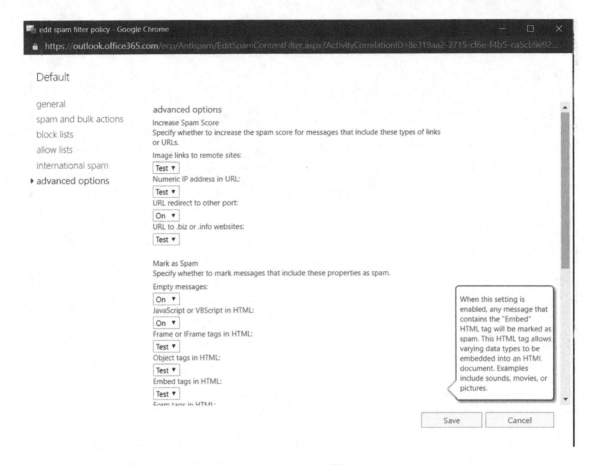

Figure 2-11. *Additional options in the spam filter*

Outbound Filter

Since Office 365 is a shared service and the resources could be shared between multiple users, it becomes really important not to tarnish the outbound IP integrity of the service.

EOP by default segregates the outbound traffic into separate IP pools. Every outbound email is scanned by the service and if a high-risk email is found, it is sent through a separate IP pool. This ensures that users sharing the resources are not affected by the outbound spam from other users in the IP pool. It also ensures that the other email security products used by the recipients will not receive emails from this high-risk IP pool. EOP will also disable an email account if it sends many spam emails.

An administrator can choose to receive emails that get marked as spam by the outbound email scanner or from an account that has gotten blocked for sending too much spam. Figure 2-12 shows the screen where you can set the preferences you want to use for outward spam.

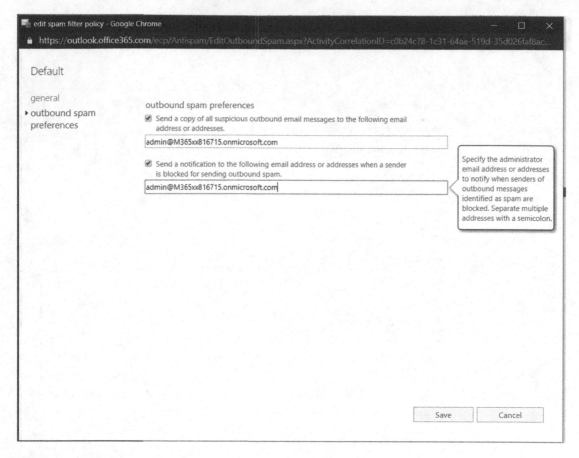

Figure 2-12. *Filter for setting outbound spam preferences*

Quarantine and Action Center/Restricted Users

The options "Quarantine" and "Action Center" can be found in the Microsoft 365
"Security & Compliance" window at `https://protection.office.com/`. In a recent
release, Microsoft introduced the Microsoft 365 Security Center and Microsoft 365
Compliance Center. However, this does not stop you from accessing the "Security &
Compliance" window directly using this link. There are also a lot of features and links
on the individual security and compliance pages that connect us to the "Security &
Compliance" center.

In Figure 2-13, you can see the most recent features that can be accessed from the
Microsoft 365 admin center.

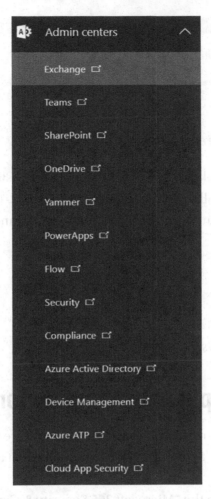

Figure 2-13. *Features available in the Microsoft 365 admin center*

You can have the "Security & Compliance" window show a list of all the email messages that have been quarantined or recognized as spam under "Threat Management - Review."

Depending on the transport rules set up in your policies and also for the high-confidence spams, your emails might get quarantined. Figure 2-14 shows a screen where you can review the emails that have been quarantined and use the filters to further your forensics if malware is found.

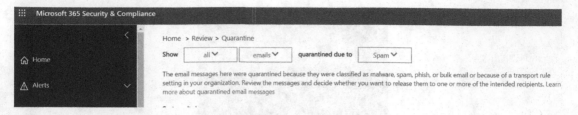

Figure 2-14. *Quarantine review tool*

You can also choose to take further action on any users listed in the "Restricted Users" section (previously called "Action Center") in Figure 2-15. You might restrict users as a result of sending bulk outbound emails or spam emails and the like.

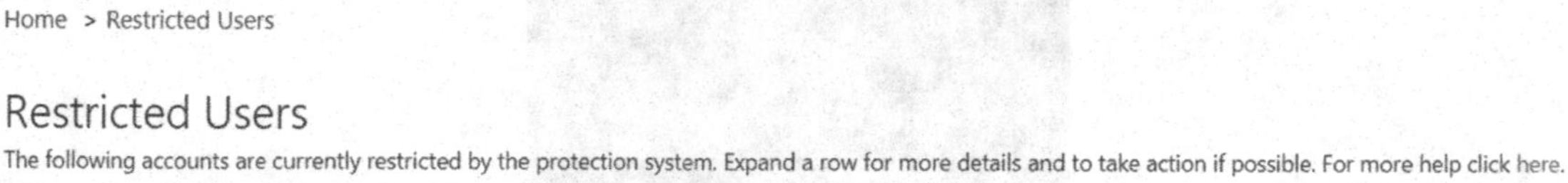

Home > Restricted Users

Restricted Users

The following accounts are currently restricted by the protection system. Expand a row for more details and to take action if possible. For more help click here.

Figure 2-15. *"Restricted Users" screen*

"Security & Compliance" Window for ATP Policies

The settings we have already reviewed, including the malware filter and spam filter, can also be configured from "Security & Compliance" page in a very similar and more streamlined way.

Here's how to do it: Go to the "Microsoft 365 Security & Compliance" section. Under "Threat management," click "Policy" and you will see a listing of these settings, as shown in Figure 2-16.

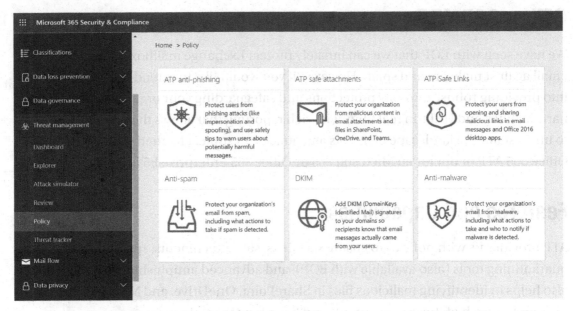

Figure 2-16. *Office EOP policies on the "Microsoft 365 Security & Compliance" page*

A detailed look at the spam filter policy reveals that the options discussed in the Exchange admin center under protection are very similar to the policies under "Security & Compliance" (Figure 2-17).

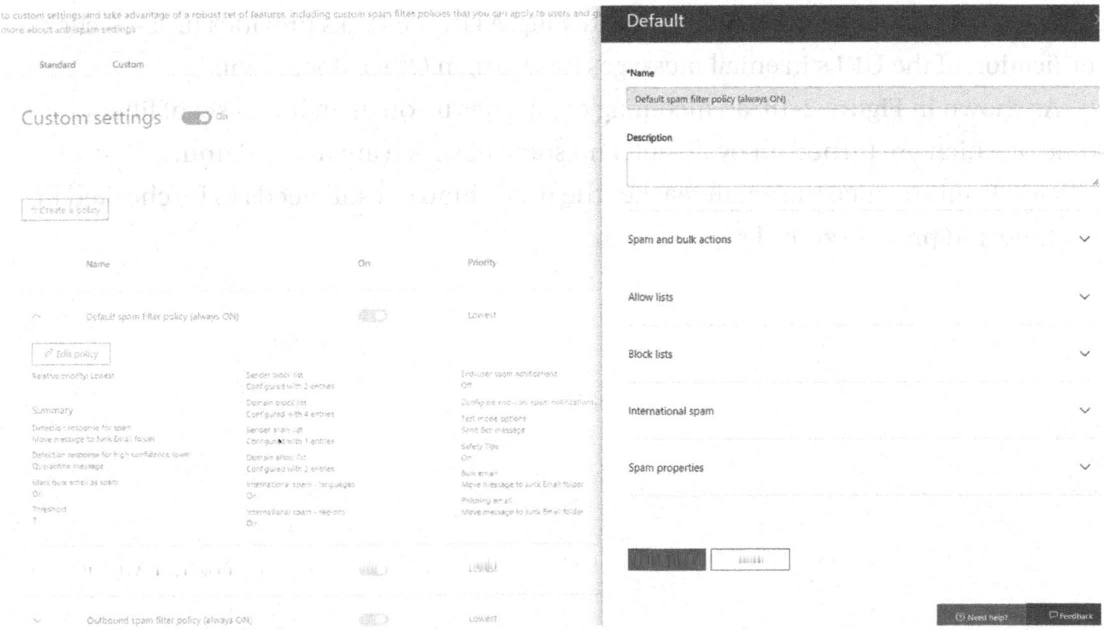

Figure 2-17. *Default Spam Filter policy in the Microsoft 365 "Security & Compliance" Center*

Office 365 ATP

We have seen with EOP that we can innately protect Exchange mailboxes and secure email against malware and spam. However, if you would like to extend those abilities into providing robust zero-day protections and safeguarding your organization against harmful links and URLs in real time, with rich reporting that allows the organization to understand the landscape of threats and attacks it's subject to, then we want to add Office 365 ATP or opt for an Microsoft 365 or Office 365 Enterprise E5 license.

Features and Capabilities

ATP provides us with policies to ensure safe links, safe attachments, spoof intelligence, quarantining tools (also available with EOP), and advanced antiphishing capabilities. It also helps in identifying malicious files in SharePoint, OneDrive, and Microsoft Teams. Let's look at each of these components and learn how to set them up.

Safe Links

The emails we receive can contain obvious and hidden links and URLs, and we do not always know where they might lead, how secure the web sites are, if they will install malware/backdoors, or cause other risky results. ATP Safe Links provides time-of-click verification of the URLs in email messages (and also in Office documents).

As shown in Figure 2-18, an incoming email goes through an initial set of filters, some of which are turned on by default and some of which are defined under EOP policies. Even so, once the email reaches the user's inbox, it still needs to be checked in real time and provide zero-day protection.

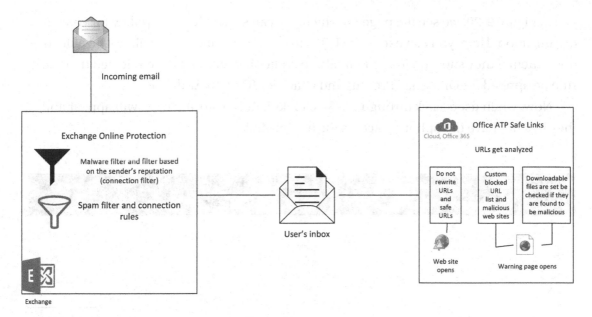

Figure 2-18. *Security process for incoming emails*

Here are some of the steps involved in setting up Safe Links in the Microsoft 365 "Security & Compliance" window: As shown Figure 2-19, under the "Threat Management" tab, click "Policy" and you will get to "Safe Links." Two sets of policies will appear. One applies to the entire organization and the second to specific groups of users.

Figure 2-19. *Accessing the "Safe Links" page*

In Figure 2-20, we see the page on which you can set a Safe Links policy for your organization. Here, you can list all the URLs to be blocked and users will not be able to open them if they show up in their emails. In addition to email, I have selected that the rule be applied for Office 365 ProPlus and Office for IOS and Android.

Now, when users click through the Safe Links URL, a warning page will appear and they will not have the option to access the original link.

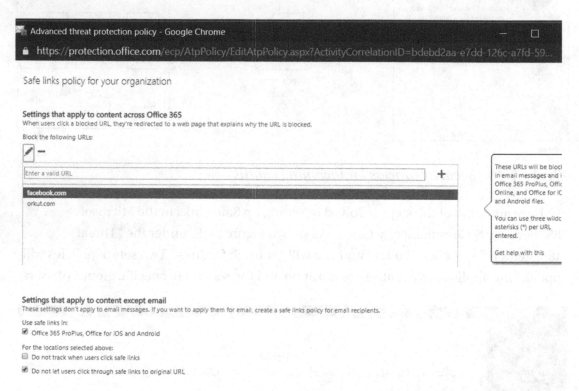

Figure 2-20. *Screen for setting a Safe Links policy for your organization*

Figure 2-21 shows a page on which we can further edit the Safe Links policy. By choosing "URLs will be rewritten and checked against a list of known malicious links when user clicks on the link," when the end user clicks links in emails and Office 365 documents, an appendage will be added to the URL that looks similar to this: `safelinks.protection.outlook.com`. After the URL is tested, it is good to go.

To ensure downloaded files are safe, we select "Use safe attachments to scan downloadable content." You can also select "Apply safe links to messages sent within the organization" to ensure that no spam is circulated within an organization.

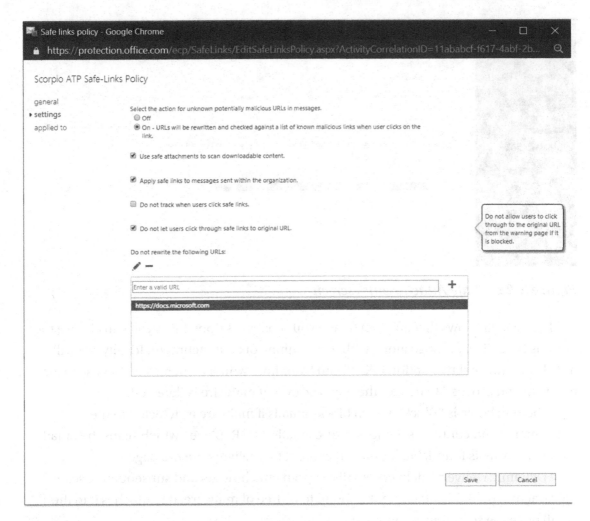

Figure 2-21. Further options for the Safe Links policy

Safe Attachments

Safe Links works hand in hand with Safe Attachments to protect your organization from malicious attacks. ATP Safe Attachments investigates the attachments to your emails for any malware or malicious content. It then takes action based on the policies set by your organization.

As we can see in Figure 2-22, you can also opt for Safe Attachments to scan the files for malicious content in SharePoint, OneDrive for Business, and Microsoft Teams. In the second half of the section, you can click "+" to either create a policy for the entire organization or separate policies for different teams.

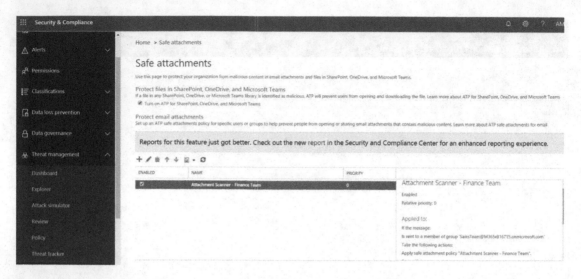

Figure 2-22. *"Safe Attachments" screen*

Figure 2-23 shows that after you name your policy, as done here, you can choose the options for delivery that go along with the scanning of an attachment. Ideally, we will not choose the first two options, "Off" and "Monitor," which respectively don't scan for malware and proceed to deliver the message even if malware is detected.

A better choice is "Block," which blocks emails if malware is detected in the attachments and continues to block future emails. Or "Replace," which scans the email and, if malware is found, blocks the attachment but delivers the message.

"Dynamic Delivery" delivers emails without attachments and subsequently scans the attachment. If the attachment is found to be free of malware, it reattaches it to the email once the scanning is complete.

You can apply this policy to a domain, user, or group.

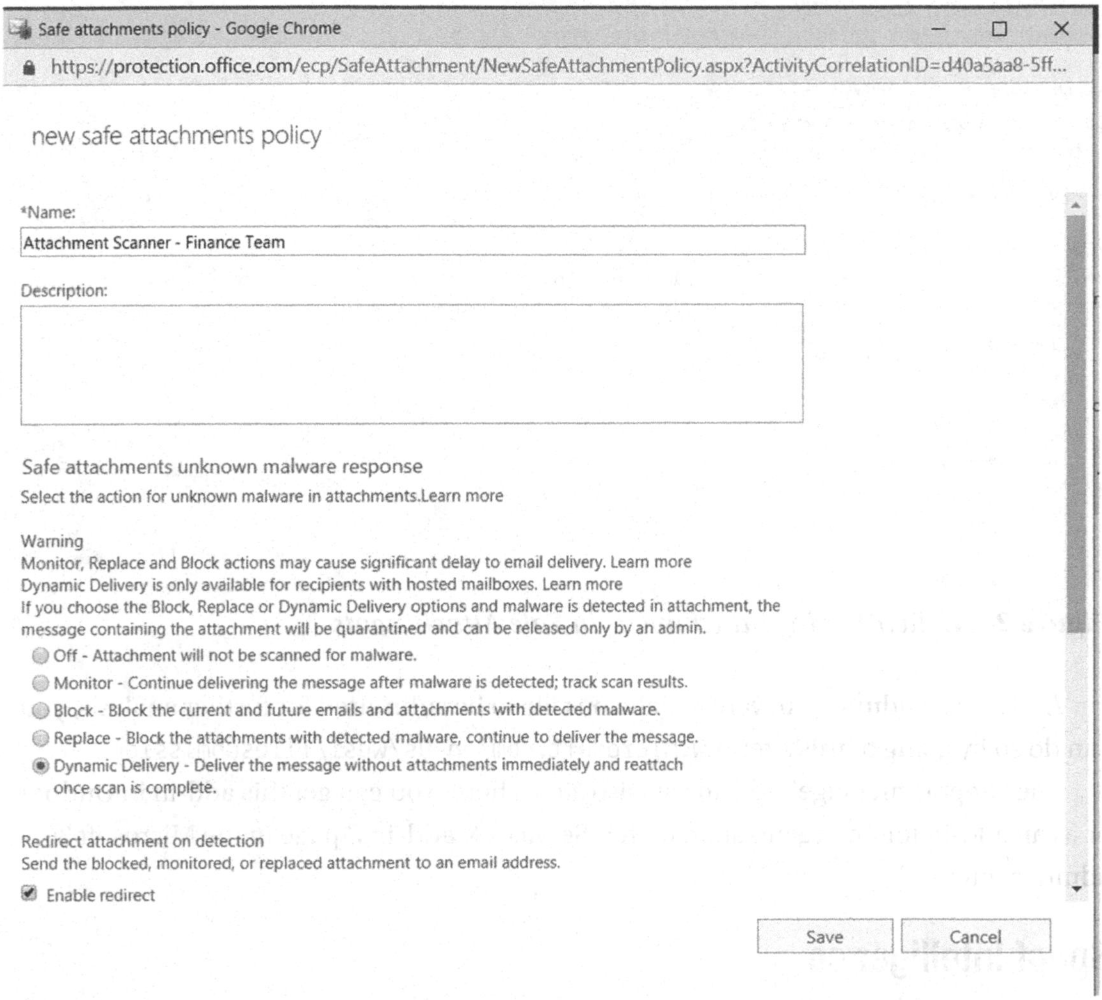

Figure 2-23. *Options for delivery in Safe Attachments*

To follow up on the previously described delivery options, we can set up a policy that will redirect the blocked, monitored, or replaced attachment to a chosen email address, as shown in Figure 2-24.

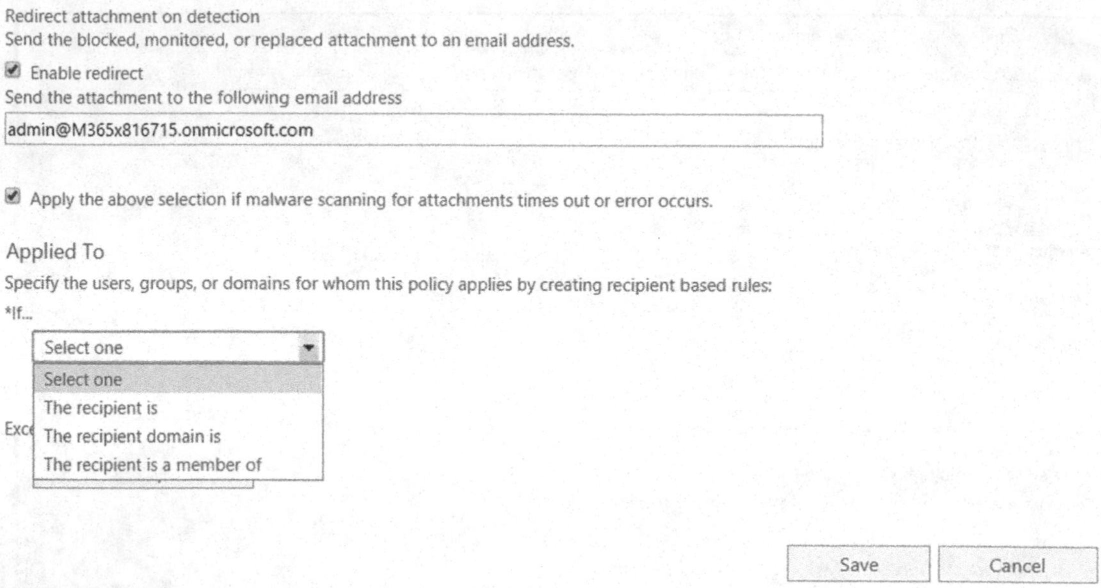

Redirect attachment on detection
Send the blocked, monitored, or replaced attachment to an email address.

☑ Enable redirect
Send the attachment to the following email address

admin@M365x816715.onmicrosoft.com

☑ Apply the above selection if malware scanning for attachments times out or error occurs.

Applied To
Specify the users, groups, or domains for whom this policy applies by creating recipient based rules:
*If...

Select one ▼
Select one
The recipient is
The recipient domain is
The recipient is a member of

Exc

[Save]   [Cancel]

Figure 2-24. *Redirecting attachments in Safe Attachments*

And if as an admin you want a malicious file to be submitted for further analysis, you can do so by going to this site: `www.microsoft.com/en-us/wdsi/filesubmission`.

The "Report message" add-in can also aid us here. You can get this add-in in Outlook or as an add-in for an organization in the "Services & add-ins" page in the Microsoft 365 admin center.

Spoof Intelligence

You do not want a spammer to spoof your domain and send out emails, nor do you want to receive emails from a spoofed domain. But in some cases you might want to allow certain senders to spoof your domain to send out bulk email on behalf of your organization (say, for company polls, sending product updates to subscribers, or an application sending notifications for your domain). And, likewise, there may be legitimate spoofers from external domains who are relaying messages for another company.

Figure 2-25 shows a Microsoft 365 "Security & Compliance" window in which you can set up a spoof intelligence policy. To do so, start by going to the "Threat management" tab, from which you will proceed to choose custom settings. On this page, you can also review any senders that you would like to permit to spoof your domain both for your own domain and an external domain.

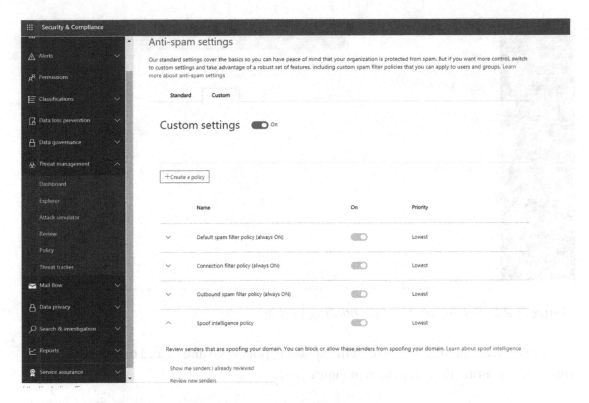

Figure 2-25. *Page for setting up a spoof intelligence policy*

Now let's get to configuring an antispoofing policy.

As shown in Figure 2-26, you can ensure that the antispoofing filter is very strict with this policy. We are here to modify that, as by default antispoofing is always on. We are still on the "Threat Management" tab. Now let's go to the "Anti-phishing" settings," create a new policy, and then edit those settings. Go to the Security and Compliance Center ➤ Threat Management ➤ Policy to select the anti-phishing policy.

Figure 2-26. *Setting up an antispoofing policy*

Since we are mainly here to edit the spoofing policy, go ahead and turn on the antispoofing protection, as shown in Figure 2-27.

Figure 2-27. *Turning on antispoofing protection*

Next let's define the action we would like to take in case the algorithm senses a user who is spoofing your domain that isn't an allowed sender. We can choose either to quarantine the email or move it to the junk folder, as shown in Figure 2-28.

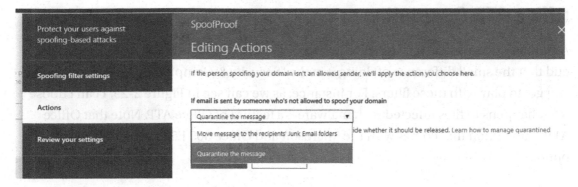

Figure 2-28. *Choosing what to do when a nonallowed sender spoofs your domain*

Along with all these options, it is highly recommended to configure SPF, DKIM, and DMARC correctly in your organization to protect against spoofs.

THREE ACRONYMS

The three policies outlined in this sidebar should be followed by most organizations even before they look into this book, hence I have not covered them in depth.

SPF

Sender policy framework (SPF) is a DNS text entry published for a domain. This is an authoritative list that has information about all the devices allowed to send email on behalf of the domain. SPF is designed to help prevent spoofing. SPF is not always used for production domains as it might not always provide the most accurate identification of spam.

DKIM

DomainKeys Identified Mail (DKIM) is an authentication system based on asymmetric cryptographic keys. The host sending the email signs the header with its private key. The receiving host verifies the signature and ensures that the email was not tampered with after it was sent by the user.

DMARC

Domain-based Message Authentication, Reporting, and Conformance (DMARC) is also a DNS text record used to prevent spoofing and phishing. DMARC needs to be enabled for outbound mails specifically as Office365 takes care of DMARC settings for inbound emails automatically.

Office ATP Quarantine

Although quarantining ATP has already been discussed as a part of EOP, I would like to add that the small difference of doing it in the "Security & Compliance" section is that you get to play with these filters. For instance, as we can see in Figure 2-29, I can choose what happens to files infected with malware—a feature of Office ATP. Note that Office ATP is an option that comes with the Microsoft and Office 365 E5 Enterprise license options.

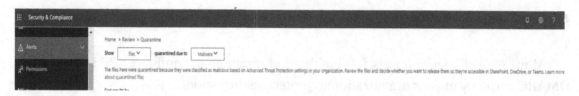

Figure 2-29. *Choosing what happens to infected files in Office ATP*

So far, we have learned that an incoming message goes through many filters before it lands in a user's inbox. However, we still see a lot commodity attacks, whaling, and spear-phishing attacks these days. To protect against them, ATP antiphishing leverages machine-learning models along with impersonation detection algorithms and applies them to incoming messages.

These machine-learning models are trained to detect phishing messages by using advanced algorithms to detect and protect against various user and domain impersonation attacks.

In ATP antiphishing policy, we can define which users and domains should be protected from impersonation attacks using a fixed list of users and domains or mailbox intelligence.

Mailbox intelligence helps with user profiling by understanding a user's email habits, contact lists, how the person communicates, and other such functions. The process is similar to building a map about a user's communication, so that message impersonations with characteristics different than those of the user can be detected.

In the "Security & Compliance" window, return to the "Threat Management" tab, choose "Policy," and you will be brought back to the "Anti-phishing" settings.

As pictured in Figure 2-30, you can choose to create a new policy and apply it either to users/groups or to your domains. Once the policy is defined, click it to edit it further.

Figure 2-30. *Creating a new antiphishing policy*

Now we will focus on the impersonation section of this antiphishing policy.

Edit the impersonation setting from the anti-phishing setting options. Click "Add users to protect" seen in Figure 2-31. These users might be high-level executives, board members, known external users, or anyone who is a likely subject of impersonation by attackers.

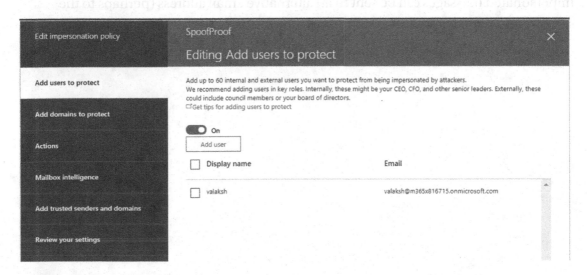

Figure 2-31. *Adding users to protect*

You can also add all the domains related to your organization and include custom domains to protect as done in Figure 2-32.

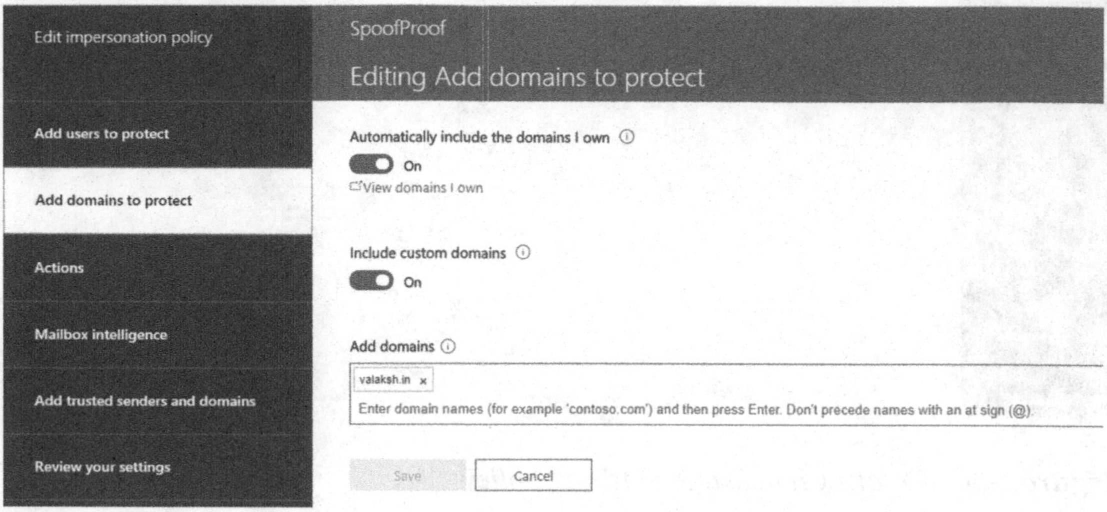

Figure 2-32. *Adding domains to protect*

Would you like to quarantine a message that was impersonated by a user or domain? If so, you can do so by clicking the "Actions" tab shown in Figure 2-33 and then choosing to "Quarantine the message." You can choose various other options as well. Impersonated messages can be sent to an alternative email address (perhaps to the security admin to do more analysis), or to a junk folder, or be deleted, and so on.

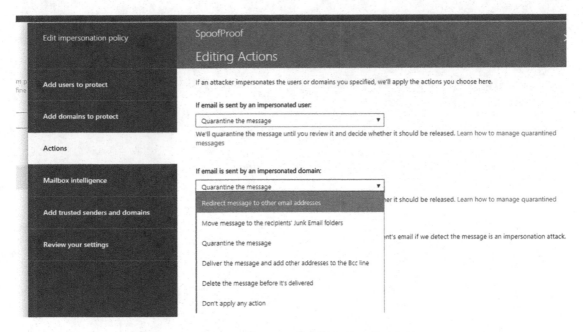

Figure 2-33. *Quarantining a message in the "Actions" tab*

You can turn on "Mailbox intelligence" in the tab under "Actions." As discussed earlier, choosing this option will help profile a user's email habits and provide enhanced impersonation results based on the map of the sender.

If you have a list of trusted senders and domains, you can white list them by going to "Add trusted senders and domains." This might help to reduce false positives if the domain and user emails are similar.

Now we have ensured that there is a strong impersonation filter powered by machine learning and advanced algorithms.

It would definitely be a tough job for a hacker to break free from all the security (the safe links, safe attachments, antiphishing software, and so on) we have now enabled for our email security. But we still need to factor in human error. It is also the responsibility of the security admin to educate all the users in your organization about recognizing illegitimate emails and phishing attacks.

And in the event that the security fails to identify an attacker, or if for some reason the attacker bypasses the email security and manages to execute a file connecting to C & C, or drops exploits in the memory, or plants malware, we need to ensure that our device security is strong, up to date, and ready to stop the attacker from progressing. We will see what the options are for tightening device-level security in Chapter 3. Let's keep our fight against these attackers going strong!

CHAPTER 3

Device-Level Security

In the life cycle of an attack, there are different stages an attacker goes through. We have already discussed in detail the first stage of an attack in our review of email security in Chapter 2. If an attacker manages to get into a user's system as a result of things like human error or a successful social-engineering attempt, we need to have the device's defenses up and running to stop the intruder from getting further into the network.

Figure 3-1 shows the multiple stages of an attack, especially those pertaining to the device. When intruders manage to get into a device by many preexploitation reconnaissance attempts followed by phishing and deliver malware to the device, their logical next steps would be to install a script and run macros and memory injections (PowerShell payload fileless attacks).

Once they have a foothold of the device, a backdoor is created and a connection to the command and control center is established. This is where the further set of actions and information gathering, or the reconnaissance, takes place. The attacker would then persist for days waiting to find a means for privilege escalation. The idea is to steal the credentials and look around for any admin credentials, or misconfigured services or systems with known vulnerabilities (no critical patches applied), or excessive admin rights. All of these will lead an attacker to privilege escalation. As attackers often make a lot of noise at each phase, every action they take can and should easily generate an alert, especially if Windows Defender ATP is enabled, as it listens for indications of compromises and attacks.

Intruders can then move further into the organization laterally by attacking more systems and servers until they achieve domain dominance and gain access to all company resources, which will require access to Kerberos tickets (remote script execution). Identity protection becomes really important to stop an attacker from gaining access to company resources by using attacks such as pass the hash, pass the attack, and the like. We will learn more about this in the next chapter.

43

© Vasantha Lakshmi 2019
V. Lakshmi, *Beginning Security with Microsoft Technologies*, https://doi.org/10.1007/978-1-4842-4853-9_3

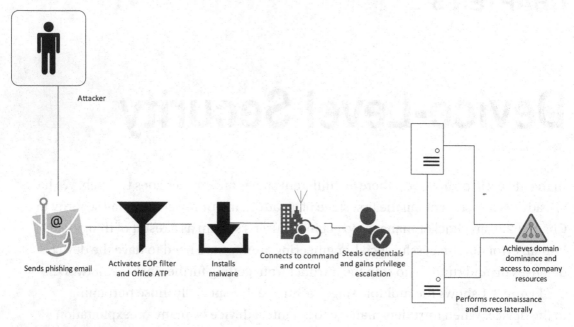

Attacker

Sends phishing email

Activates EOP filter
and Office ATP

Installs
malware

Connects to command
and control

Steals credentials
and gains privilege
escalation

Achieves domain
dominance and
access to company
resources

Performs reconnaissance
and moves laterally

Figure 3-1. Life cycle of an attack

We will start by looking at device-level security from two perspectives: prebreach
and postbreach.

Prebreach

In the past, we saw a mindset that mostly focused on security of the perimeter by using
firewall rules to enhance security. This is effective in a world where the end users worked
from corporate offices and only that perimeter had to be protected. Now, we have all
broken this perimeter and work is taken care of irrespective of where the user works from
and which device they work from.

Endpoint security incorporates EPP and EDR. Both components are required for
solving the device security puzzle for any organization. They have cloud-powered
intelligence (leveraging machine learning) to identify the attacks and also to understand
the context of an attack. Understanding the context of an attack will further aid in
providing an alert when new malware or malware that has an unknown signature is
found, or if there is unknown or even fileless attacks.

The advent of Windows 10 has added depth to the device-level security, bringing such features as Device Guard (which is more of an advanced security mode than a feature, consisting of Windows Defender Application Control and Windows Defender Exploit Guard); the Device Health Attestation (DHA) service in its integration with MDM and checks for BitLocker; secure boot and ELAM (early launch antimalware); and Windows Defender antivirus, which provides real-time protection against viruses, malware, spyware, and the like. Windows 10 also has features such as Credential Guard, Windows Hello for Business, and Microsoft Passport. We will look at these features in the in the next chapter on identity protection. With all this progressive technology in place, we are moving toward a unified endpoint protection.

Let's delve into these features now so that we can understand how to contribute to device security and destroy the playbook of attackers by making all known current attack methods outdated.

Advanced Security Mode: Device Guard

Locking down an operating system is very critical and we have been doing so for many years with traditional/legacy options. Some of these options are still good to use, such as group policy, application locker, access control lists (ACLs), and role-based access control (RBAC). However, the security that was once considered sufficient in Windows 7 will not stop an attacker from breaching your device security measures today. To keep our systems tamper-free, we must not only rely on the software-based security offered by the OS but also leverage hardware-based security. Hardware-based security helps maintain and validate system and hardware integrity. Earlier, especially in Windows 7, we could install any application and the default nature of the OS was to trust the application. It is not so in Windows 10 and the application is required to earn trust.

Let's look at the two components of Device Guard: Windows Defender Application Control (WDAC) and Windows Defender Exploit Guard (WDEG).

Windows Defender Application Control

Traditionally, most applications were trusted to run on a device by default (as was the case with Windows 7). What should be questioned is that when such access to applications is automatically provided, their level of access on the device is the same as that of the user running the application. This can lead to sensitive information being transmitted out of the system if a user runs malicious software.

45

WDAC can help thwart threats that are generally found in executable file-based malware (e.g., `.dll`, `.exe` files). Application Control helps block the applications that users are allowed to run on their systems, so that not all the code/script has access to the system kernal. We can create WDAC policies to block unsigned scripts and Microsoft Installers (MSIs), and run Windows PowerShell in the constrained language mode. This tool is not only limited to applications but also can be used for add-ins, plug-ins, and modules that only specific applications are supposed to run (may be a line of business application).

Note   Constrained language mode permits the running of all Windows and PowerShell cmdlets, and the execution is limited to only permitted types such as Microsoft signed and certified apps. It supports User Mode Code Integrity (UMCI) policies to protect the systems (Windows RT).

To create WDAC policies, we can use Windows 10 Professional, Windows 10 Enterprise, or Windows Server 2016.

Distribution of WDAC policies can be taken care of by MDM solutions such as Microsoft Intune or even by group policies.

Here are some of the planning considerations:

- In a real-world scenario where you would like to apply WDAC, extensive planning might be required if you want to stay in control of each and every application in your organization. So, it is advisable to have a manageable number of applications in your organization. That sounds simple enough and like all you need to do is white list all these applications.

- The scenario can get convoluted if you would like to white list certain applications based on their departments. You can also create an exception list of applications you would like to avoid being installed. These policies can be applied to different organizational units through group policies as well.

- You can choose to control classic Windows apps or universal Windows apps or both.

- If you need to identify all the applications being used in your organization, you can run WDAC in audit mode. This will let you monitor any applications that are not defined or recognized by an administrator in the policies, or run by end users in event logs. You can also choose this as the method for doing the initial few pilot tests with the end users without affecting their productivity or blocking any applications.

Let's look at two hypothetical scenarios where we can apply WDAC today. (You can definitely use it for a lot more than these two scenarios, depending on how much you want to lock down your organization.)

- Your organization has been running a traditional or even hybrid management solution with Active Directory on the premises and has a lot of Windows 10 systems joined to the local domain. Business applications used by the end users are highly dependent on the group they belong to, such as the finance department, the marketing department, the IT department, and so on. You would like to enforce the use of signed drivers as well. The System Center Configuration Manager, or SCCM, can also be involved and any managed application installed from SCCM should be marked as an approved app. The organization likes to plan its deployment and be in control of its applications and how they are distributed across various groups.

- Your organization is a born-in-the-cloud organization. Azure Active Directory (AD)–joined, and in turn Intune- or MDM-joined, Windows 10 devices. And your organization would like to leverage best-in-class policies and is not very strict about the applications that are allowed to run. Your organization also might not be interested in taking control centrally to create a whitelisted set of applications allowed to run or a strict locked-down environment. In such a case, the organization might be interested in leveraging the cloud-powered Microsoft Intelligent Security Graph (ISG). ISG allows the execution of reputable and well-known applications, and blocks that of unknown and bad software. This way the end user is still empowered and gets to decide his or her application needs.

Traditional Scenario

Let's start with the first scenario. To address such a scenario, we will create a golden image from a Windows 10 computer, and it should be malware- and virus-free.

Creating a WDAC Policy from a Reference Computer

It is highly recommended that you have a list of all the applications (user mode) required by an organization or a group of users in the organization along with the drivers that you plan to create a golden image with.

Note   A golden image is a base image of Windows 10, with business applications and driver-installed standardizing images, that helps with reducing administrative workload.

I've installed WordWeb (the free dictionary) and Adobe Reader for my golden image. We will get started by initializing variables on the Windows 10 system. We would be saving the `initialscan.xml` in the desktop as per these commands:

```
$CIPolicyPath=$env:userprofile+"\Desktop\"
$InitialCIPolicy=$CIPolicyPath+"InitialScan.xml"
$CIPolicyBin=$CIPolicyPath+"DeviceGuardPolicy.bin"
New-CIPolicy -Level FilePublisher -FilePath $InitialCIPolicy -ScanPath C:\
-UserPEs -Fallback Hash 3> CIPolicyLog.txt
```

The initial scan will take a while (can be hours) to run, and the use of -UserPEs ensures that the policy captures user mode executables (applications) along with kernel mode binaries such as drivers. We could have passed the -Option (0-16) argument in the command line as well. And by default, option 3 is enabled, which puts us in audit mode. For more see: `https://docs.microsoft.com/en-us/windows/security/threat-protection/windows-defender-application-control/select-types-of-rules-to-create`.

Figure 3-2 shows a copy of the `initialscan.xml` file. It is clear that our policy is still an unsigned system integrity policy. It is in audit mode. Preboot users will have the F8 menu enabled for them. The policy is also enabled for all universal Windows applications. As you can see, the hashes of the applications and the drivers are all captured. We are working at the hash level to ensure security.

Figure 3-2. Initial scan XML file

After we have captured the initial image with apps and drivers, we will convert the WDAC policy to a binary format as follows:

```
ConvertFrom-CIPolicy $MergedCIPolicy $CIPolicyBin
```

In Figure 3-3, you can see both the binary file and the `initialscan.xml` file.

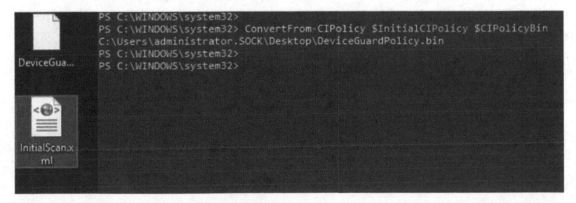

Figure 3-3. Converting to a binary format

> **Note**   You can either create a code-signing certificate for WDAC or use a publicly
> issued code-signing certificate. Should you choose to use an internal CA, I would
> recommend using `signtool.exe` to sign your WDAC Policy. You can use this
> command line to integrate the certificate with your WDAC Policy: `Add-SignerRule`
> `-FilePath <policypath> -CertificatePath <certpath> -User`.

Now that we have created a new WDAC policy on a Windows 10 system with
applications installed (part of base image or golden image) let's look at the options we
have for deploying these policies. We can use:

- group policies

- Microsoft Intune

- System Center Configuration Manager, or SCCM, Current Branch
  (managed installer scenario)

Group Policies

On the local computer you would like to apply this on, go to `gpedit.msc.`

Under "Computer Configuration," go to "Administrative Templates," then "System,"
and "Device Guard." Edit the "Deploy Windows Defender Application Control." As
shown in Figure 3-4, reference the `.bin` file created in the previous steps. You can also
have this `DeviceGuardPolicy.bin` file under the `C:\Windows\System32\CodeIntegrity`
folder. This, however, must be done on all systems and you can choose to have this bin
file in a shared folder location, too.

The group policy in Figure 3-4 references the p7b file in its explanation. Even if we
were referencing a bin file in this group policy, Windows 10 would automatically convert
the bin file to a p7b file.

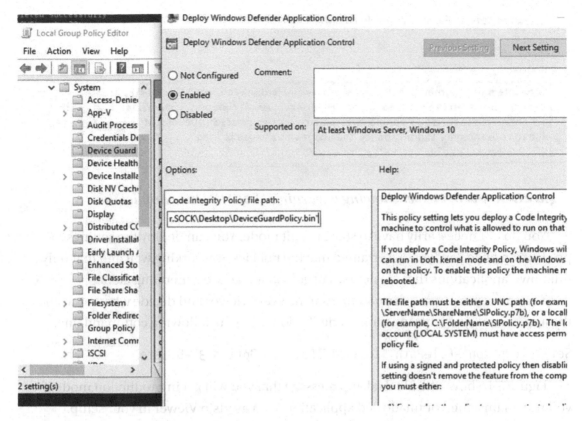

Figure 3-4. *WDAC group policy*

You can update the group policy on the system, and for the policy to take effect just reboot your computer. To test the settings, install an application that was not already part of your golden image. Since the policy is available in audit mode only, you will be able to see alerts in the event log (shown in Figure 3-5) by going to "Applications and Services Logs," "Microsoft," "Windows," and "CodeIntegrity."

You will then see a warning (for event 3076) in the event viewer that the new application installed does not meet the company standards and violates the code integrity.

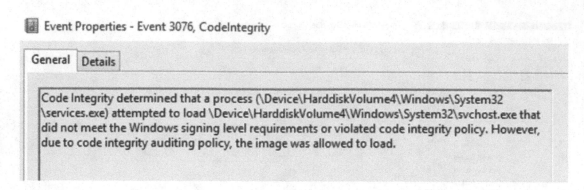

Figure 3-5. *Event viewer showing a warning about the new application*

You do not necessarily have to stay in audit mode. You can deploy the settings to production once you have ascertained that the policies are working well and that only unknown applications that are not part of golden image are generating alerts.

You can capture this information from the event viewer and decide whether to allow the app or continue in production mode. To do so, use the following command line:

```
Set-RuleOption -FilePath $InitialCIPolicy -Option 3 -Delete
```

Figure 3-6 shows the blocked app message that you will get in production mode if you run an unsigned or unallowed application such as Visio Viewer in your setup.

Figure 3-6. *Blocked app message*

If you choose to integrate a new application to be signed and allowed by the WDAC policy, you can merge the auditscan.xml file with initialscan.xml file using the Merge-CIPolicy command.

Intune Settings

The Code Integrity policy can be deployed from Intune through Open Mobile Alliance Uniform Resource Identifier (OMA-URI) settings:

1. Intune - Device Configuration - Profile - Create Profile
2. Platform - Windows 10 & Later, Profile Type - Custom

As shown in Figure 3-7, I am using the AppLocker CSP (configuration service provider) in the OMA-URI setting. The path for the Open Mobile Alliance Uniform Resource Identifier (OMA-URI) setting is:

`./Vendor/MSFT/AppLocker/EnterpriseDataProtection/Grouping/CodeIntegrity`

We need to ensure that the data type is a Base64 encoded blob. You can use the `certutil-encode` command line to convert the p7b file to Base64:

`certutil -encode WinSiPolicy.p7b WinSiPolicy.cer`

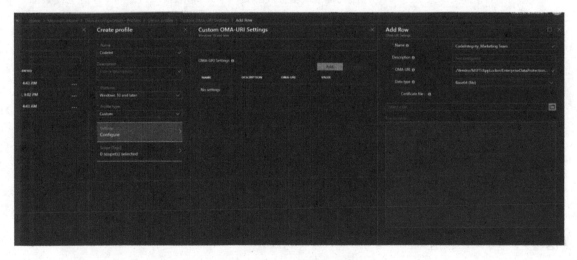

Figure 3-7. AppLocker CSP in the OMA-URI setting

SCCM Current Branch

Let's look at the SCCM settings for enabling WDAC. WDAC is still a prerelease feature in most versions of SCCM and you have to turn on pre-release features to enable the WDAC option. We can do this by going to "Administration," "Overview," "Updates and Servicing," and "Features." Then turn on the "Windows Defender Application Control" prerelease feature as shown in Figure 3-8.

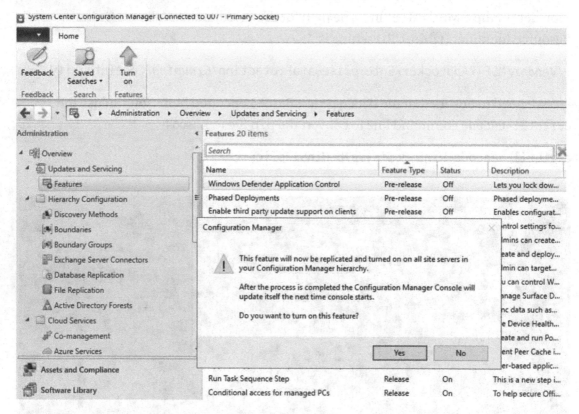

Figure 3-8. *Turning on the SCCM WDAC feature*

Now when you go back to "Assets & Compliance"/"Endpoint Protection," you will see the WDAC policy as well (Figure 3-9). Right click and create a new one.

You can choose to restart the system once the policy has been enabled. Enforcement mode and audit mode are both available.

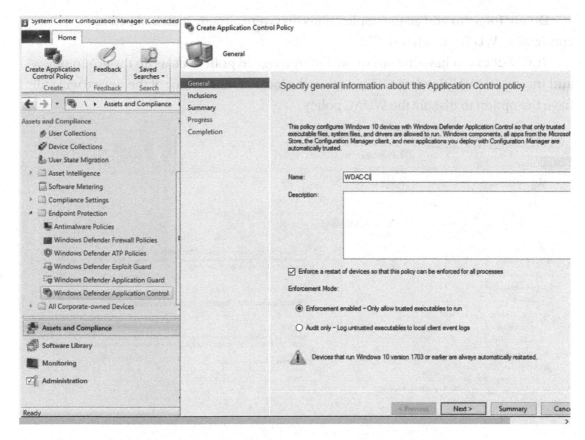

Figure 3-9. *Creating a new WDAC policy in SCCM*

In the next step, shown in Figure 3-10, we will add all the files and folders we want to be identified as part of our organization's policy (trusted files or folders), especially if they can't be deployed from SCCM. SCCM is recognized as a managed installer once the WDAC policy gets enabled and the software automatically deployed from SCCM is trusted. We can also choose to authorize the trusted software of Microsoft ISG, which will help with the cloud scenario, too. However, it would be ideal to use ISG in our second scenario as well, where we don't create a separate policy, golden image, or managed installer.

Once the policy is created, we can target it to the collections.

Note   SCCM uses the AppLocker policy to be set up as the managed installer. However, all the other policies are enforced through WDAC itself.

Do not forget to add all the applications that were already installed before configuring WDAC through SCCM.

SCCM does not have the option to deploy a signed policy yet, as do the group policy and Intune OMA-URI policies. Due to this, the local administrator of the device will still have the option to disable the WDAC policy.

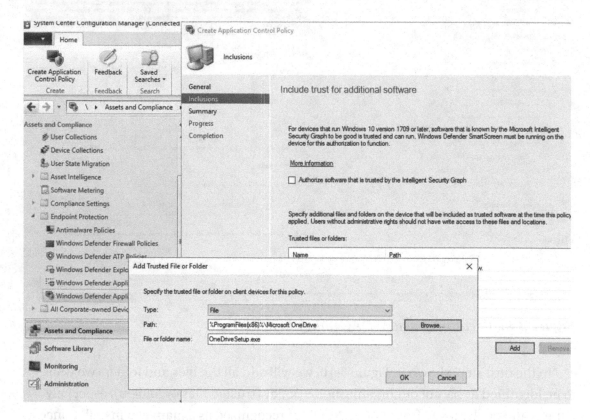

Figure 3-10. *Adding trusted files or folders*

We have now learned quite a few of the uses of WDAC for an organization wishing to exert control over its devices and distribute centralized policies to an entire organization, or to decentralize and multiply the policies and apply them to multiple collections, Organizational Unit (OU), and so forth.

Cloud Scenario

Next, how about a cloud-born organization or a hybrid company that no longer relies heavily on its on-premise technology? In such cases, an Azure AD–joined device can utilize the appropriate policies from Intune. We have already looked at Microsoft ISG in detail in Chapter 1. We will now see how to use it for the WDAC security policy that will be implemented on devices.

As simple as it looks, Intune lets me put the WDAC policy in enforcement or audit mode and choose to trust the Universal Windows Apps, Windows components, and reputable apps as defined by ISG.

Once the policy is created, it can be easily deployed to groups. This is best for MDM-joined devices.

The code integrity policy can be deployed from Intune through the OMA-URI settings as follows:

> Intune Portal-Device Configuration- Profile -Create Profile.
> Platform - Windows 10 & Later, Profile Type -Endpoint Protection-
> Windows Defender Application Control - Application Control
> Code integrity- Enforce/Audit

Be sure to choose to trust apps with a good reputation. This way, you can guarantee that the ISG ensures that only trusted apps are allowed to be executed.

So far, we have seen:

- the scenarios WDAC can be applied to
- the different ways to create code integrity policies
- the options available to deploy these policies

How about the devices? Do they need to have certain hardware features enabled as well?

Hardware Requirements for WDAC and WDEG

Device Guard was split into two features, WDAC and WDEG, mainly so that the setup of these features could be clarified separately. The device itself can be challenging for some organizations that are still running old hardware. It is important for these organizations to know that WDAC does not have any explicit hardware requirements for the devices it will be installed on. But that does not mean that the devices' hardware will have no significance. For companies that have invested or are about to invest in new devices, it might be a good idea to choose components that will promote device security.

WDAC with HyperVisor Code Integrity (HVCI) turned on will benefit from increased kernel memory protections. The Kernel Mode Code Integrity checks occur in virtualization-based security, or VBS, and the User Mode Code Integrity checks run in kernel, too. This protects the device from kernel memory exploits.

WDEG (whose implementation we will learn about shortly) requires some of these hardware features to be turned on:

- CPU virtualization extensions (Intel VT-x or AMD-V)

- Second-Level Address Translation (SLAT)

- input-output memory management units (IOMMU)

The CPU virtualization extensions and SLAT enable the code integrity service to run alongside the kernel in a protected HyperVisor container (as part of VBS).

Note   OEMs should definitely make note of these hardware features, as they can inherently enhance the security of the device when the device is being sold to enterprises.

WDEG leverages VBS to isolate the process that performs integrity validation and authorization of kernel mode codes.

Here are some of the requirements for WDEG:

- secure boot

- Trusted Platform Module (TPM)

- UEFI (Unified Extensible Firmware Interface)

- VBS

To ensure that all the requirements are met, Microsoft has released the Device Guard and Credential Guard hardware readiness tool.

The following is an example of running it on a device to ensure that the features are turned on and, if they are not, enabling them.

```
PS C:\Users\valaksh\Desktop\dgreadiness_v3.6> .\DG_Readiness_Tool_v3.6.ps1
###########################################################################
Readiness Tool Version 3.4 Release.
Tool to check if your device is capable to run Device Guard and Credential
Guard.
###########################################################################
How to read the output:
 1. Red Errors: Basic things are missing that will prevent enabling and
 using DG/CG
 2. Yellow Warnings: This device can be used to enable and use DG/CG, but
 additional security benefits will be absent. To learn more please go
 through: https://aka.ms/dgwhcr
 3. Green Messages: This device is fully compliant with DG/CG requirements

###########################################################################
Hardware requirements for enabling Device Guard and Credential Guard
 1. Hardware: Recent hardware that supports virtualization extension with SLAT
###########################################################################

Usage: DG_Readiness.ps1 -[Capable/Ready/Enable/Disable/Clear] -[DG/CG/HVCI] -
[AutoReboot] -Path
Log file with details is found here: C:\DGLogs

To Enable DG/CG. If you have a custom SIPolicy.p7b then use the -Path
parameter else the hardcoded default policy is used
Usage: DG_Readiness.ps1 -Enable OR DG_Readiness.ps1 -Enable -Path <full
path to the SIPolicy.p7b>

To Enable only HVCI
Usage: DG_Readiness.ps1 -Enable -HVCI

To Enable only CG
Usage: DG_Readiness.ps1 -Enable -CG

To Verify if DG/CG is enabled
Usage: DG_Readiness.ps1 -Ready

To Disable DG/CG.
Usage: DG_Readiness.ps1 -Disable
```

```
To Verify if DG/CG is disabled
Usage: DG_Readiness.ps1 -Ready

To Verify if this device is DG/CG Capable
Usage: DG_Readiness.ps1 -Capable
To Verify if this device is HVCI Capable
Usage: DG_Readiness.ps1 -Capable -HVCI
To Auto reboot with each option
Usage: DG_Readiness.ps1 -[Capable/Enable/Disable] -AutoReboot
############################################################################
Readiness Tool with '-capable' is run the following RegKey values are set:
HKEY_LOCAL_MACHINE\SYSTEM\CurrentControlSet\Control\DeviceGuard\Capabilities
CG_Capable
DG_Capable
HVCI_Capable
Value 0 = not possible to enable DG/CG/HVCI on this device
Value 1 = not fully compatible but has sufficient firmware/hardware/
software features to enable DG/CG/HVCI
Value 2 = fully compatible for DG/CG/HVCI
############################################################################
```

Now run the following:

```
DG_Readiness_Tool_v3.6.ps1 -capable
```

This checks if the device is capable of running both Device Guard and Credential Guard. This command line also requires that you reboot the system and execute the same command again.

The second executed command line after the reboot gives us information about all the features required to run Device Guard and Credential Guard.

The listing above provides information about all the command lines that are available.

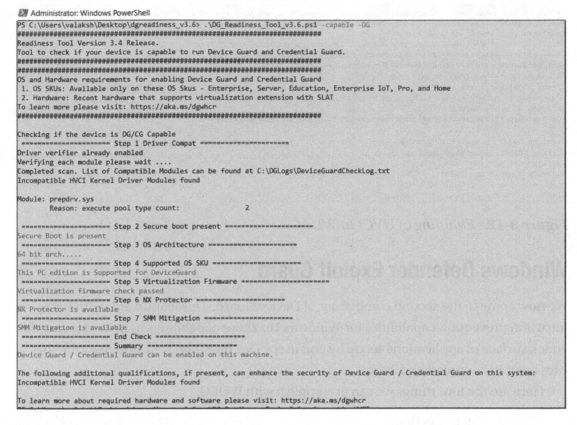

```
Administrator: Windows PowerShell
PS C:\Users\valaksh\Desktop\dgreadiness_v3.6> .\DG_Readiness_Tool_v3.6.ps1 -capable -DG
####################################################################
Readiness Tool Version 3.4 Release.
Tool to check if your device is capable to run Device Guard and Credential Guard.
####################################################################
####################################################################
OS and Hardware requirements for enabling Device Guard and Credential Guard
  1. OS SKUs: Available only on these OS Skus - Enterprise, Server, Education, Enterprise IoT, Pro, and Home
  2. Hardware: Recent hardware that supports virtualization extension with SLAT
To learn more please visit: https://aka.ms/dgwhcr
####################################################################

Checking if the device is DG/CG Capable
====================== Step 1 Driver Compat ======================
Driver verifier already enabled
Verifying each module please wait ....
Completed scan. List of Compatible Modules can be found at C:\DGLogs\DeviceGuardCheckLog.txt
Incompatible HVCI Kernel Driver Modules found

Module: prepdrv.sys
        Reason: execute pool type count:               2

====================== Step 2 Secure boot present ======================
Secure Boot is present
====================== Step 3 OS Architecture ======================
64 bit arch.....
====================== Step 4 Supported OS SKU ======================
This PC edition is Supported for DeviceGuard
====================== Step 5 Virtualization Firmware ======================
Virtualization firmware check passed
====================== Step 6 NX Protector ======================
NX Protector is available
====================== Step 7 SMM Mitigation ======================
SMM Mitigation is available
====================== End Check ======================
====================== Summary ======================
Device Guard / Credential Guard can be enabled on this machine.

The following additional qualifications, if present, can enhance the security of Device Guard / Credential Guard on this system:
Incompatible HVCI Kernel Driver Modules found

To learn more about required hardware and software please visit: https://aka.ms/dgwhcr
```

Figure 3-11. *WDAC hardware requirements*

Turning on HVCI becomes vital to leverage hardware/HyperVisor-based security. Figure 3-12 shows the enabling of HVCI with the command line.

```
PS C:\Users\valaksh\Desktop\dgreadiness_v3.6> .\DG_Readiness_Tool_v3.6.ps1 -enable HVCI
#########################################################################
Readiness Tool Version 3.4 Release.
Tool to check if your device is capable to run Device Guard and Credential Guard.
#########################################################################
#########################################################################
OS and Hardware requirements for enabling Device Guard and Credential Guard
 1. OS SKUs: Available only on these OS Skus - Enterprise, Server, Education, Enterprise IoT, Pro, and Home
 2. Hardware: Recent hardware that supports virtualization extension with SLAT
To learn more please visit: https://aka.ms/dgwhcr
#########################################################################

Enabling Device Guard and Credential Guard
Setting RegKeys to enable DG/CG
Copying user provided SIpolicy.p7b
Enabling Hyper-V and IOMMU
Enabling Hyper-V and IOMMU successful
Please reboot the machine, for settings to be applied.
```

Figure 3-12. *Enabling of HVCI in WDAC*

Windows Defender Exploit Guard

We now come to the second component of Device Guard. This feature aids with host intrusion prevention capabilities for Windows 10. These capabilities help in reducing the attack surface of applications set up by end users. Our intention is to stop malware that uses exploits to spread and infect.

Here are the four things we can accomplish with WDEG:

- exploit protection
- attack surface reduction rules
- network protection
- controlled folder access

Exploit Protection

Exploit mitigation techniques can be applied on both operating systems and individual apps. They work well with third-party antivirus solutions as well as with Windows Defender Antivirus.

There are multiple options for mitigation within exploit protection. And it can be used for system-level settings as done in the following screenshots. Note that audit mode is available for app-only mitigations.

As shown in Figure 3-13, go to the Windows Defender Security Center/"Windows Security" app, then "App & Browser Control," "Exploit protection," and "System settings."

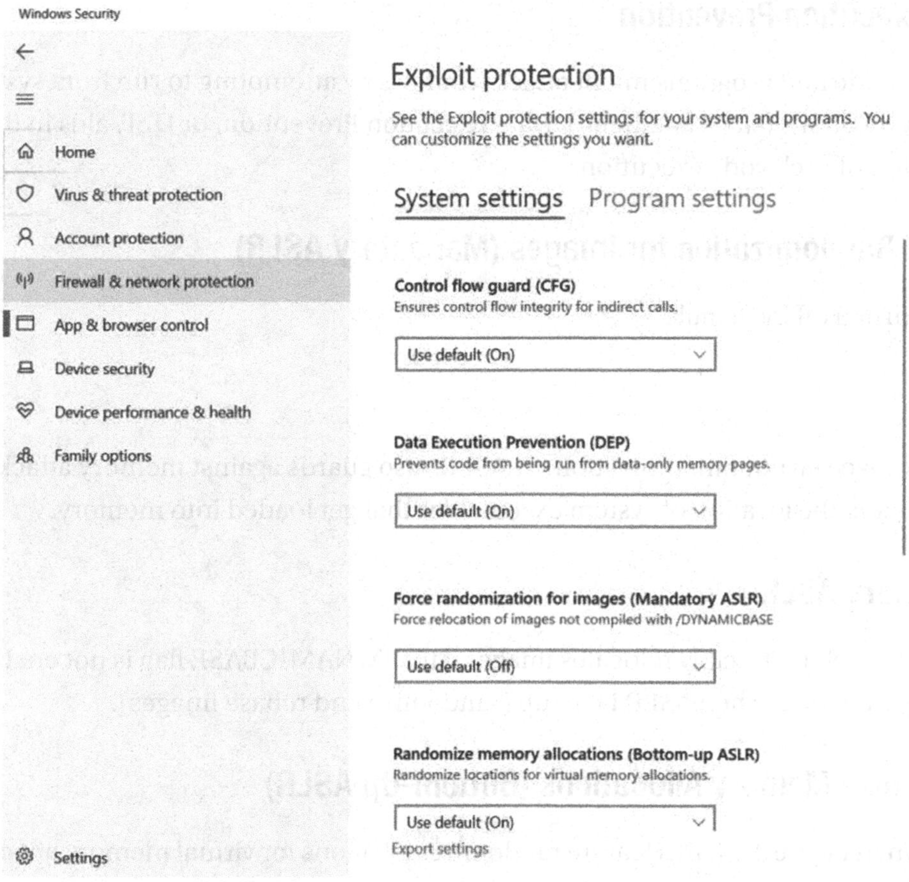

Figure 3-13. *Setting up exploit protection in Windows Security*

Let's go through these steps one at a time.

Control Flow Guard

We define tight restrictions on where an app can execute code from. This ensures code integrity for indirect calls for the execution of code, thus making it hard for exploits to execute arbitrary code through vulnerabilities like buffer overflow.

With Windows 10 (versions 1703 and above), the Windows kernel gets compiled with Control Flow Guard, or CFG, and uses HyperVisor to do so. This prevents malicious kernel code from overwriting a CFG bitmap.

Data Execution Prevention

Harmful code and programs might attack windows by attempting to run from system memory locations (stack and heap). Data Execution Prevention, or DEP, aids in the prevention of such code execution.

Forced Randomization for images (Mandatory ASLR)

This is turned off by default.

ASLR

Address space layout randomization, or ASLR, also guards against memory attacks by randomizing the location of system executables that get loaded into memory.

Mandatory ASLR

Mandatory ASLFR forcibly relocates images if the DYNAMICBASE flag is not enabled. The flag is enabled when ASLR is set up (randomize and rebase images).

Randomize Memory Allocations (Bottom-Up ASLR)

As shown in Figure 3-14, this feature randomizes locations for virtual memory allocations and searches for free regions for execution from the bottom of the address space.

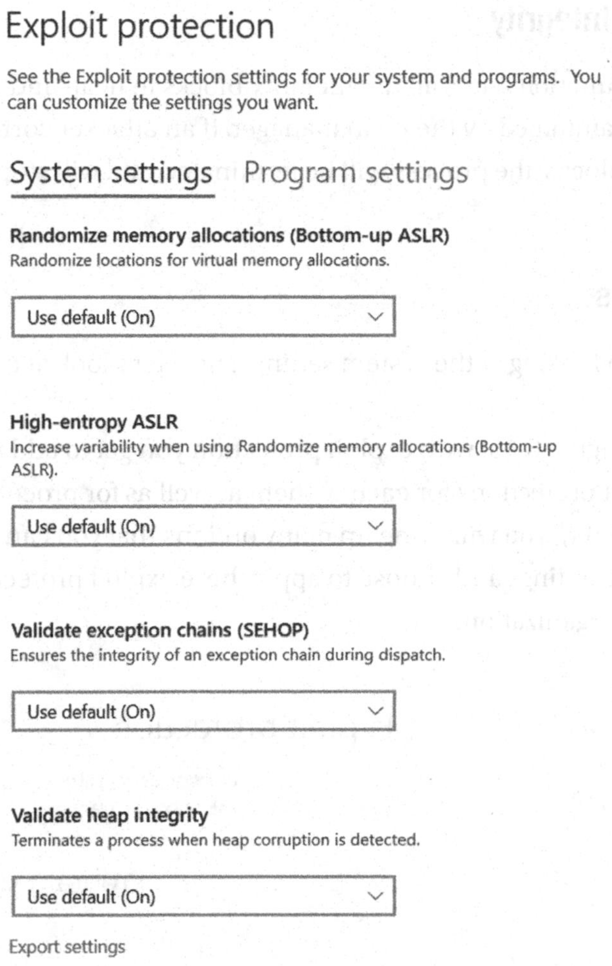

Exploit protection

See the Exploit protection settings for your system and programs. You can customize the settings you want.

System settings   Program settings

Randomize memory allocations (Bottom-up ASLR)
Randomize locations for virtual memory allocations.

```
Use default (On)                          ⌄
```

High-entropy ASLR
Increase variability when using Randomize memory allocations (Bottom-up ASLR).

```
Use default (On)                          ⌄
```

Validate exception chains (SEHOP)
Ensures the integrity of an exception chain during dispatch.

```
Use default (On)                          ⌄
```

Validate heap integrity
Terminates a process when heap corruption is detected.

```
Use default (On)                          ⌄
```

Export settings

Figure 3-14. *"Randomize memory allocations" setting*

High-Entropy ASLR

The randomization of address space becomes more effective when more entropy is present in random offsets. It is applicable for 64-bit processes.

Validate Exception Chains (Structured Exception Handler Overwrite Protection)

Attackers are known to exploit the Structured Exception Handler (SEH) overwrite exploitation technique. They usually target browser-based vulnerabilities.

Validating Heap Integrity

The HeapValidate function scans all the memory blocks in heap and validates that they are consistent as maintained by the heap manager. If an attacker corrupts or changes the heap memory blocks, the process will be terminated and will stop him or her from proceeding further.

Program Settings

So far we have been looking at the system settings; now let's look at exploit protection in program settings.

As pictured in Figure 3-15, with exploit protection you get to add individual applications and set protections for each of them as well as for processes.

When you hit "Edit," you will bring up many options that you can tweak. You can also override the default settings and choose to apply these exploit protections in audit mode if required by your organization.

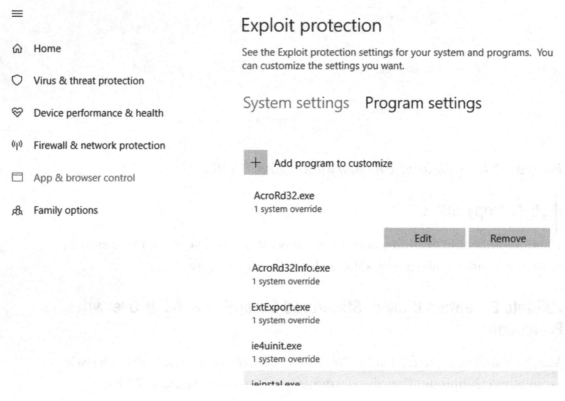

Figure 3-15. *"Exploit protection" page*

Figure 3-16 shows the settings for exploit protection. Although only a few options are pictured, we can also choose the behavior of other mitigation components such as CFG, DEP, and many more.

Note   Arbitrary Code Guard prohibits remote code execution and kernel code injections when enabled. WannaCry ransomware used these methods to attack devices. With ACG enabled, unreliable code execution can be averted.

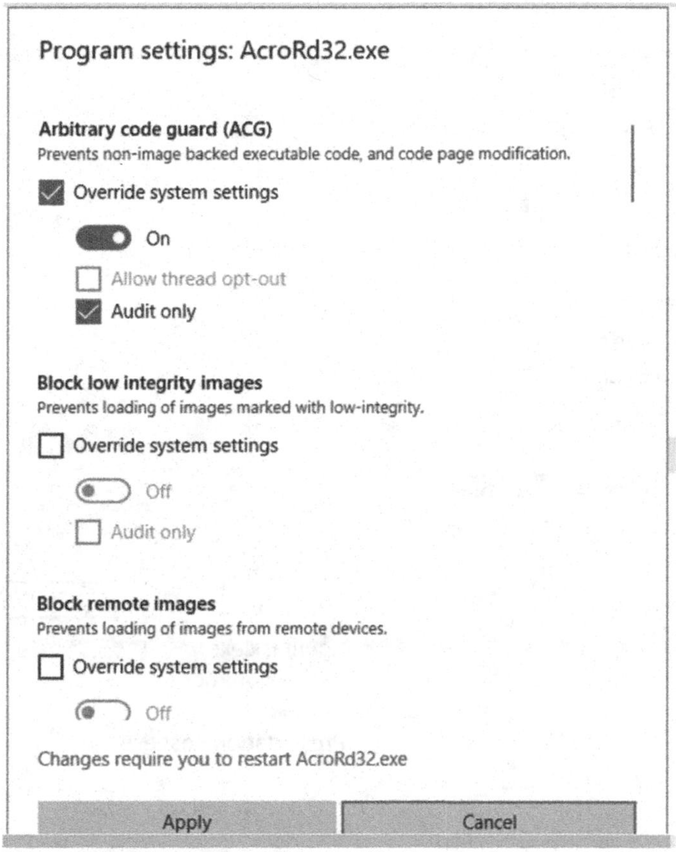

Program settings: AcroRd32.exe

Arbitrary code guard (ACG)
Prevents non-image backed executable code, and code page modification.
☑ Override system settings
　　⬤ On
　　☐ Allow thread opt-out
　　☑ Audit only

Block low integrity images
Prevents loading of images marked with low-integrity.
☐ Override system settings
　　⬤ Off
　　☐ Audit only

Block remote images
Prevents loading of images from remote devices.
☐ Override system settings
　　⬤ Off

Changes require you to restart AcroRd32.exe

Apply	Cancel

Figure 3-16. *Exploit protection settings*

I am not including topics involved with Enhanced Mitigation Experience Toolkit (EMET), as it does not work with Windows 10, version 1709.

The settings we have been looking at are all configured on a single system. Now let's see the way to deploy them across an organization. To do so, once all the settings have been configured, start by clicking the "Export setting" option on the Windows Security app to export the XML file, as shown in Figure 3-17.

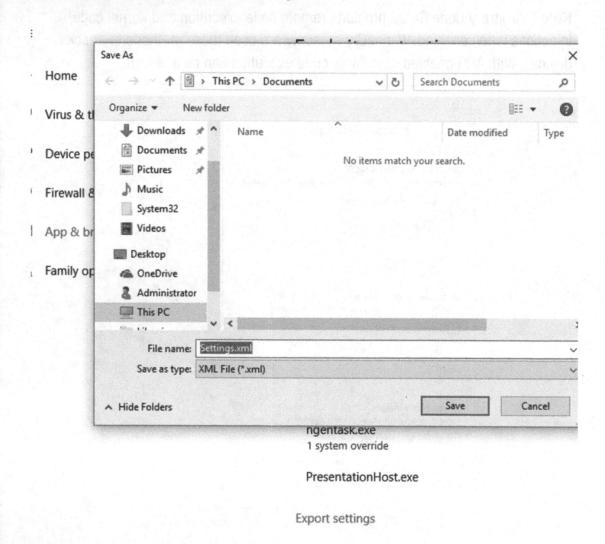

Figure 3-17.   *Exporting the XML file*

Then, you can use group policies to deploy onto multiple devices, at the OU level, or in other ways. To do so, as shown in Figure 3-18, go to "gpedit," "Computer configuration," then click "Administrative templates," "Windows components," "Windows Defender Exploit Guard," and "Exploit Protection,"

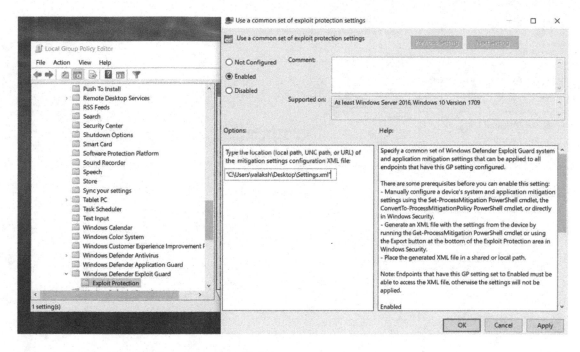

Figure 3-18. *Deploying group policies*

From Intune in the Azure portal, go to "Device configuration," "Profiles," "Create new profile for Windows 10 & Endpoint Protection," "Windows Defender Exploit Guard," and "Exploit protection."

Add the XML file exported from your Windows 10 system.

Here's the way to deploy the same policy from SCCM. As shown in Figure 3-19, in the SCCM Console, go to "Assets&Compliance," "Endpoint Protection," "Windows Defender Exploit Guard," then "Create new policy." I've selected only "Exploit Protection" for this example, but in a real-world scenario where you are applying the policy organization-wide, you can also have attack surface reduction, controlled folder access, network protection, and so on.

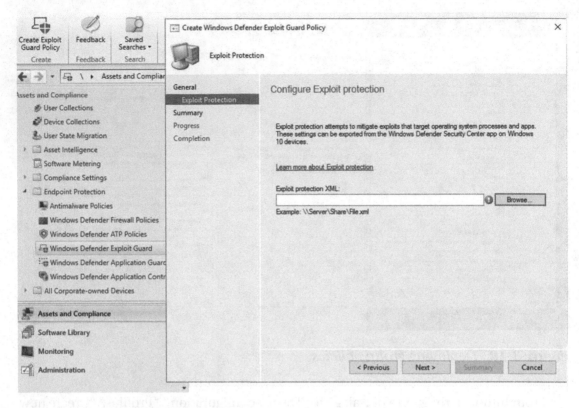

Figure 3-19. *Deploying from SCCM*

Note   Some of these exploit mitigation techniques might cause compatibility issues with certain applications. It is highly recommended that you thoroughly test these policies before widely deploying them in any organization.

Attack Surface Reduction Rules

The usual attack vectors we see are Office, script, mail-based malware, and so on. To stop these vectors, we can use attack surface reduction rules along with WDAV.

This is a Windows 10 Enterprise E5 or Microsoft 365 Enterprise E5 feature and works very closely with Windows Defender ATP (our post-breach solution).

Attack surface reduction rules can be applied in these scenarios:

- Office apps and web mail have executable files and scripts that attempt to download malicious files

- obfuscated scripts

- anomalous behavior from applications and the like

Let's learn more about these settings from the policies under the Intune console as shown in Figure 3-20.

To get there, go to:

- Intune Portal-Device Configuration- Profile -Create Profile.

- Platform - Windows 10 & Later & Profile Type - Windows Defender Exploit Guard - Attack Surface Reduction.

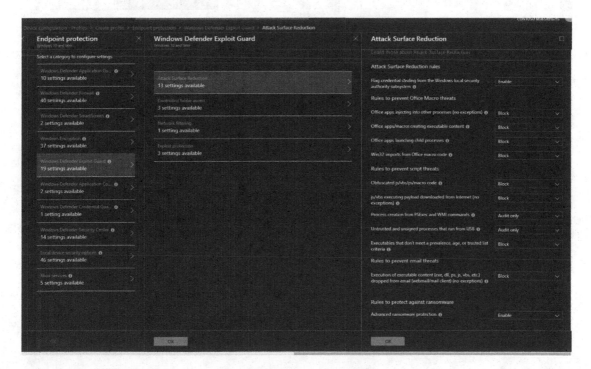

Figure 3-20. *Attack surface reduction rules on Intune*

To set up attack surface reduction rules in group policy, go to gpedit-Computer configuration and click Administrative templates- Windows components - Windows Defender antivirus-Windows Defender Exploit Guard & attack surface reduction.

The difference between Intune/SCCM and group policy is that in group policy each rule has a GUID (global unique identifier) format, the set of which you can find clearly documented in the Microsoft attack surface reduction rules. For example, as shown in Figure 3-21, the GUID to block executable content from email clients and web mail is `be9ba2d9-53ea-4cdc-84e5-9B1eeee46550`.

The values used also depict the action selected for the rule as follows:

- *Value 0*: disable

- *Value 1*: block

- *Value 2*: use audit mode

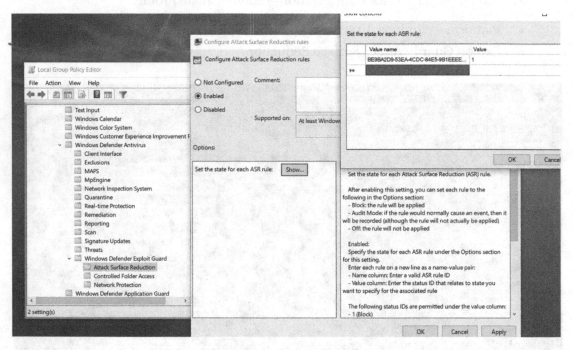

Figure 3-21. *GUID for an attack surface reduction rule shown in group policy*

Figure 3-22 shows the same setting in SCCM.

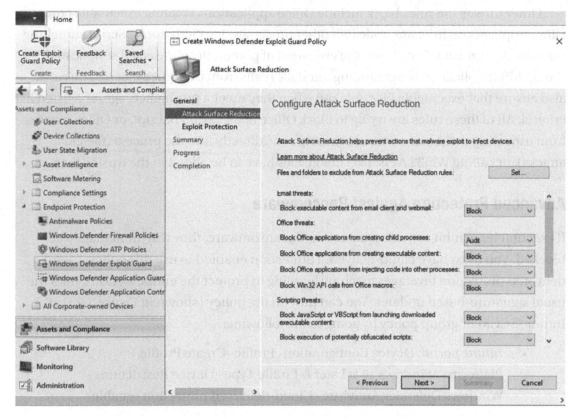

Figure 3-22. *SCCM setting for attack surface reduction rules*

Now let's look into these policies more precisely to understand how attack surface reduction rules help keep anomalous files and executables at bay.

Executable Content from Email Clients and Web Mail

Attack surface reduction rules block executable files such as .exe, .msi, .scr, .dll, and so on. They also block scripts files such as .ps and .vbs from getting executed from an email client such as Outlook, Outlook Web App (OWA), and Gmail.

Office and Scripting Threats

Another threat the attack surface reduction rules block is Office applications creating child processes. Creating a child process is a typical malware behavior. It might run a macro and, secretly in the background, run a command line to create a backdoor. The rules don't allow such processes to be created in Word, Excel, PowerPoint, OneNote, and Access (not applicable for Outlook).

Other threats the rules block include Office applications creating executable content; Office applications injecting code into other processes; JavaScript or VBScript launching downloaded executable content; the execution of potentially obfuscated scripts; and Win32 API (application programming interface) calls from the Office macro. The rules also ensure that executable files only run when they meet a prevalence, age, or trusted list criteria. All of these rules are trying to block Office apps, Java/VBScript, or Office macros from executing malicious content, injecting code directly into the process (fileless attacks), or calling Win32 APIs. Executable files have to be added in the trusted list.

Advanced Protection Against Ransomware

If executables exhibit activities that resemble ransomware, they will immediately be blocked. You must have cloud-delivered protection enabled to use this policy. Cloud-delivered protection leverages machine learning to protect the endpoint faster than the usual signature-based updates. You can turn on the policy (shown in Figure 3-23) at Intune/SCCM or group policy by going to the following:

- *Intune portal*: Device Configuration- Profile -Create Profile. Platform - Windows 10 & Later & Profile Type- Device Restrictions - Windows Defender Antivirus - Cloud-delivered protection- enable

- *Group policy to enable cloud-delivered protection*: gpedit-Computer configuration and click Administrative templates- Windows components - Windows defender antivirus- MAPS- Join Microsoft MAPS

For the cloud-enabled protection to apply, the policy will need to be at least basic or advanced (though the two mean the same thing in the Windows 10 OS; the differences only apply to the older OSs).

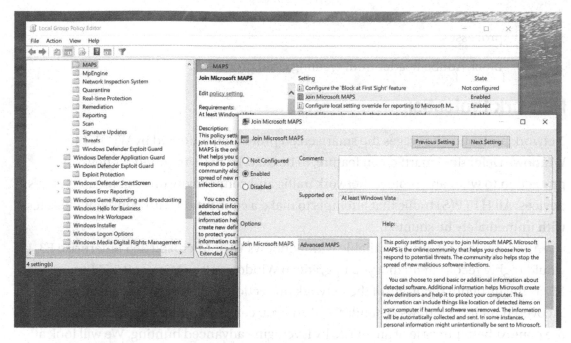

Figure 3-23. *Cloud-delivered group policy protection against ransomware*

Credential Stealing from the Windows Local Security Authority Subsystem (lsass.exe)

Tools such as Mimikatz can steal clear-text passwords and NTLM (Windows New Technology Lan Manager) hashes from LSASSs (Local Security Subsystem Services). Advanced Protection Against Ransomware will aid us in prohibiting credential stealing. This is especially helpful in organizations that are not able to deploy Credential Guard.

Other Processes

Finally, all the following rules can assist in blocking processes in known/trusted tools, such as PsExec and Windows Management Instrumentation, or WMI (which can be applied from Intune/GP but not from SCCM as it will block SCCM WMI commands); USB; Outlook; and Adobe Reader.

- Block process creations originating from PSExec and WMI commands.

- Block untrusted and unsigned processes that run from USB.

- Block Office communication application from creating child processes.

- Block Adobe Reader from creating child processes.

Network Protection

Network protection leverages the smartscreen protection rendered by WDAV (a Windows Defender SmartScreen feature, to be exact). This is required for network protection to work and protects network traffic and connectivity on your organization's devices. All HTTP(S) traffic that attempts to make a connection with nonreputable sites with immediately be shunted.

Although this feature is available with Windows 10 or Microsoft 365 Enterprise E3, I would highly recommend that you upgrade to Windows 10 or Microsoft 365 Enterprise E5, as the in-depth reporting of the network protection feature with the newer systems is covered under Windows Defender ATP and you can create queries to understand the context better in case of an attack, by leveraging advanced hunting. We will look at Windows Defender ATP in detail later in the chapter.

We also get audit mode and production(block) mode with network protection.

To get started enabling network protection, as in Figure 3-24, we can use group policy/MDM-Intune or even PowerShell scripts.

From group policy editor:

1. Go to gpedit-Computer configuration and click Administrative templates- Windows components - Windows defender antivirus- Windows Defender Exploit Guard - Network Protection - "Prevent users & apps from accessing dangerous websites."

2. We are given the options of "Block," "Disable (Default)," and "Audit Mode."

3. If you would like to test this feature and not impact the users during the testing phase, you can stay in audit mode.

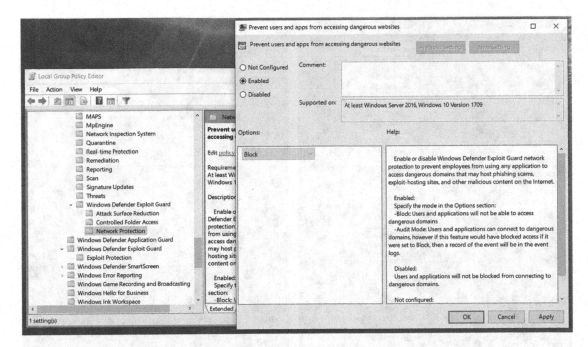

Figure 3-24. *Turning on network protection in group policy*

To turn on network protection in Intune, as shown in Figure 3-25, use these settings:

- Intune Portal-Device Configuration- Profile -Create Profile

- Platform - Windows 10 & Later

- Profile Type - Device Restrictions - Windows Defender Smart Screen - malicious site access - Block

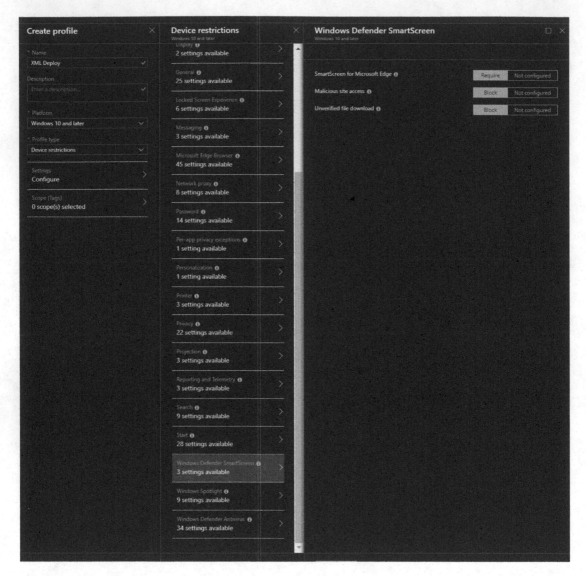

Figure 3-25. *Turning on network protection in Intune*

As shown in Figure 3-26, here's how to enable network protection in SCCM:

- SCCM Console - Assets & Compliance - Endpoint Protection - Windows Defender Exploit Guard - Network Protection - Block

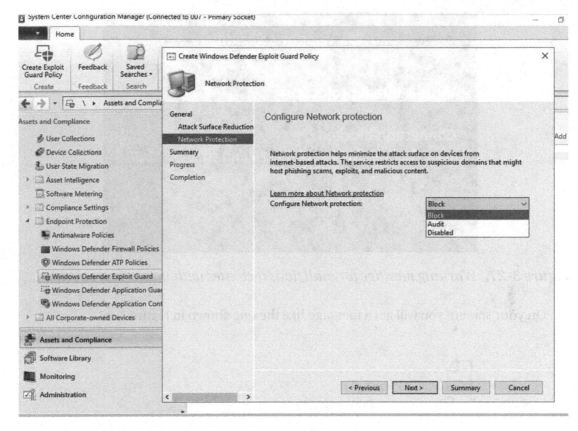

Figure 3-26. *Turning on network protection in SCCM*

Once you have implemented the network protection settings on your devices, you can test them on this web site:

https://smartscreentestratings2.net/

After the policy is enforced, your system will automatically sense malicious sites and block your connection to them, giving you the message "Connection blocked," as shown in Figure 3-27.

Figure 3-27. *Warning message for malicious web sites with network protection*

On your screen, you will get a message like the one shown in Figure 3-28.

This site can't provide a secure connection

smartscreentestratings2.net uses an unsupported protocol.

ERR_SSL_VERSION_OR_CIPHER_MISMATCH

Details

Figure 3-28. *Screen that appears when you try to access malicious web sites*

If you choose to evaluate network protection in audit mode, the web site will not be blocked but an event will be generated relating to it in the event viewer:

- Under Event Viewer - Applications & Service Logs - Microsoft
  -Windows - Security-Mitigations - Kernel Mode

Event ID 10 is used for block mode as shown in Figure 3-29. Ideally you should see Event ID 9 in audit mode.

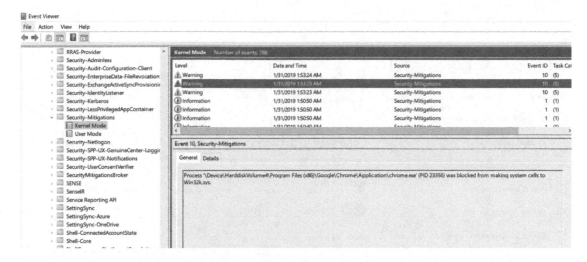

Figure 3-29. *Network protection in block mode*

Controlled Folder Access

Malicious apps, including those installed by file-encrypting ransomware, try to change the key system files and folders. For this reason, we need to provide access to these files and folders in a very controlled way. This feature also requires the use of WDAV.

All apps (`.exe`, `.dll`, etc.) are tested by WDAV to see if they contain malicious files. Any malicious file that is detected will not be allowed to make changes to files and folders. This will make it very difficult for an attacker to ask for ransom through encrypting your files. We can enable controlled folder access from Security Center apps, MDM/Intune, group policy, SCCM, and more.

As in Figure 3-30, we can enable and customize controlled folder access in the Security Center/Windows Security app by doing the following:

1. Go to "Windows Security," "Virus & threat protection," "Ransomware protection," and turn on "Controlled folder access."

2. To customize the settings, click "Protected folders" and add the list of folders you want to protect.

3. If you would like to enable access to the controlled folder list for an application you trust, you can do so by clicking "Allow an app through Controlled folder access."

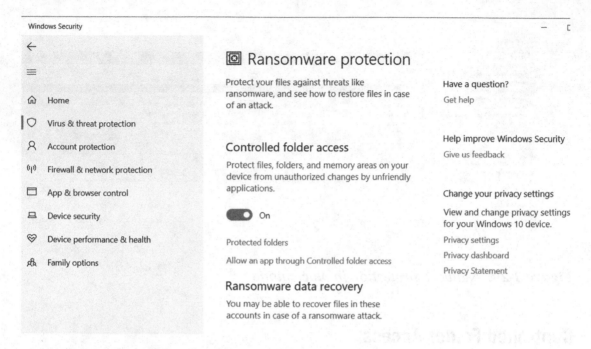

Figure 3-30. Enabling controlled folder access in the Windows Security app

We can establish these settings from group policy as well:

- Go to gpedit-Computer configuration and click Administrative templates- Windows components - Windows Defender antivirus- Windows Defender Exploit Guard - Controlled Folder Access - Configure Controlled folder access - Enabled

- We can block the access of these sensitive folders by selecting "Block." You can test this policy in audit mode.

- If you choose to block disk modification only, it will block attempts by untrusted apps to write disk sectors but not block the modification/ delection of data by untrusted apps.

- You can also choose to audit disk modification only. You can find event log alerts under applications and Services Logs ➤ Microsoft ➤ Windows ➤ Windows Defender ➤ Operational ➤ ID 1124 for attempts by untrusted apps to write disk sectors.

We can also enable controlled folder access from Intune by taking the following steps. We will be using OMA-URI policies here.

1. Intune Portal-Device Configuration- Profile -Create Profile. Platform - Windows 10 & Later & Profile Type - Custom - Add new policy - Give it a name

2. For OMA-URI policy, go to:

```
./Vendor/MSFT/Policy/Config/Defender/
EnableControlledFolderAccess
```

3. Value should be an integer that ranges from 0 to 2

   - Default (Disabled): 0

   - Block: 1

   - Audit mode: 2

4. To add protected folders, use this OMA-URI policy:

```
./Vendor/MSFT/Policy/Config/Defender/
ControlledFolderAccessProtectedFolders
```

Data Type is a string and the value will be the folders that are to be protected from unwarranted access. Multiple values can be separated by the "|" symbol.

To white list or give controlled folder access to trusted applications, we can use the following policy. The value type used again is a string. This step is not always necessary, as WDAV recognizes trusted apps automatically.

```
./Vendor/MSFT/Policy/Config/Defender/ControlledFolderAccessAllowedApplications
```

If SCCM is deployed in your organization, here is the setting to enable controlled folder access (in this case, I've chosen to block the access of any untrusted apps, as shown in Figure 3-31):

SCCM Console - Assets & Compliance - Endpoint Protection - Windows Defender Exploit Guard - Controlled Folder Access - Block

As you can see in the figure, we can also allow trusted apps to permit access to a protected folder.

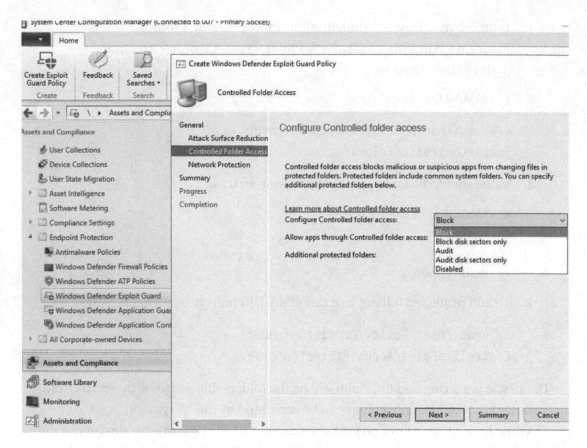

Figure 3-31. *Blocking controlled folder access from SCCM*

Windows Defender Application Guard

One of the original ideas behind introducing security features for Windows 10 was to make the attacker's playbook obsolete. The features are especially designed for Microsoft Edge (providing yet another reason to use the Edge browser) and Internet Explorer, and they leverage hardware isolation.

The concept here is simple: Instead of trying to catch up with the attacker, we are trying to isolate the browser using hardware isolation (i.e., opening the browser in an isolated Hyper-V–enabled container) and let the malicious code run its course. The attacker will never be able to gain access to the core kernel files/infect the OS and not be able to access internal network, either. When the user's task is completed (i.e., when he or she closes the Edge browser), traces of malware will be removed without infecting the OS.

Enterprise desktops, enterprise mobile laptops, BYOT (bring your own technology) devices, and personal devices are all capable of using Application Guard.

Some of the prerequisites to get WDAG up and running are:

- a 64-bit CPU

- CPU virtualization extensions (SLAT, Intel VT-x, or AMD-V for VBS)

- 8 GB of RAM

- 5 GB free

- IOMMU (highly recommended)

WDAG can be installed in:

- *Stand-alone mode*: The user will access the Edge browser in isolated mode, which is not managed by an administrator.

- *Enterprise managed mode*: The administrator defines the corporate boundaries and trusted domains, and the user will get redirected to open the browser in isolated mode/container if it is a nontrusted domain.

As shown in Figure 3-32, here's how to turn on WDAG for your users in stand-alone mode :

1. Turn on "Windows Defender Application Guard" from "Programs & Features" in Control Panel.

2. Reboot the system for it to function in hardware isolation mode.

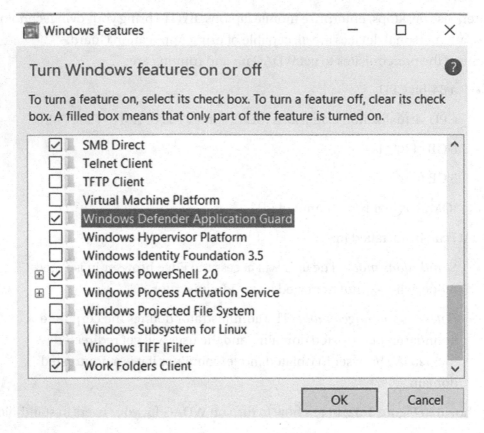

Figure 3-32.   Turning on Windows Defender Application Guard

3. Check your Edge browser in "More settings" and you will see "New Application Guard window" as shown in Figure 3-33.

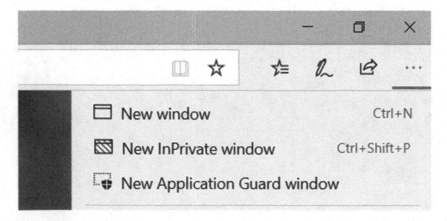

Figure 3-33.   WDAG for Edge browser

As shown in Figure 3-34, you will then see a message indicating a new Edge browser is being opened in Application Guard mode.

Figure 3-34. *Message about Edge opening in Application Guard mode*

Figure 3-35 shows how the protected browser will look in Edge.

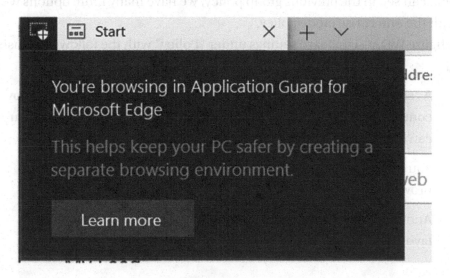

Figure 3-35. *Protected browser for Application Guard*

To install WDAG in enterprise managed mode:

1. Follow all the steps in the stand-alone mode.

2. Add the trusted list of domains in the group policy: Go to gpedit-Computer configuration and click Administrative templates-Network - Network Isolation. Enable the policy and indicate the domains you trust and are enterprise resources.

You also have another policy in the same location called "Domains characterized as both work and personal." Add any domains such as Bing that you trust and can be used for personal as well as business purposes.

Now it's time to turn on WDAG.

To do so, Go to gpedit-Computer configuration and click Administrative templates-Windows components - Windows defender application guard. Turn on WDAG in enterprise mode. You can choose to apply this setting to the Edge browser only, to Microsoft Office only, or to both.

Once these policies are enforced, the trusted and neutral sites will be opened in the regular Edge browser, while the untrusted sites will be opened in a WDAG enterprise mode–enabled browser.

As you can see in the previous group policy, we have many more options we can add along with the enterprise mode policy.

Configure WDAG clipboard settings under "Policy" with the following considerations in mind:

- As shown in Figure 3-36, I have chosen to allow the clipboard to copy content from the WDAG browser to the host, and not vice-versa. You can choose the setting that works best for your organization.

- You can set up a similar policy to allow or disable printing from the browser.

- Another setting allows you to maintain the data, such as cookies, favorites, and like, to use in the next or subsequent WDAG sessions.

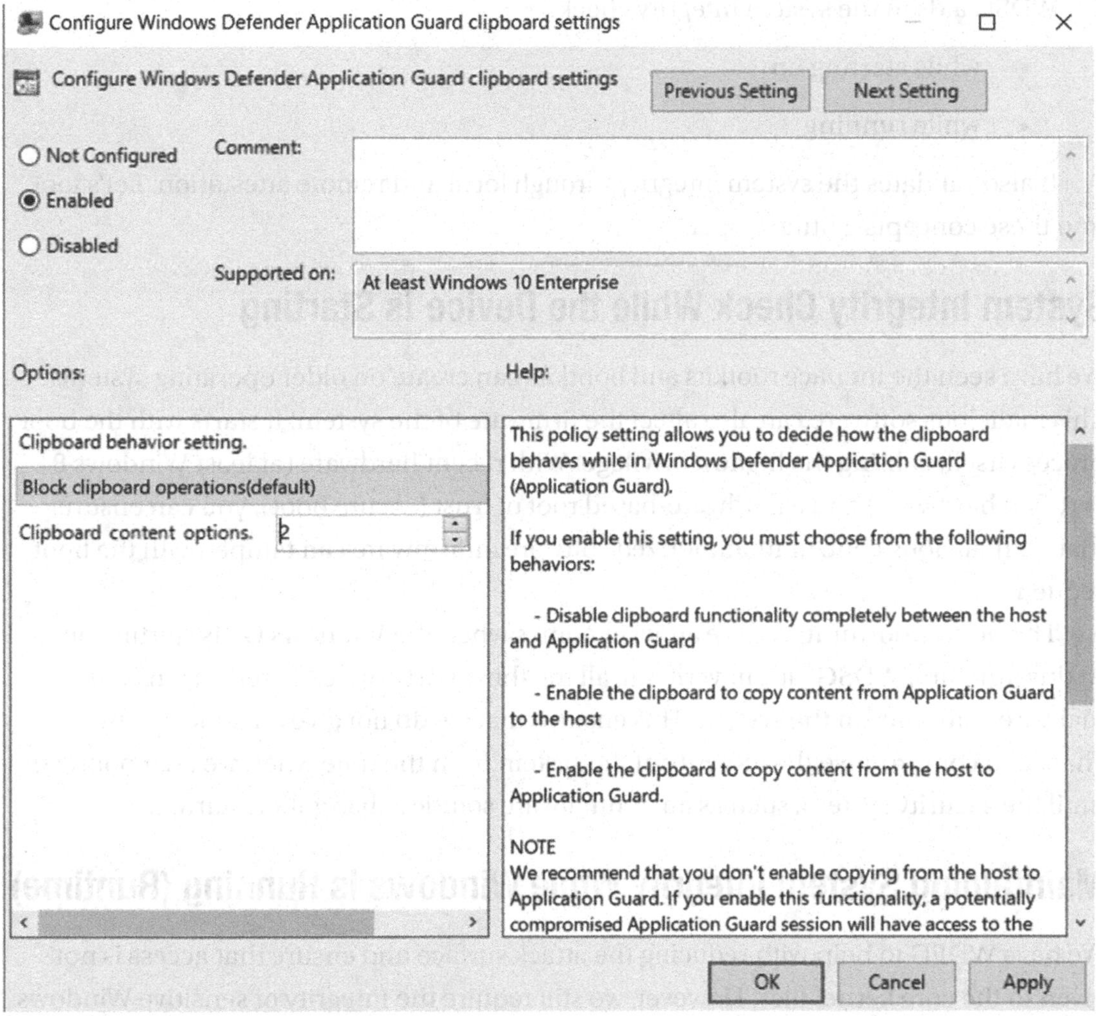

Figure 3-36. *Configuring WDAG clipboard settings*

Windows Defender System Guard

With the advent of Windows 10 and the security features that it brought along with it came a lot of resources that cannot be compromised, such as single sign-on tokens, Windows authentication stack, the virtual trusted platform module, Windows Hello biometric staff, and many more. WDSG was introduced to ensure system and resource integrity.

WDSG aids in the system integrity check:

- while starting up

- while running

It also validates the system integrity through local and remote attestation. Let's look into these concepts a little deeper.

System Integrity Check While the Device Is Starting

We have seen the menace rootkits and bootkits can create on older operating systems. This malicious software can also affect the firmware of the system. It starts with the boot process itself, gaining the highest privilege. With recent hardware (at least Windows 8–certified hardware) and a hardware-based root of trust (secure boot), you can ensure that no malicious code or unauthorized software or firmware can tamper with the boot sequence.

The next opportunity for the attacker comes when the Windows OS is starting up. At this juncture, WDSG aids in verifying all the third-party drivers after starting anti-malware solutions on the system. This ensures that we do not give an attacker any chance to compromise the integrity of the system from the time when we are booting up until the security system, such as an antimalware solution, has gotten started.

Maintaining System Integrity While Windows Is Running (Runtime)

We have WDEG to help with reducing the attack surface and ensure that access is not given to the core kernel files. However, we still require the integrity of sensitive Windows services such as Credential Guard, Device Guard, and the virtual trusted platform module (TPM) to be maintained even when the attacker gains the highest privileges in the system. We leverage VBS to ensure hardware isolation of these critical services for the system.

Validation of Platform Integrity (Runtime): Device Health Attestation

Adopting an assume breach mentality helps us validate the security services that have been implemented in an organization. WDSG aids in remote analysis of the device's integrity. TPM 2.0 takes integrity measurements by using WDSG. This data is hardware isolated and tamperfroof.

Measurements include checking the integrity of the device firmware, the hardware configuration state, and the Windows boot-related components. WDSG seals these data after the boot.

We can use SCCM/Intune for managing and collecting information if these data are changed, or if there is lack of integrity access to company resources can be blocked or denied.

Windows Defender Antivirus

We have all used WDAV at some point in time. This antimalware solution is a built-in feature in Windows 10 and Windows servers. Over the years, we have seen WDAV improve on various parameters, such as its protection score, performance score, and usability score. Instead of mentioning each and every detail, I would suggest visiting www.av-test.org/en/antivirus/business-windows-client/ to check the scores. AV-TEST is a third-party web site that compares all the antivirus products and gives them scores based on many parameters.

WDAV comprises cloud-delivered protection for near-instant detection, getting the information for detection from leveraging machine learning and ISG. (But we already know this, don't we? We read about it while reviewing the setup of the attack surface reduction rules. We saw that WDAV is required to turn on cloud-delivered protection for advanced protection against ransomware.)

We have seen so far that we can turn on cloud-delivered protection with various tools such as group policy, MDM/Intune, and SCCM. Now, let's get into finding out what always-on scanning means. The monitoring of files, processes, behaviors, and other heuristics provides real-time protection. It looks out for malicious activities, such as processes making unusual changes to files or adding start-up registry keys (e.g., Run and RunOnce keys) and start-up locations.

As shown in Figure 3-37, to enable always-on scanning through group policy:

- Go to gpedit-Computer configuration and click Administrative templates- Windows components - Windows defender antivirus- Real-time Protection.

Real-time protection helps monitor files (e.g., file writes and edits) and program activities (e.g., if the program is opened or if a child program is called). It also helps scan all files and apps (as does the smartscreen filter, which already scans files before and while downloading). We can also turn on process scanning and look for any suspicious changes in the processes. Behavior monitoring and raw-volume write notifications help access files and registries and process changes.

Turning on the heuristics will aid in immediately suppressing malware and providing alerts. This is done in the "Scan" section.

We also have policies to choose the priority of the defender service (helps in lightweight deployments).

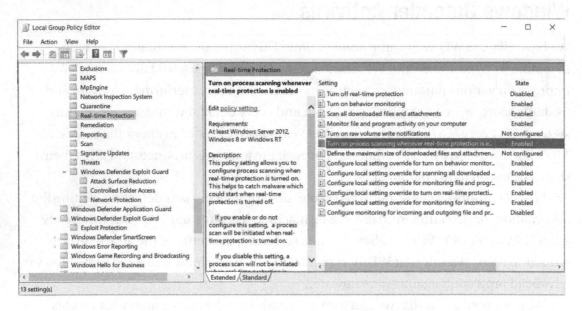

Figure 3-37. *Enabling process scanning with real-time protection*

The same can be achieved from Intune, as shown in Figure 3-38.

- Intune Portal-Device Configuration- Profile -Create Profile.

- Platform - Windows 10 & Later & Profile Type - Device Restrictions - Windows Defender Antivirus- Turn on Real-time/behavior monitoring, and other related policies as previously explained based on your organization's requirements.

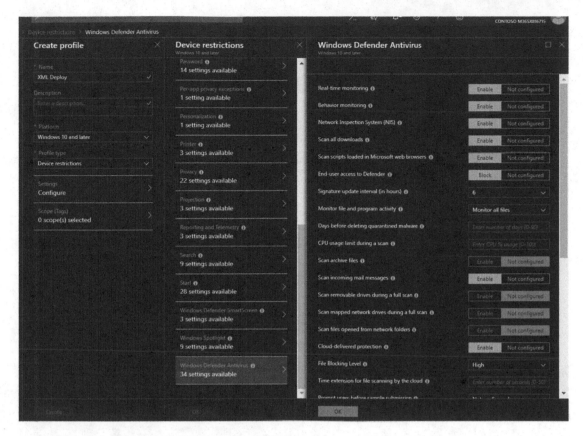

Figure 3-38. *Using WDAV in Intune*

And for those of you who are fond of SCCM, here's how to use WDAV with the configuration manager, as shown in Figure 3-39.

- In the SCCM console, go to "Assets and Compliance," "Endpoint Protection," and "Antimalware Policies." Then create a new policy or edit a default antimalware policy to enable real-time protection and monitoring.

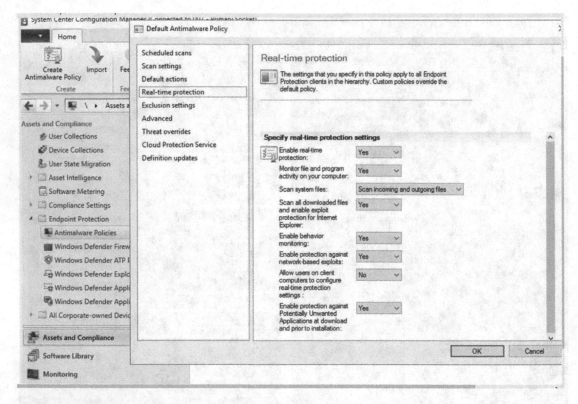

Figure 3-39.   *Using WDAV with SCCM*

Managing WDAV Updates and Applying Security Baselines

There are two types of updates you can use to ensure the highest level of protection for your endpoints: protection updates and product updates.

Protection updates:

- leverage cloud-delivered protection (Microsoft Advanced Protection Service-MAPS) (requires an active connection to the Internet).

- download security intelligence updates (protection updates) once a day to protect the device.

Product updates:

- WDAV requires monthly engine and platform updates.

- SCCM and Windows Server Update Service (WSUS) can help to distribute these updates.

There are five locations from which we can apply the protection updates:

- Microsoft Update

- SCCM

- WSUS

- a network file share

- Microsoft Malware Protection Center (MMPC)

This does not mean that you need to have just one source; there are multiple options mentioned through our management tools:

- Go to gpedit-Computer configuration and click Administrative templates- Windows components - Windows defender antivirus- Signature Updates - Define the order of sources for downloading definition updates.

Figure 3-40 shows the screen allowing you to define the order of sources for downloading updates. I've selected the following sequence: InternalDefinitionUpdateSe rver|MicrosoftUpdateServer|MMPC.

WSUS, SCCM, and MMPC will deliver less frequent updates. However, the size of the information updated may be slightly larger than the size of the frequent updates. MMPC, by default, downloads the updates every two days.

If you are selecting internal file share as one of your source locations, you will also have to mention the UNC (universal naming convention) path of the location in the group policy setting at "Define file shares for downloading definition updates."

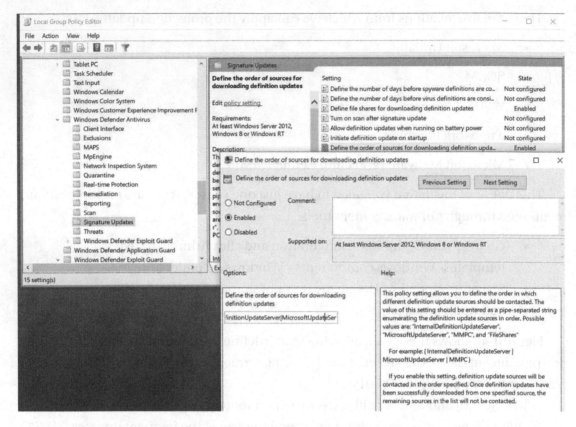

Figure 3-40. *Screen for defining the order of sources for downloading updates*

To deploy updates from UNC files shares using SCCM:

- As shown in Figure 3-41, in the SCCM Console under the "Assets
  & Compliance" bar, go to "Endpoint Protection," "Antimalware
  Policies," and you will be taken to the "Definition updates" screen.
  Here you can create a new policy or edit a default antimalware policy.

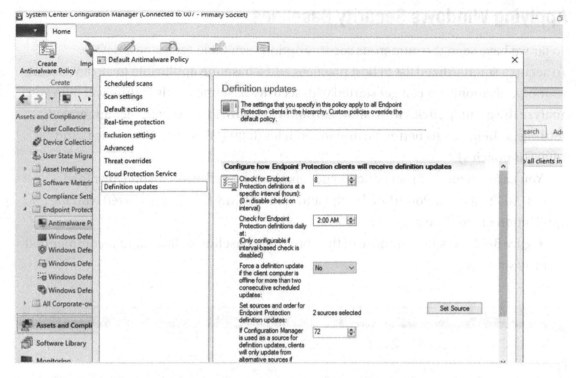

Figure 3-41. *Implementing definition updates with SCCM*

The same can be accomplished with an Intune policy as well with OMA-URI as follows:

- *Intune Portal*: Device Configuration- Profile -Create Profile. Platform - Windows 10 & Later & Profile Type - Custom - Add new policy - Give it a name

- *OMA-URI policy*:

  `./Vendor/MSFT/Policy/Config/Defender/SignatureUpdateFallbackOrder`

  Data Type is a string and Value entered:

  `InternalDefinitionUpdateServer | MicrosoftUpdateServer | MMPC`

Applying Windows Security Baselines

So far we have seen the numerous security options available for a single device. To set up a standardized list of best practices and a baseline applicable to all devices in your organization, you can get started with security baselines. This feature will help you analyze the group policies in your organization and provide you with recommended settings. It helps us to better assimilate policies 3000 (Windows 10 policies) and 1800 (IE policies).

You can download these policies and templates from the Microsoft Download Center. You will use a PowerShell script and some ADMX files to get started with the application of baseline policies.

Figure 3-42 gives us a glimpse of the applicable baseline policies and recommended security settings.

Figure 3-42. *Baseline policies and recommended security settings*

Postbreach

We have already seen a plethora of Windows Security products that prohibit a breach of device security. But what if we have a scenario where the attacker is already on the premises or in an organization's network/device? We need to be on the lookout for any indications of attacks to be able to send, or alert, or even better remediate this issue, say by isolating the system. This will make us ready for a postbreach scenario. Also, in our previous look at device security topics, we only saw the application of policies but not much on the reports or even a dashboard with valuable information about your organization.

Windows Defender ATP

Windows Defender ATP helps enterprise networks prevent, detect, investigate, and respond to advanced threats.

Windows 10 has embedded sensors, so you do not have to deal with installing agents and the system slowing down due to them. These sensors process behavioral signals and send them to a private, isolated cloud where the customer telemetry is secure.

Windows Defender ATP also leverages cloud security analytics. Machine learning and big data help with analyzing the context of the user with data from Office 365 and other cloud assets, help in generating alerts, and provide recommendations for further forensic analysis.

Threat intelligence that provides the required information to aid in the detection of threats is usually the result of Microsoft hunters, security teams, and partners.

Windows Defender ATP is a Windows 10 or Microsoft 365 Enterprise E5 feature. It works collectively with all the Windows Security features discussed earlier, as those features help in setting the context (better reports and dashboard) and sending signals through the sensors. Let's look at some of these features:

- *Attack surface reduction*: We have already discussed this when we were looking at WDEG features. This is also a Windows 10 or Microsoft 365 Enterprise E5 feature.

- *Next generation protection*: We discussed this as part of WDAV.

- *Endpoint detection and response*: EDR helps with detection, investigation, and remediation/response. For security admins, the Windows Defender ATP console offers protection against an aggregation of attacks (incidents) by the same attacker and its movement within the systems, network activity, deep optics into kernel, memory manager, user login activities, registry, and file changes, as well as against the processes that the attacker triggered (cybertelemetry). This cybertelemetry is inspired by an assume breach mentality.

Let's peek at the "Security operations" dashboard shown in Figure 3-43. To get there, go to `https://securitycenter.windows.com/`, log in, and the dashboard will automatically load.

Figure 3-43. *"Security operations" dashboard*

As we can see, it is a very intuitive dashboard that shows us the severity of the incidents/alerts in detail and then a view of the users and machines at risk. The sensors on the Windows/Linux/Mac devices are healthy and connected. The number of machines connected and reporting on a day-to-day basis is seen in the daily machines reporting section. You can also view a list of suspicious activities collected from Firewall, Antivirus, Exploit Guard, and Device Guard. You will additionally see a list of active automated investigations (which can provide cues for your security team's internal analysis) and statistics, such as whether the alert was automatically or partially remediated.

Incident Queue

Windows Defender ATP gives you a clear picture of the activities that are happening in your company and which require your attention. Windows Defender uses correlation analytics and aggregates all alerts to produce an attack timeline or story of an attack.

The incident queue helps in creating an informed cybersecurity response.

By default, we can view the incidents that have happened for up to 30 days, and as you can see, we have a lot of columns, filtering options, multiple views, and so on. The incidents are also color coded to help identify their severity. Red is used for advanced persistent threats, orange for suspicious files or registry changes and rarely observed threats in the organization, yellow for prevalent malware and threats associated with hack tools and the like, and grey for informational messages. One look at the category should provide a lot more information about the type of attack and its phase in the kill chain.

You have the option to manage the incidents page, as shown in Figure 3-44, and assign the activities or further investigate, classify, and perform other actions for them.

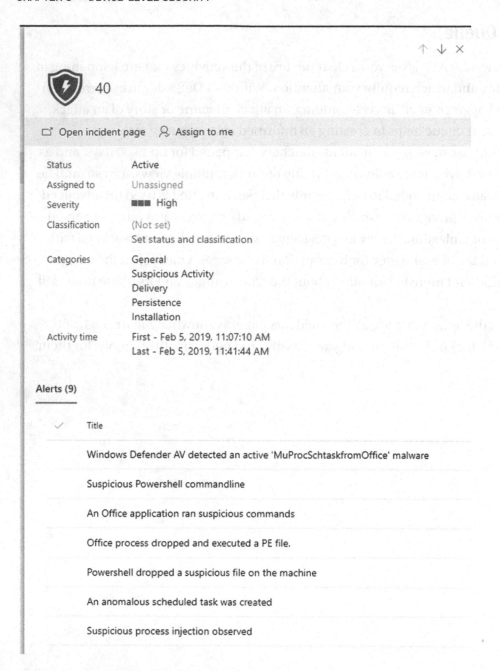

Figure 3-44. *Managing the incidents page*

Your goal as a head of security is to find out more about the source of alerts and such things as how many systems they affected. You will want to do your own investigation as well as get as much information as you can from the investigation done by Windows Defender ATP. It produces information using machine learning and data for identifying threats/malware/suspicious activity from Microsoft Intelligent Security Graph.

The investigation view shows all the alerts on a system and provides information about the category of each alert. We can find out, for instance, what phase of an attack the attacker is in (sending a phishing email, installing malware, connecting command and control, privilege escalation, and so forth). The machine view gives us information about the systems affected.

Windows Defender ATP's investigation can give us information about the security component on the device that helped detect the alert. For reports on Antivirus and to manage the alerts centrally, it is highly recommended that you upgrade to an Enterprise E5 license.

Note   Intune on Azure does not showcase malware/alerts as it did in the old version of Intune.

Similar to this, our other sources such as alerts from Windows Defender Exploit Guard, Credential Guard (which we will look at in the next chapter), and Application Guard are also centrally coordinated by Windows Defender ATP and thus can provide bigger and better context to help you or your organization thwart any attacks.

Figure 3-45 is a screen showing the "Evidence" tab for file investigations and alerts letting us know we need to take action on a rogue file (by, say, quarantining it).

Figure 3-45. *"Evidence" tab for investigations and alerts*

This beta graph in Figure 3-46 shows an attacker's activity and movement. We can see clearly how noisy it is being as it executes all its suspicious activities and how easily Windows Defender ATP catches on to its movement.

In the figure, the macro-enabled `winword.exe` is executing a PowerShell script on the client system (cliwx01) and creating a backdoor to the public IP/command and control center at 204.79.197.203. You can highlight every file and action on your screen to find out more information about each.

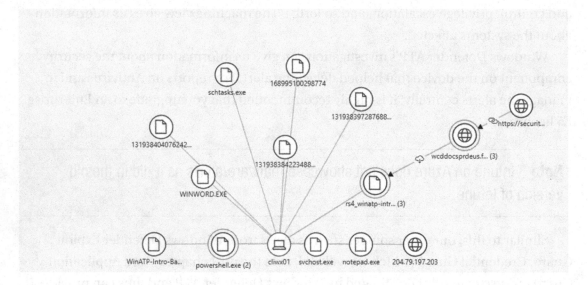

Figure 3-46. *Windows Defender ATP graph of an attack*

Alerts Queue

The alerts queue lists all the alerts in an organization chronologically and shows all the machines on which they were detected, providing information about the severity of each.

As we look further at an alert, we will find out more information about the automatically investigated process. The actions we can take on an alert (in the machine timeline view, incident page view, etc.); recommendations; descriptions; and process trees showcase evidence that occurred within the same execution context and time period. The incident graph helps us understand the sequence of events or triggers on the machine. The artifact timeline provides information for your investigation by letting you know information such as whether the evidence was on the device before it triggered any alerts.

As pictured in Figure 3-47, for an alert Windows Defender ATP shows you the problem, the description, the context and status, and some recommended actions you can take to proceed with your investigation. The process tree depicts the processes involved in executing the compromised executable and brings you nearer to finding out the source of the alert.

Figure 3-47. *"Alerts" screen in Windows Defender ATP*

The "Incident graph" in Figure 3-48 provides more context for the executable file and shows how many systems it affected in your organization. You can also find out when this compromised file was first found in your environment.

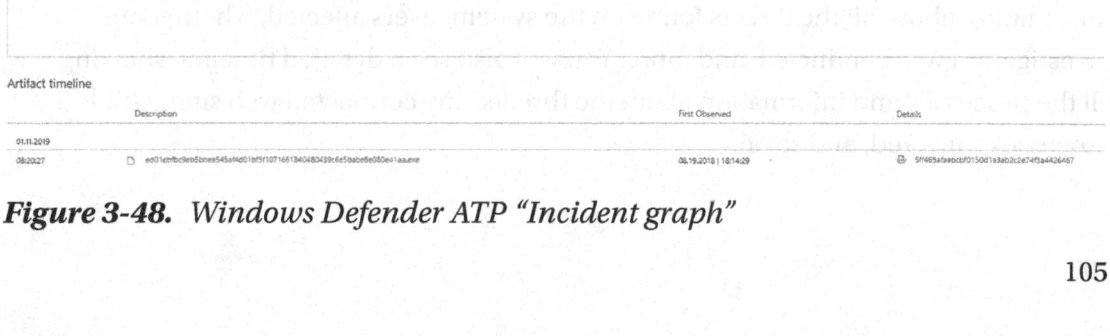

Figure 3-48. *Windows Defender ATP "Incident graph"*

Figure 3-49 shows a screen on which you can investigate the files further by selecting the rogue file or executable. You can choose to "Stop and Quarantine file" or "Block file" or submit the file for further analysis. You can also find more about the attack worldwide, such as the multiple machines on which this file was found. The example on the screen is of a well-known ransomware attack, WannaCrypt, which was found on multiple systems but was immediately detected by WDAV and quarantined before it able to be executed and the files encrypted.

Windows Defender ATP is a well-integrated solution, and if Office 365/Azure ATP are connected, it will provide more details and context for your investigation. The screenshot in the figure gives us information about how prevalent the attack is within the organization and if it was found to have affected email as well.

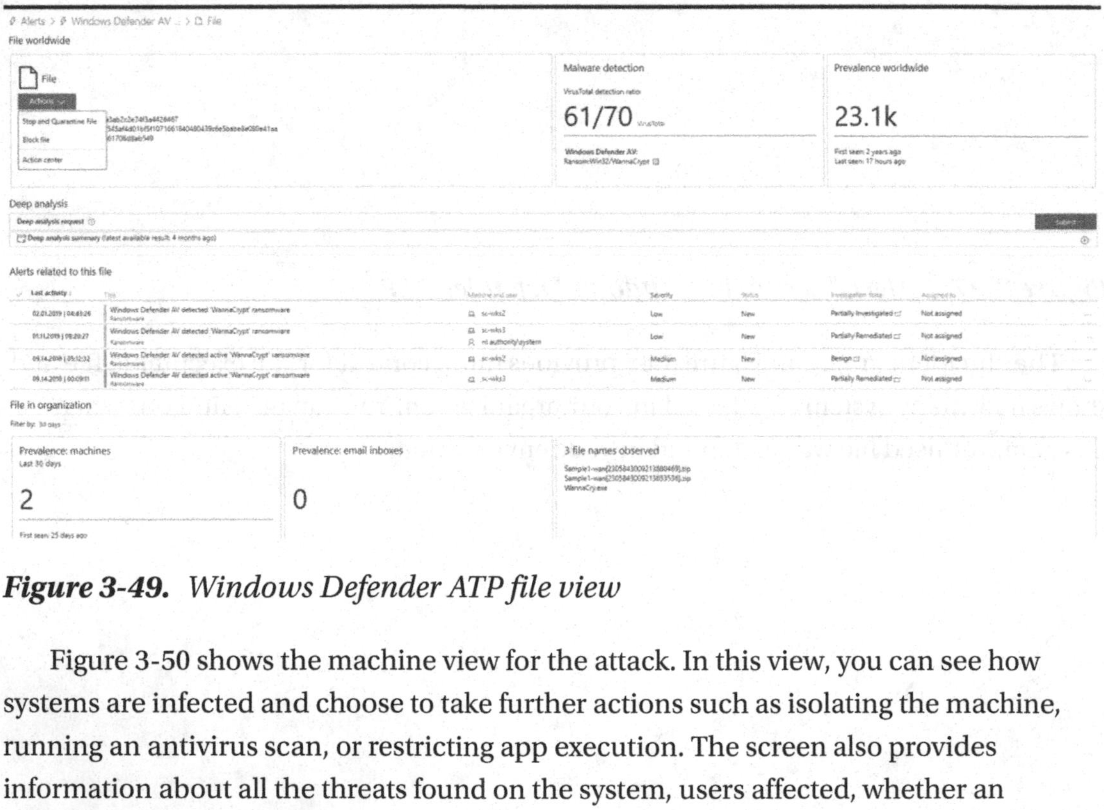

Figure 3-49. *Windows Defender ATP file view*

Figure 3-50 shows the machine view for the attack. In this view, you can see how systems are infected and choose to take further actions such as isolating the machine, running an antivirus scan, or restricting app execution. The screen also provides information about all the threats found on the system, users affected, whether an investigation was conducted, and more. You will also see a detailed timeline showing all the processes and information about the threats, any connected web sites, child processes triggered, and so on.

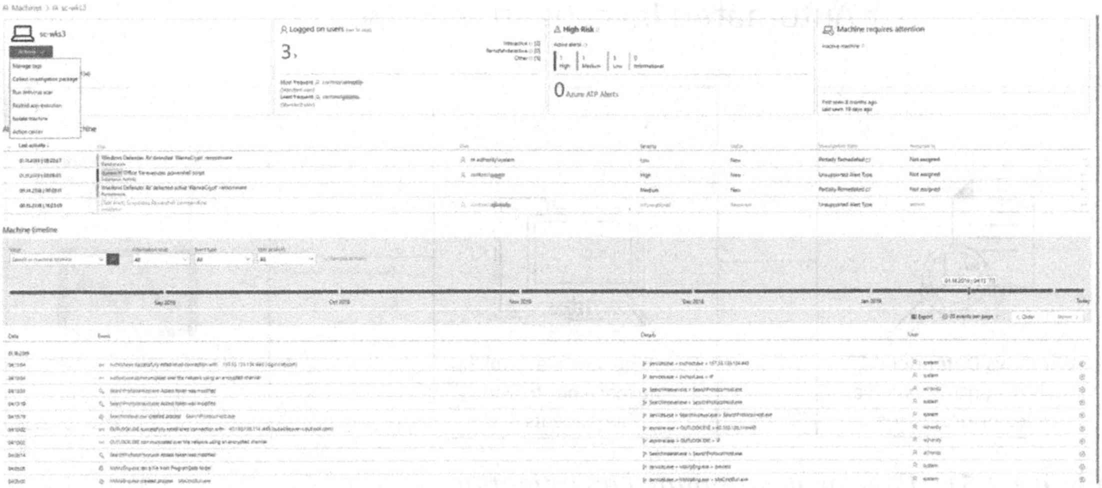

Figure 3-50. *Windows Defender ATP machine view*

Likewise, you can investigate an IP, find out who the IP belongs to, where it is located, how many machines are accessing it, and so forth.

We can also find out more about domain and user accounts along with helpful information about the domains and accounts to help us with further forensic investigation.

Automated Investigation and Remediation

We have seen in the multiple views—machine view, alert view, file view, and so on—that Windows Defender ATP attempts automatic and partial investigations to aid in further analysis. Because it can be very challenging for the security team of any organization to address all the alerts on its own, it leverages various inspection algorithms and processes as shown in Figure 3-51.

Automated investigations work on Windows 10, version 1803 and above, while memory investigations require Windows 10, version 1809.

Automated Investigation Flow

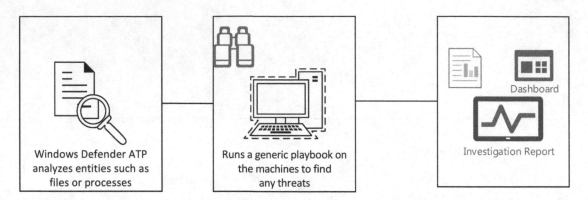

Windows Defender ATP
analyzes entities such as
files or processes

Runs a generic playbook on
the machines to find
any threats

Dashboard

Investigation Report

Figure 3-51. *Flow of an automated investigation*

Figure 3-52 provides a detailed view of an automated investigation. It includes an "Investigation graph" and a detailed analysis consisting of the number of entities (files, processes, drivers, and IPs) on the machines; relative alerts on the particular systems; the time it took to conduct each of the analyses; and the final outcomes. We can go to individual "Alerts," "Machines," "Key findings," and other tabs to find out more about co-related alerts, the investigated machine, and if there is any particular reason for the attack, such as the execution of a file. We have a list of each and every entity scanned. In the figure, 540 entities were scanned, consisting of 5 files, 145 processes, 384 drivers, and 6 IP addresses. The steps taken during the investigation and the entities analyzed are detailed in the logs along with the time taken to execute these steps and a description of them.

If a similar threat is detected on another machine, that will automatically be added to the investigation. When this goes over 10 machines, an approval will be required.

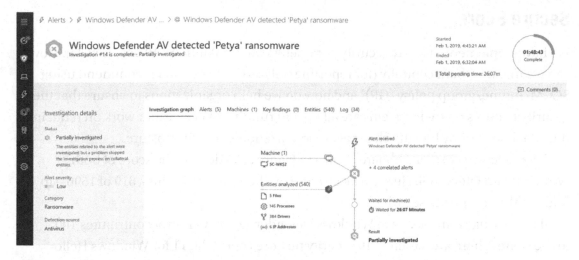

Figure 3-52. *WDAV automated investigation*

As shown in Figure 3-53, you get to select how you want to remediate your systems. You can create multiple machine groups and have different levels of autoremediation applied.

For critical systems, you can choose "Semi—require approval for core folders remediation."

For test systems, you can go with "Semi—require approval for any remediation." This will allow you to analyze more on the system manually and then decide if you would like to remediate the issue automatically. Make sure you don't have a lot to lose if you choose not to remediate immediately.

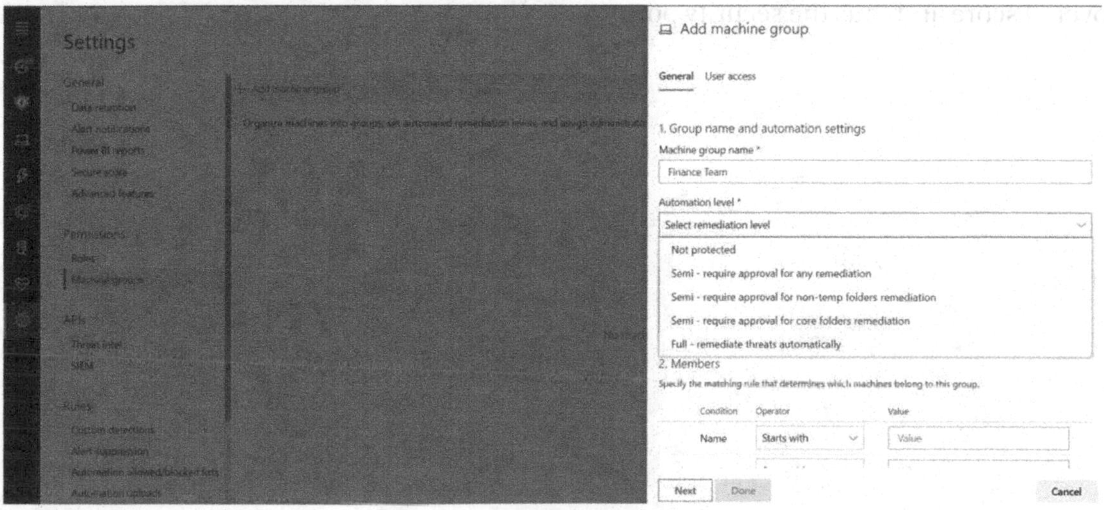

Figure 3-53. *Creating machine groups for remediation*

Secure Score

We have implemented many security parameters on the Windows 10 device so far. How can we manage them centrally (for reporting only as deployment, I recommend using SCCM/Intune/group policy (GP)) and how do we help organizations to ensure that the security features on their systems are all up and running? Let's further work on reducing the attack surface by looking closer at an organization's security posture.

The "Secure score" dashboard shown in Figure 3-54 depicts the score of both Windows and Office 365. Here we focus more on the Windows score—619 of 1596—to find out the composite security.

The scoring is simple. Each Windows Defender security control contributes 100 to the score. There are a total of 10 security postures here (the 11 for Windows Hello for Business are not shown). We then multiply the 10 postures by 100, as each security posture contributes 100 to the score. A total score of 1,000 is achieved.

If both the Windows Defender ATP sensors are turned on at the same time, EDR is given a score of 100; if one system is turned on and the other off, a score of 50 is given, and so on. If you notice, the Antivirus security posture only has a score of 88 out of 100, as one of the systems has failed to turn on Potentially Unwanted Applications (PUA) protection. To get a maximum score, organizations can look at some of the top recommendations. In the example shown in the figure, turning on Credential Guard can bring the score up 50 points (since we just have two systems). As you will remember from the start of the chapter, Exploit Guard has many subfeatures and each of these features contribute 33 percent to the weight of the score. You can turn them on to increase the overall score and thus the security posture.

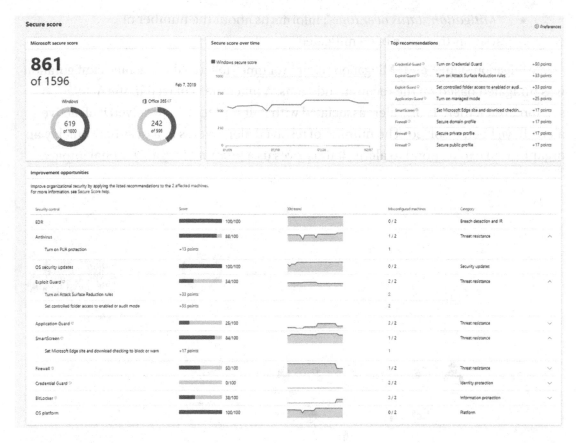

Figure 3-54. *"Secure score" dashboard*

Threat Analytics

The Windows Defender ATP research team identifies emerging threats and outbreaks and publishes these reports in its Threat Analytics evaluations. These help assess the impact of threats and offer a recommended list of actions to restrict them.

As we can see in Figure 3-55, the site's threat analysis provides a detailed summary of where the threat is coming from, where it's been, the techniques and tools used for the attack, and so forth. Some of the items analyzed include:

- *"Machines with alerts"*: shows machines that need attention.

- *"Machines with alerts over time"*: shows whether there has been an increase or decrease in the threat.

- *"Mitigation status"*: informs us about systems in which the threat has been mitigated.

111

- *"Mitigation status over time"*: informs us about the number of systems that have been mitigated.

"Mitigation status" and "Mitigation status over time" tell us if the machine configuration was mitigated based on the recommendations. A machine is placed in the Active section even if there is one alert associated with it. It is placed in Resolved if all active alerts have been resolved. The number of resolved alerts helps to assess how quickly an organization can respond to alerts. It thus gives us a picture of organizational impact.

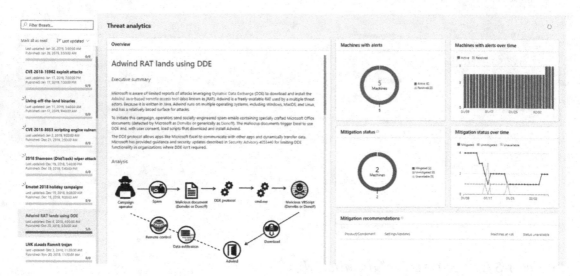

Figure 3-55. *Windows Defender ATP threat analytics*

The threat analytics of Spectre and Meltdown (critical vulnerabilities in CPUs that allow attackers to steal data from kernel memory) should definitely pique your interest, as they were quite the talk of the town (or was it only cybertown?). You can look this up in Threat Analytics and you will find a detailed summary of the threat and the mitigation recommendations. One reason I mention this is because it requires that you install critical updates not only from Microsoft (Windows and browsers) but also from the original equipment manufacturer, or OEM, and CPU vendors.

Currently, Windows Defender ATP can check for microcode mitigations from Intel processors only.

Advanced Hunting

Advanced Hunting is based on the Azure Kusto query language. It is a powerful search and query tool that helps you with creating your own detection rules (custom rules).

It leverages:

- *Powerful query language with IntelliSense*: gives us more flexibility and helps us focus on threat hunting.

- *Query-stored telemetry*: allows us to query the telemetry data gathered by Windows Defender ATP as well as events such as process creation, network communication, and so forth.

- *Links to portal*: If we get machine names/IP/files as results in the query, Advanced Hunting will take us directly to the portal for further investigation, combining the existing portal investigation experience.

- *Query Examples*: helps us with some examples in the welcome page called "Let's start hunting," as shown in Figure 3-56.

Figure 3-56. *Welcome page in Advanced Hunting*

The data model for Advanced Hunting is made up of 10 tables in total. You can leverage this query language better if you understand columns in the Advanced Hunting schema and build queries that span multiple tables.

Let's try running some simple queries: In the following example, I am trying to see the number of processes created a day ago (can be 1 hour, 12 hours, or whatever you choose). I can see that 2 systems and 169 processes were involved. The files responsible for causing these processes are also listed here:

```
ProcessCreationEvents
| where EventTime > ago(1d)
```

Let's run a more specific query to find any events/processes that have run the PowerShell script from the Word documents in the last 30 days:

```
ProcessCreationEvents | where InitiatingProcessFileName in~ ("winword.
exe","excel.exe","powerpnt.exe")
| where FileName =~ "powershell.exe"
| where EventTime > ago(30d)
```

As a result of this, I can find out that a system in my organization was seen executing PowerShell scripts and the source of it was MS documents. This can be a suspicious behavior and allows the security team to start a further investigation of it. We can also create a detection rule around it and any future events will be tracked.

Overview of Management and APIs

Although we have been mainly talking about the Windows client devices (7,8,8.1, and 10), Windows Defender ATP is capable of working on so much more than those. It can also detect threats on Windows servers (2012 R2, 2016, 2019, Windows 10, version 1803); Linux; MacOS; iOS; and Android, as shown in the drop-down in Figure 3-57.

Since every customer is different and companies can range from a small and medium sized to enterprises, Windows Defender ATP can also be integrated with various management tools, such as SCCM, group policy, local script, Intune, VDI (virtual desktop infrastructure) and onboarding.

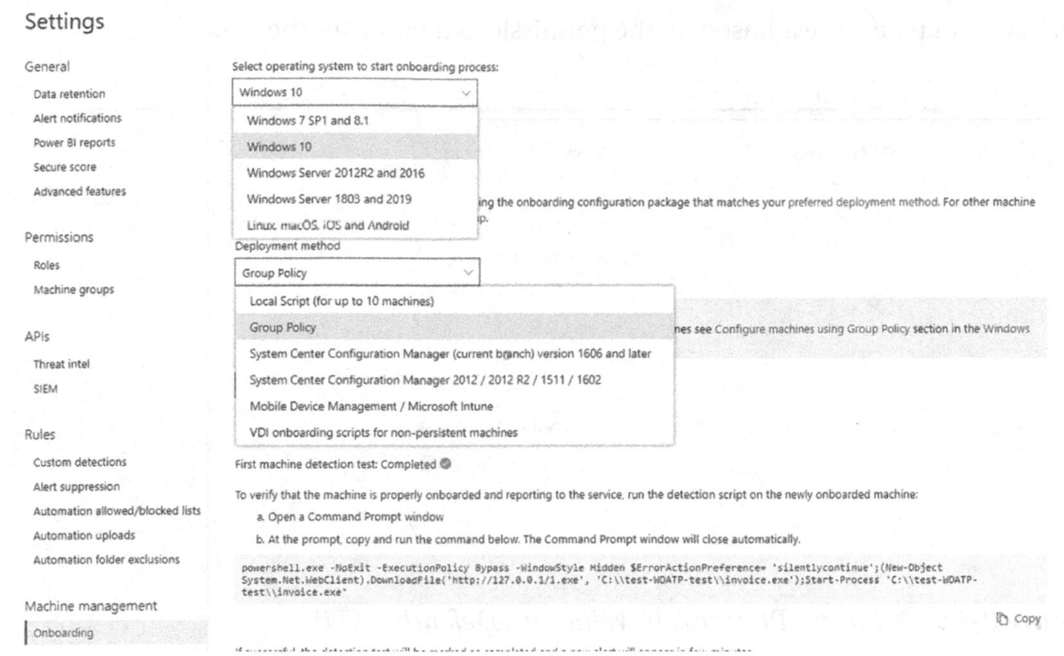

Settings

General
- Data retention
- Alert notifications
- Power BI reports
- Secure score
- Advanced features

Permissions
- Roles
- Machine groups

APIs
- Threat intel
- SIEM

Rules
- Custom detections
- Alert suppression
- Automation allowed/blocked lists
- Automation uploads
- Automation folder exclusions

Machine management
- Onboarding

Select operating system to start onboarding process:

Windows 10

- Windows 7 SP1 and 8.1
- Windows 10
- Windows Server 2012R2 and 2016
- Windows Server 1803 and 2019
- Linux, macOS, iOS and Android

...ing the onboarding configuration package that matches your preferred deployment method. For other machine ...p.

Deployment method

Group Policy

- Local Script (for up to 10 machines)
- Group Policy
- System Center Configuration Manager (current branch) version 1606 and later
- System Center Configuration Manager 2012 / 2012 R2 / 1511 / 1602
- Mobile Device Management / Microsoft Intune
- VDI onboarding scripts for non-persistent machines

...nes see Configure machines using Group Policy section in the Windows

First machine detection test: Completed ⊘

To verify that the machine is properly onboarded and reporting to the service, run the detection script on the newly onboarded machine:

  a. Open a Command Prompt window
  b. At the prompt, copy and run the command below. The Command Prompt window will close automatically.

```
powershell.exe -NoExit -ExecutionPolicy Bypass -WindowStyle Hidden $ErrorActionPreference= 'silentlycontinue';(New-Object
System.Net.WebClient).DownloadFile('http://127.0.0.1/1.exe', 'C:\\test-WDATP-test\\invoice.exe');Start-Process 'C:\\test-WDATP-
test\\invoice.exe'
```

⧉ Copy

Figure 3-57. *Windows Defender ATP's range of threat detection*

Windows Defender ATP API

Windows Defender ATP exposes some data and actions through programmatic APIs. These APIs help in automating both workflows and innovation. It leverages OAuth 2.0.

You can create an APP in Azure AD-APP Registrations for exposed Windows Defender ATP APIs, as shown in Figure 3-58. You can select the level of permission the application will have. The developer can be decided along with this, too. You can also set read and write IOC (inversion of control) permissions, run advanced query permissions, and even isolate machine permissions.

You can get access to a token and use that token to access Windows Defender ATP APIs.

With delegated permissions, once the application with relevant permissions for Windows Defender ATP APIs is created with tokens and permissions, the user logging in to this app can access some features of Windows Defender ATP depending on the permissions provided on the app. Since this is enabled with delegated permissions, it also becomes important that the user has the right permissions, such as the alert investigation permission to, let's say, investigate a system.

With application permission, when a user is not involved, Windows Defender ATP will have complete access based on the permissions defined for the app.

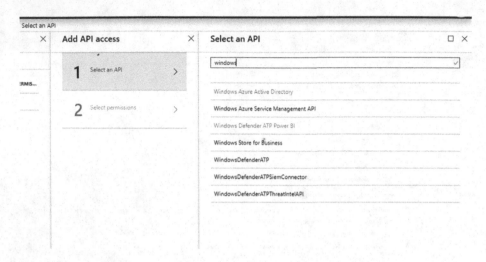

Figure 3-58. *Adding API access in Windows Defender ATP*

In Figure 3-59, it is selected that permissions be applied to Windows Defender ATP API. You should select only the application that will be required by the APIs or for your customized application or project.

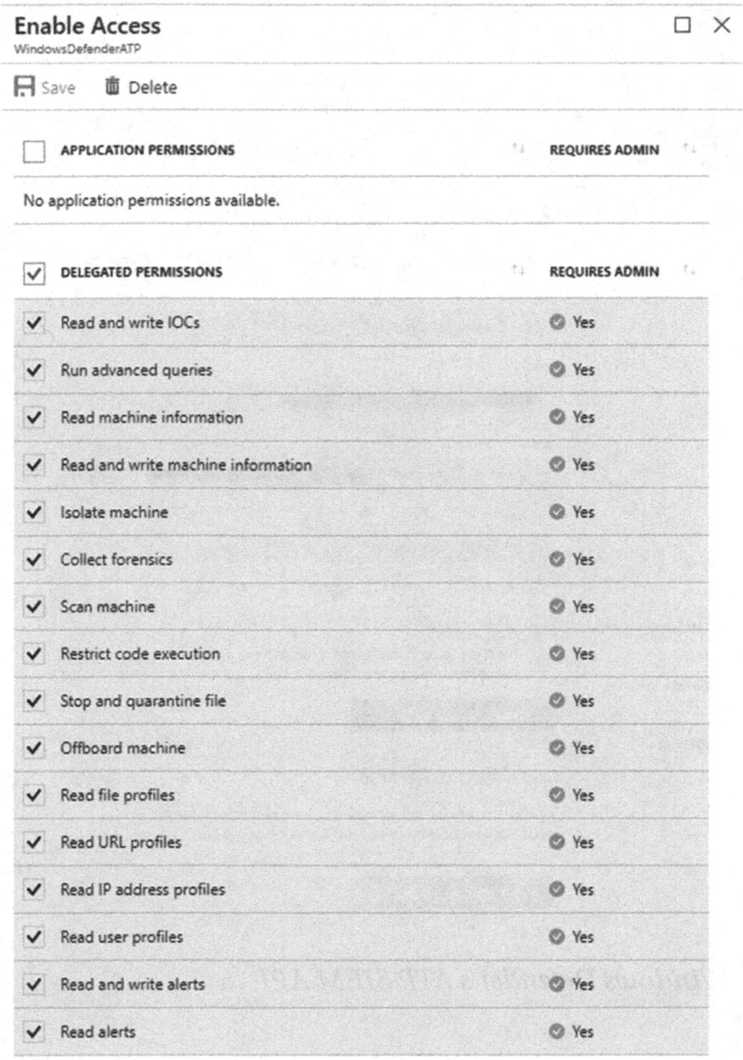

Enable Access   □ ✕
WindowsDefenderATP

🖫 Save   🗑 Delete

	APPLICATION PERMISSIONS	↑↓	REQUIRES ADMIN	↑↓

No application permissions available.

✓	DELEGATED PERMISSIONS	↑↓	REQUIRES ADMIN	↑↓
✓	Read and write IOCs		✓ Yes	
✓	Run advanced queries		✓ Yes	
✓	Read machine information		✓ Yes	
✓	Read and write machine information		✓ Yes	
✓	Isolate machine		✓ Yes	
✓	Collect forensics		✓ Yes	
✓	Scan machine		✓ Yes	
✓	Restrict code execution		✓ Yes	
✓	Stop and quarantine file		✓ Yes	
✓	Offboard machine		✓ Yes	
✓	Read file profiles		✓ Yes	
✓	Read URL profiles		✓ Yes	
✓	Read IP address profiles		✓ Yes	
✓	Read user profiles		✓ Yes	
✓	Read and write alerts		✓ Yes	
✓	Read alerts		✓ Yes	

Figure 3-59. *Windows Defender ATP APIs permission*

Now that we have learned how to create an app in Azure AD, we can use the same information in multiple scenarios—one of them being creating and linking custom threat intelligence alerts in the Windows Defender ATP console to manage custom indicators of compromise.

As shown in Figure 3-60, we can also leverage the Windows Defender ATP's SIEM (security information and events management) API to create an APP that gives permission to pull alerts from the Windows Defender ATP environment into the SIEM database itself.

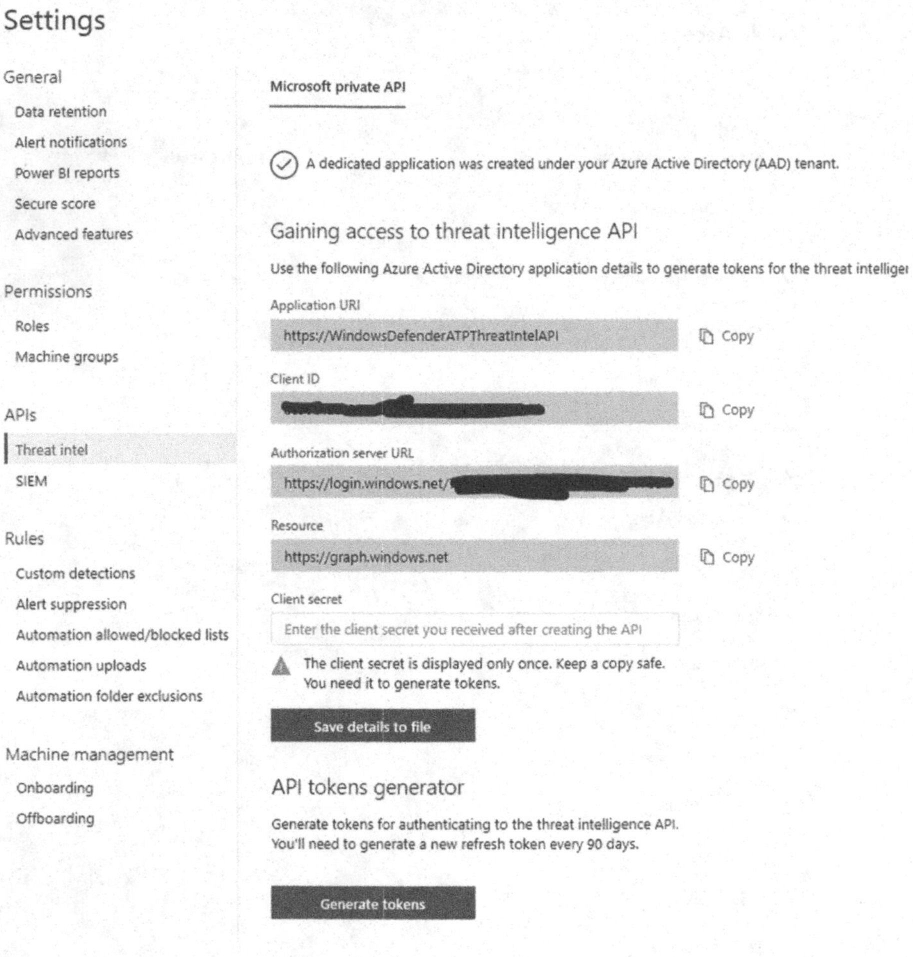

Figure 3-60. *Windows Defender's ATP SIEM API*

Microsoft Threat Protection

Microsoft Threat Protection is the entire threat protection solution that is available with Office 365 Advanced Threat Protection. Windows Defender ATP is just a subset of it. The other products under this umbrella are:

- Azure Advanced Threat Protection

- Office Advanced Threat Protection

- Azure Information Protection

- Azure AD conditional access

- Microsoft Cloud App Security

- Skype for Business

Threat protection works better if all these components can be deeply integrated. Doing so will set a better context, better alerts, better investigations, and so on. We will look at most of these components in the upcoming chapters.

Before we wind up this chapter, I recommend you browse the tutorials section of Windows Defender ATP to test some of the responses to the basic attacks, which can be found at:

`https://securitycenter.windows.com/tutorials`

You can test other features like Exploit Guard, Windows Defender ATP, and Windows Defender Smartscreen features at this web site:

`https://demo.wd.microsoft.com/`

Those are some of the plethora of options we have today to protect our devices and there are loads more currently being released. It's not only Windows Defender ATP that's available anymore; Microsoft has broadened its platform to be applicable for Mac as well, and hence you will hear a lot about Microsoft Defender ATP. And that's not all— Threat & Vulnerability Management (TVM) is being introduced (it's in preview as I write this book) to discover, prioritize, and remediate threats and vulnerabilities by leveraging Intune and SCCM.

But we will not stop at device protection! In Chapter 4, we will learn what protection we have available when an attacker moves laterally into an organization's network and attempts to compromise its identity.

CHAPTER 4

Identity Protection

When attackers have managed to compromise a device with a phishing email and user interaction or any other attack vector, they will then look for a privileged account. If they manage to elevate their user privileges, they will be at liberty to traverse an organization's network and further execute remote scripts and compromise systems and servers. They will continue to laterally move until they finally reach the domain controllers and achieve domain dominance. Our goal here is to thwart these attacks by providing identity protection.

In this chapter, we will learn about the available options that can be leveraged to protect identities at an enterprise level. Since an attacker's first step is to compromise user credentials before moving laterally into an organization's network, going passwordless would ideally be a step forward for all organizations and one they should all consider. Credential Guard plus Windows Hello for Business/Virtual or physical smart cards (such as the modern-day smart card FIDO) can help protect corporate data by leveraging hardware-level security provided by TPM. Some organizations can also choose to implement two-factor or multifactor authentication to access corporate services. This can also aid in identity protection to a great extent.

As we see in Figure 4-1, Credential Guard protects credentials at the device level. Before the user is authorized to gain access to the corporate network, his or her credentials will be verified by Credential Guard. If the user's credentials are already compromised before the implementation of Credential Guard, the extra hardware-level protection does not aid in protecting the user's identity. So, it is highly recommended that you implement Credential Guard as soon as possible.

© Vasantha Lakshmi 2019
V. Lakshmi, *Beginning Security with Microsoft Technologies*, https://doi.org/10.1007/978-1-4842-4853-9_4

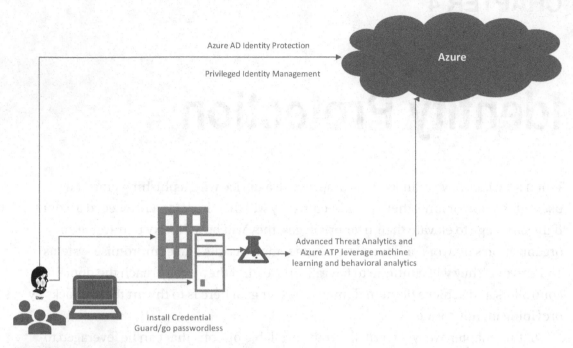

Azure AD Identity Protection

Privileged Identity Management

Azure

Advanced Threat Analytics and
Azure ATP leverage machine
learning and behavioral analytics

User

Install Credential
Guard/go passwordless

Figure 4-1. *Identity protection process*

Once the attacker compromises the attacker's credentials, it can execute remote
scripts to gain further hold on the organization, including pass the hash, pass the ticket,
reconnaissance, skeletal key, and golden ticket. It is necessary for an organization to
keep track of whether there is any deviation from the normal user/entity behavior since
the activities performed by an attacker in compromising a user's identity will deviate
from the user's regular behavior (an anomaly) and a compromised user's activity can
be used to achieve domain dominance. To detect an alert and suggest remediation/
recommended steps, it is a great idea to work with Advanced Threat Analytics and Azure
ATP. Both of these resources have gateways and listeners to detect the traffic coming
toward a domain controller. So, they can help an enterprise with full-fledged, on-premise
infrastructure with forests, domains, and so forth, as well as with servers on Azure.

An enterprise can also have corporate resources on Azure that leverage Azure
identity for authentication into cloud apps, and for this reason, we will have to secure
Azure identities using Azure AD Identity Protection and Privileged Identity Management
(PIM). Identity Protection helps with accessing the risks involved in user logins. If there
is any unusual behavior (could be a brute force attack or an attempt to compromise the
credentials) exhibited by the user, it is immediately tracked and an alert is sent out. PIM
caters to privileged accounts, such as those of administrators of various types, and helps

to control and manage them and keep track of the number of admin accounts without providing any extra privileges.

Windows Defender Credential Guard

By giving access to a privileged software system to access system secrets such as credentials, we can ensure that user credentials are protected. Windows Defender Credential Guard protects the NTLM password hash, kerberos tickets, and credentials stored as domain credentials by applications. Implementing Credential Guard can keep at bay attacks such as pass the hash and pass the ticket, which steal user credentials, hash values, Kerberos tickets, and ticket-generating tickets to authenticate on remote servers and services.

Malware with administrative privileges cannot breach the virtualization-based security provided by the hardware (TPM, Secure Boot, and virtualization). This approach works well with Windows Defender Device Guard, as discussed in detail in Chapter 3.

Prior versions of Windows used an LSA (Local Security Authority) process to store passwords in memory. With Credential Guard enabled, LSA communicates with the LSA Isolated (LSAIso) process. LSA uses remote procedure calls to communicate with the LSAIso process, which is protected by VBS. The LSAIso process does not host any device drivers. Only a subset of (certified and validated) system binaries that are especially required for security are hosted. This process is depicted in Figure 4-2.

Note   NTLMv1 (New Technology LAN Manager version 1), MSCHAPv2 (Microsoft Chap version 2), Digest, and CredSSP (Credential Security Support Provider) cannot use the sign-in credentials for SSO (single sign-on) purposes when Credential Guard is on. Unconstrained Kerberos delegation or DES (Data Encryption Standard) encryption will not work with Credential Guard enabled for both signed-in and prompted credentials.

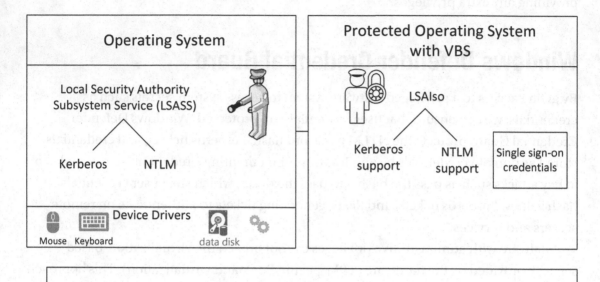

Figure 4-2. *Credential Guard*

Requirements:

- 64-bit architecture OS

- Virtualization extensions (AMD-v and Intel VT-x) and extended page tables such as SLAT for turning on VBS

- TPM 1.0 or 2.0 for protecting VBS-encrypted keys

- UEFI (Unified Extensible Firmware Interface) for Secure Boot to ensure only signed boot processes are loaded

- Secure firmware update process

- Windows 10 Enterprise, Education or Windows Server 2016/2019, or Windows 10 IoT Enterprise

Enabling Windows Defender Credential Guard

There are multiple ways to enable Credential Guard on the Enterprise systems, such as with group policy, Intune, the 111 SCCM-DISM command, and the Windows Defender Device Guard and Credential Guard hardware readiness tools.

Once the previous requirements are set up on the systems, we can enable them in any of the following ways.

Group Policy

As shown in Figure 4-3, here's how to turn on virtualization-based security in group policy:

- Goto Computer Configuration in gpedit ➤ expand Administrative Templates ➤ Expand System ➤ You will find Device Guard- edit the "Turn On Virtualization Based Security"

In the screenshot, I've enabled the highest security option by selecting "Secure Boot and DMA [Direct Memory Access] Protection." Code integrity policy with UEFI lock is enabled specifically for Device Guard and can also be enabled to provide VBS for code integrity.

Next, I've enabled "Virtualisation-based protection of code integrity" with UEFI lock, as it will not allow disabling of Credential Guard remotely. The admin must be present at the device.

You can also secure the boot chain by enabling Secure Launch configuration.

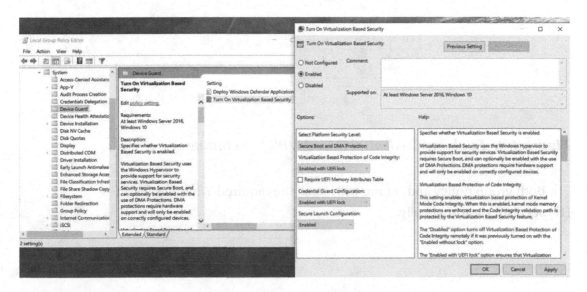

Figure 4-3. *Turning on virtualization-based security*

Intune

Earlier we had to set up policies using CSP/OMA-URI; now have a direct policy to enable Credential Guard/VBS policies from Intune, as shown in Figure 4-4.

To do so:

- Go to Intune Portal-Device Configuration, "Profile," and "Create Profile." For the "Platform," choose "Windows 10 and later." For the "Profile type," choose "Endpoint protection." In "Windows Defender Credential Guard," choose "Enable with UEFI Lock."

Note that just as in the example using group policy, I have set up Credential Guard with UEFI lock.

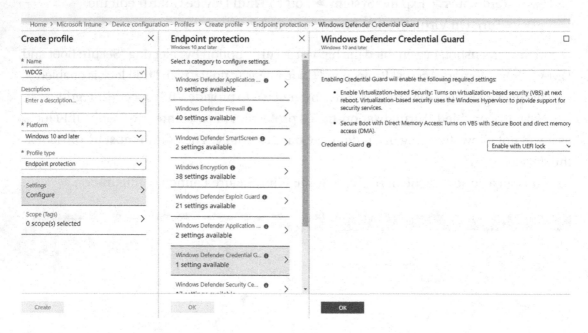

Figure 4-4. *Enabling Credential Guard/VBS from Intune*

Both group policy and Intune will install the required Windows features (HyperVisor) automatically.

Windows Defender Device Guard and Credential Guard

Just like in Device Guard/application control, we can leverage Windows Defender
Device Guard and Credential Guard hardware readiness tools. Here is a brief example of
how to enable Credential Guard:

```
PS C:\Users\valaksh\Desktop\dgreadiness_v3.6> .\DG_Readiness_Tool_v3.6.ps1
-Enable -CG
############################################################################
Readiness Tool Version 3.4 Release.
Tool to check if your device is capable to run Device Guard and Credential Guard.
############################################################################
############################################################################
OS and Hardware requirements for enabling Device Guard and Credential Guard
  1. OS SKUs: Available only on these OS SSKs - Enterprise, Server,
     Education, Enterprise IoT, Pro, and Home
  2. Hardware: Recent hardware that supports virtualization extension with
     SLAT
To learn more please visit: https://aka.ms/dgwhcr
############################################################################

Enabling Device Guard and Credential Guard
Setting RegKeys to enable DG/CG
Enabling Hyper-V and IOMMU
Enabling Hyper-V and IOMMU successful
Please reboot the machine, for settings to be applied.
```

You can also verify if Credential Guard is running:

From msinfo32.exe in System Summary:

Virtualization-based security	Running
Virtualization-based security Required Security Properties	Base Virtualization Support, Secure Boot
Virtualization-based security Available Security Properties	Base Virtualization Support, Secure Boot, DMA Protection, ...
Virtualization-based security Services Configured	Credential Guard, Hypervisor enforced Code Integrity, Secu...
Virtualization-based security Services Running	Credential Guard
Device Encryption Support	Elevation Required to View
A hypervisor has been detected. Features required for Hyper-...	

From the PowerShell script:

```
PS C:\Users\valaksh\Desktop\dgreadiness_v3.6> .\DG_Readiness_Tool_v3.6.ps1
-Ready -CGCG
#########################################################################
Readiness Tool Version 3.4 Release.
Tool to check if your device is capable to run Device Guard and Credential Guard.
#########################################################################
#########################################################################
OS and Hardware requirements for enabling Device Guard and Credential Guard
  1. OS SKUs: Available only on these OS Skus - Enterprise, Server, Education,
     Enterprise IoT, Pro, and Home
  2. Hardware: Recent hardware that supports virtualization extension with SLAT
To learn more please visit: https://aka.ms/dgwhcr
#########################################################################

Now, Credential Guard is enabled and running.
```

Advanced Threat Analytics

ATA is an enterprise-level solution that identifies various advanced cyberattacks and insider threats. It operates on premises with full domain-based infrastructure.

Traditionally, looking through the network logs was the way to proceed—it was similar to searching for a needle in the haystack. Any security solution still based on only this approach can fail and provide false alerts for attacks such as pass the hash, pass the attack, and the like. A new concept and understanding were required and they came with the assume breach strategy. ATA works with a combination of deep packet inspection, information about entities from AD (uses an UEBA [user and entity behavioral analysis] algorithm), and an analysis of specific events.

ATA focuses on several different phases of a cyber–kill chain and on TTPs (tactics, techniques, and procedures) of an attacker's attack playbook:

- Internal Reconnaissance ➤ privilege escalation ➤ Compromised Credentials ➤ Admin Reconnaissance ➤ Remote code execution ➤ Domain admin Credentials ➤ Domain dominance

In the previously described phases, the attacker repeats multiple steps and can slowly traverse an organization laterally. This can occur for many weeks.

However, domain dominance won't be the end of the process for an attacker; it can proceed as follows:

- Remote code execution ➤ Asset ReconnaissanceReconnaissance ➤ Privilege escalation - Asset access - Exfiltration

The point here is that ATA will have a keen understanding of these phases, which it gathers from machine learning and real-time detection powered by UEBA and deterministic engines as follows:

- *UEBA*: analyzes and creates a profile with information about users and their usual behavior. A user being active for eight or nine hours every day, his or her location, any laptops used, and servers accessed (entities) are all included in this profile. It might initially take 30 days from the setup of ATA to collect the data for this analysis.

- *Deterministic engine*: helps to detect advanced attacks and security risks. The security team along with threat hunters come up with the intelligence, which also helps in recognizing signs of some advanced attacks.

ATA can detect:

- *Abnormal user behavior*: This is where UEBA comes into the picture, helping ATA to detect attack indicators such as anomalous logins, abnormal working hours, password sharing, lateral movement, and so on.

- *Advanced attacks*: ATA uses rule-based analysis (deterministic algorithms/detection) to detect advanced attacks such as pass the ticket, pass the hash, over pass the hash, golden ticket, skeleton key, and the like.

- *Known security configuration issues and risks*: ATA utilizes world-class security research work to identify security issues such as broken trusts, weak protocols, and known protocol vulnerabilities.

Architecture

ATA monitors domain controller traffic by using either ATA Lightweight Gateway (installed on Domain Controller (DC)) or port mirroring. One of the main differences between the two is the traffic handled by the Gateways. Lightweight Gateway can handle up to 10,000 packets per second (with 16 CPU cores and 24 GB of memory), while Gateway with port mirroring enabled can handle up to 50,000 packets per second (with 16 CPU cores and 48 GB of memory).

You can have both of the Gateways configured in your organization, as some domains can leverage port mirroring with ATA Gateway and some domains can have Lightweight Gateway installed. SIEM can be integrated with ATA to forward any security events and Windows Event Forwarding can also send events for further analysis by ATA, as it relies on analyzing multiple network protocols.

While these events are collected through the ATA Gateways, they are processed in the ATA center. The very first time you install ATA, it can take up to 30 days to understand the entire infrastructure. The ATA center logs all the events and notes the standard behavior of the entities to help detect any abnormal behavior. This is all shown in Figure 4-5.

Note   Do not forget to plan the capacity of your ATA Gateway and ATA centers.

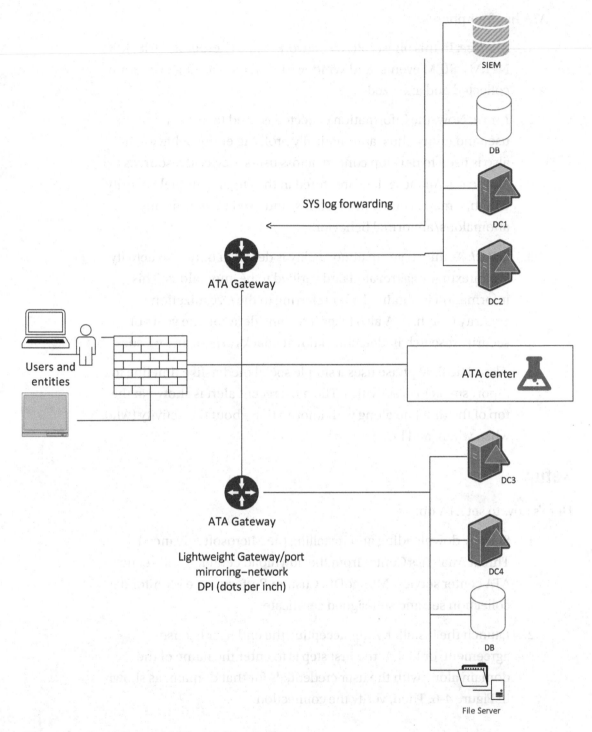

SIEM

DB

DC1

SYS log forwarding

DC2

ATA Gateway

Users and
entities

ATA center

DC3

ATA Gateway

Lightweight Gateway/port
mirroring–network
DPI (dots per inch)

DC4

DB

File Server

Figure 4-5. *Advanced Threat Analytics*

ATA has four phases:

1. *Analyze*: In this phase, all AD network traffic (Kerberos, DNS, RPC, NTLM); SIEM events; and Windows Event Forwarding events are collected and analyzed.

2. *Learn*: Now, the information collected is used to learn about the user and entity; thus, automatically profiling entity behavior. It also is used to develop context across users, devices, resources, and so on. All these data are stored in the Organizational Security Graph, a map of entity interactions, and used to identify any anomalous/abnormal behavior.

3. *Detect*: At this stage, an abnormality is detected only if an activity is contextually aggregated and verified to be anomalous. This information is obtained after referring to the Organization Security Graph. ATA also takes into consideration the years of security research in detecting known attacks and security issues.

4. *Alert*: The final phase uses a simple social media–like timeline to report suspicious activities. The most recent alert is shown at the top of the timeline along with information about the activity (who, what, when, and how).

Setup

Here's how to set ATA up:

1. Start by downloading and Installing the Microsoft Advanced Threat Analytics Center from the download center. It will set up ATA center service, MongoDB, Custom Performance Monitor data collection set, and self-signed certificates

2. Launch the installer. After accepting the end user license agreement, or EULA, the first step is to enter the name of the domain along with the user credentials for that domain, as shown in Figure 4-6. Then, verify the connection.

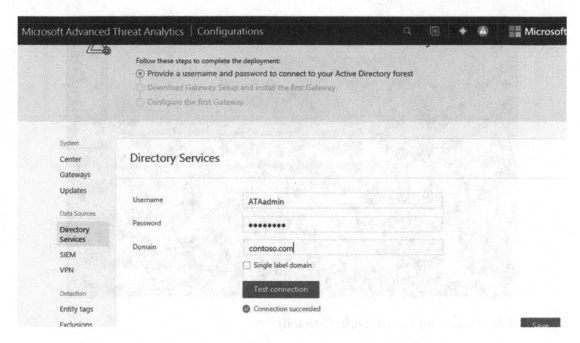

Figure 4-6. *Entering the domain and user credentials to install ATA*

3. Next, download the Gateway setup as shown in Figure 4-7.

Figure 4-7. *ATA Gateway download*

4. Figure 4-8 shows that I've selected Lightweight Gateway to be installed on the domain controller. If you choose to have port mirroring configured for DC traffic, then you should enable the Gateway option as well. Once you select the Gateway option, the next steps for installation are straightforward: it will install the ATA Gateway service, the Microsoft Visual C++ 2013 Redistributable Package, and Custom Performance Monitor data collection set in Windows Performance Monitor.

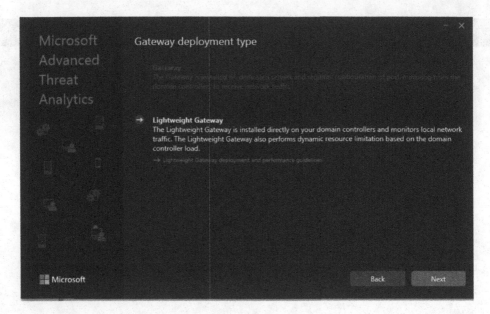

Figure 4-8. *Installing Lightweight Gateway*

5. Once the installation of Lightweight Gateway is complete, the
    Gateway details are populated in the ATA console. You can further
    configure Gateway and it is advised that you enable at least one
    Gateway as the domain synchronizer candidate, as shown in
    Figure 4-9, to keep ATA and the AD domain in sync.

Figure 4-9. *Enabling Gateway as a domain synchronizer candidate*

6. If you have the SIEM DB/Syslog server or even simple Windows Event Forwarding, you can configure them to receive events such as 4776, 4732, 4733, 4728, 4729, 4756, and 4757, as well as additional information on network-related activities on DC and on sensitive group modifications. Click "SIEM" to under "Data Sources" to activate it.

At the configuration level, you can integrate ATA with a virtual private network (VPN) and also exclude the IP address (for known security scanners using DNS) as well as configure a honey token account (a usually dormant account set up to trap malicious actors).

Since we are at the configuration stage, we might as well also look at setting up SAM (Security Account Manager) Remote Protocol. Doing so is required for lateral movement path detection, as it depends on queries to identify local admins on specific machines.

SAM account is a special account required to identify lateral movement of an attacker.

To configure SAM Remote Protocol, go to the client group policies as shown in Figure 4-10:

- "Computer Configuration," "Windows Settings," "Security Settings," "Local Policies," and "Security Options"

Then, enable remote access to the ATA service account created in the previous steps by selecting the policy "Network access: Restrict clients allowed to make remote calls to SAM."

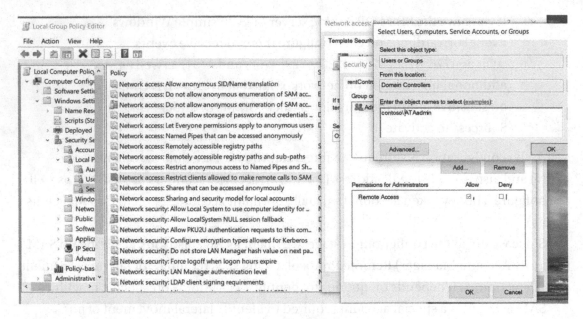

Figure 4-10. *Configuring a SAM Remote Protocol account*

ATA Timeline

Figure 4-11 gives an example of what the ATA timeline looks like. As you can see, there are multiple options for navigation. We are starting with this timeline that is in a social feed–like format, but we can also go to the health center, which provides us with the overall health information of the ATA system, such as if the Gateway is down or outdated or the ATA service is not active, and produces reports as well. The reports might feature a summary of dashboard activities (e.g., suspicious activities, health issues); the modification of sensitive groups; passwords exposed in clear text; and lateral movement paths to sensitive accounts.

All the detected threats and suspicious activities are listed/alerted On the timeline. As we can see in Figure 4-11, the alerts are color coded, with red for high alerts, yellow for medium alerts, and grey for low alerts. As we can see on the screen, suspicious DNS activity was observed on two systems, CLIENTs 1 and 2, and a brute force attack was also noticed on CLIENT2.

Figure 4-11. *Example of an ATA timeline*

Since the purpose of this chapter is not to highlight how attacks take place but to see the various types of attacks that can be detected by ATA, it is useful to take a look at a cyber–kill chain showing the threats that can be identified by ATA.

- *Reconnaissance*:
  - account enumeration
  - session enumeration
  - AD enumeration
- *Compromised credentials*:
  - brute force attacks
  - unusual protocol implementation
  - abnormal behavior

- *Lateral movement*:

    - pass the ticket

    - pass the hash

    - overpass the hash

    - abnormal behavior

- *Domain dominance*:

    - golden ticket

    - malicious replication requests

Figure 4-12 shows another example of alerts for high-priority attacks, such as pass the hash and pass the ticket, that target the key distribution center, or KDC, of a domain controller in an attempt to gain access to the Kerberos ticket-granting tickets (TGTs) password hash. These TGTs can be used to request Kerberos service tickets on other systems as well or to gain access to network resources.

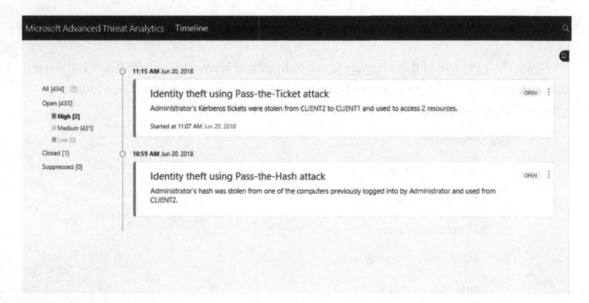

Figure 4-12. *ATA timeline showing high-priority alerts*

Azure Advanced Threat Protection

Although the functionality of Azure ATP is similar to Advanced Threat Analytics, it is different in its approach, as it is a cloud-based service. Azure ATP helps identify, detect, and investigate advanced threats.

With Azure ATP sensors having to be deployed instead of the ATA gateways and traffic sent to Azure ATP for detection and alerts, we have to choose between Azure ATP and ATA. One of these tools will work well for an organization, as both of them are based on UEBA algorithms.

Azure ATP helps detect advanced attacks in hybrid environments to:

- monitor user and entity behavior using analytics—UEBA is leveraged and a profiling of users and entities takes place.

- protect user identities and credentials in AD - Azure ATP's visual lateral movement paths help us protect sensitive accounts and prohibit lateral movement as well.

- identify and investigate (integration with WDATP enhances the context-based detection) suspicious activities and threats in the cyber–kill chain (the kill chain explained in ATA applies here as well).

Incident information is clearly seen in the timeline. This also helps reduce false positives.

Architecture

So far we have seen that Azure ATP is a cloud service and the Azure ATP sensor should parse the traffic going toward the domain controller and send it to the cloud service for further analysis and investigation. Figure 4-13 is a diagram illustrating this interconnection.

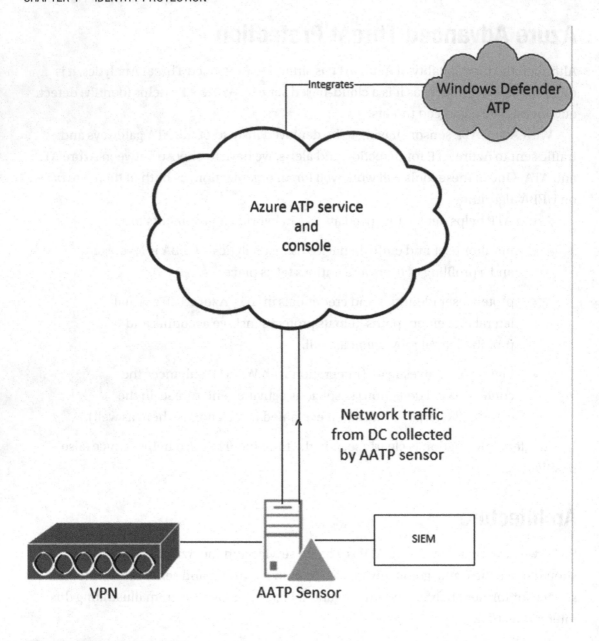

Figure 4-13. *Azure ATP*

The Azure ATP sensor can receive RADIUS (Remote Authentication User Dial-in Server or Service) accounting information from a VPN provider as well as from the network parsing it does. It can also receive Windows events (4776, 4732, 4733, 4728, 4729, 4756, 4757, and 7045) from the domain controller directly (also explained in relation to ATA). It retrieves data about users and computers and performs resolution of network entities and more.

After one (or many) Azure ATP sensors is set up as a domain synchronizer candidate, it will be responsible for synchronizing all entities from a specific AD. The Azure ATP sensor also ensures that it has 15 percent of memory and domain resources available at all points in time.

Setup

To set up Azure ATP:

1. Go to https://portal.atp.azure.com and log in with your organization's admin credentials. Ensure that you have Microsoft 365 Enterprise E5 or Enterprise Mobility and Security (EMS) E5 licenses activated.

2. Ensure that you are using a global admin or security admin account to log in to the Azure ATP portal. Enter your domain credentials to install the Azure ATP sensor as shown in Figure 4-14. Unlike in the ATA console, we do not have the test connection feature to examine the credentials supplied here. The credentials have to be correct to get the Azure ATP sensor up and running.

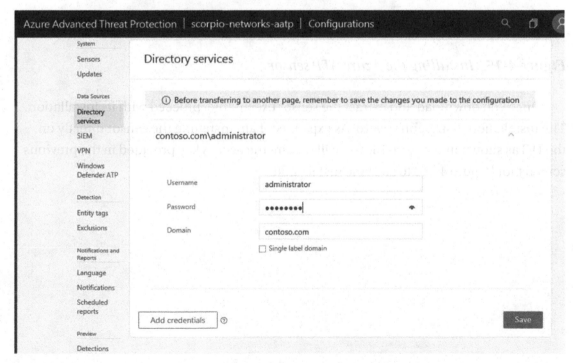

Figure 4-14. Entering your account credentials in the Azure ATP setup

3. Download the Azure ATP sensors. This is where we will have to choose to install either a stand-alone Azure ATP sensor on a dedicated server and configure the network adapters to receive mirrored domain controller traffic. Or for a simple setup without port mirroring, install the Azure ATP sensor on the DC itself as in Figure 4-15.

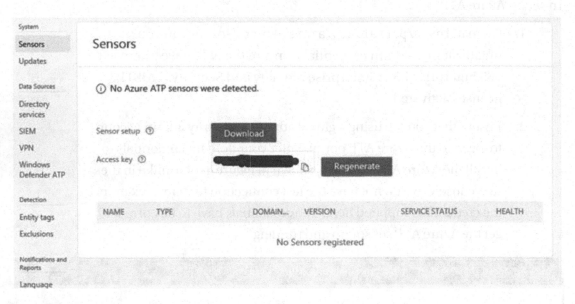

Figure 4-15. *Installing the Azure ATP sensor*

Once you download and extract the sensor executable, proceed with its installation. The installation is straightforward. As explained, I am installing the sensor directly on the DC as shown in Figure 4-16. You will require the access key provided in the previous screenshot (Figure 4-15) to start the installation.

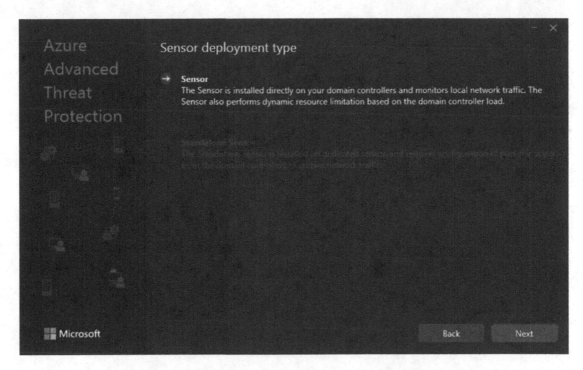

Figure 4-16. *Installing the sensor on the DC*

You will then be able to see the sensor up and running as in Figure 4-17.

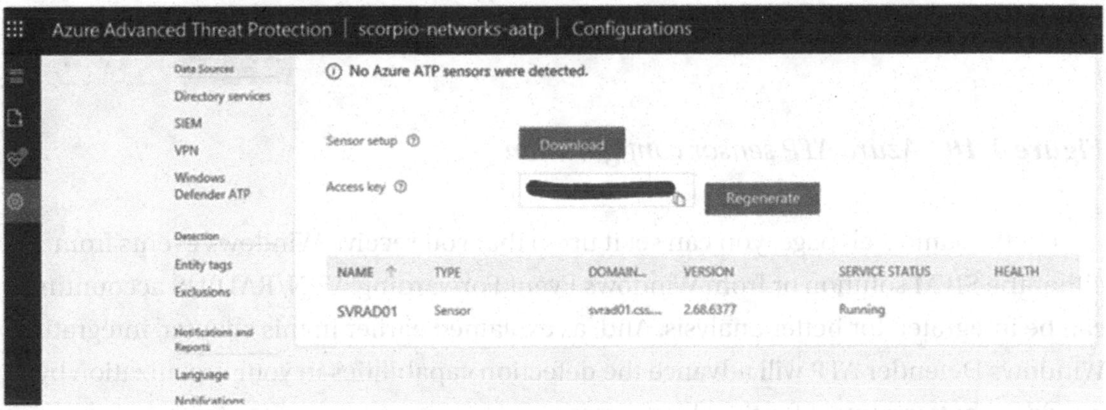

Figure 4-17. *Sensor activated in Azure ATP*

To futher configure the sensor (if using a stand-alone sensor) and to ensure that all the relevant network adapters are selected, as shown in Figure 4-18, check that the all the DCs are mentioned and that at least one is a global catalog server that can aid in resolving objects. Also ensure that network adapters configured as destination mirror port is selected. You also need to have the domain synchronizer candidate turned on for at least one of your sensors.

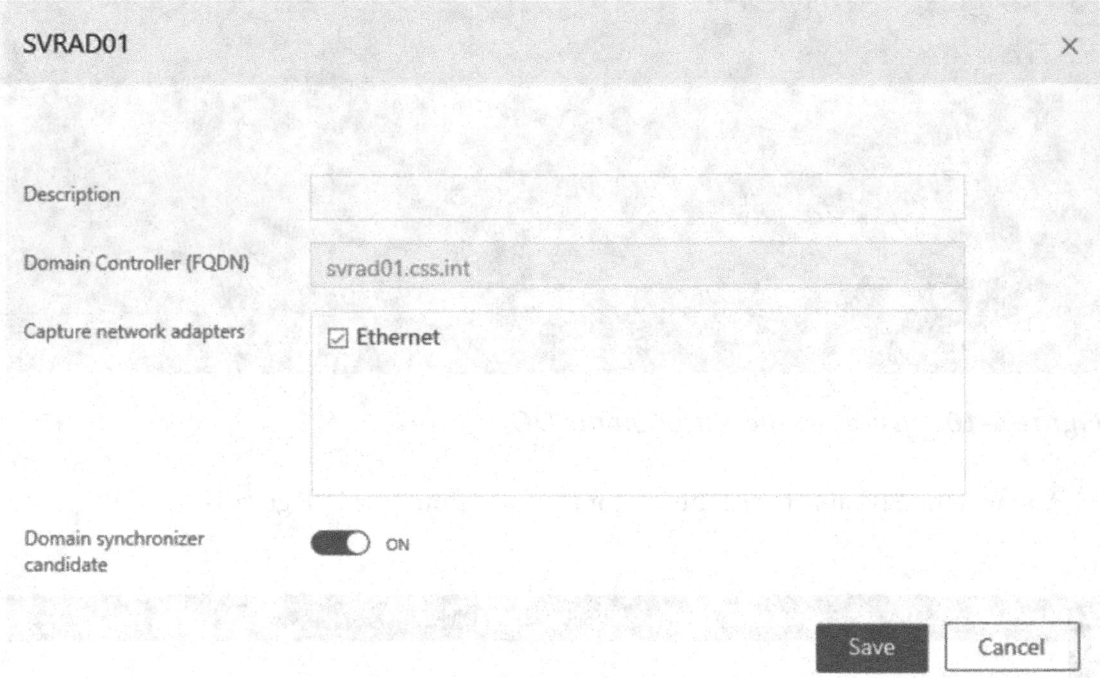

Figure 4-18. *Azure ATP sensor configuration*

On the same web page, you can set it up so that you receive Windows events from either the SIEM solution or from Windows Event Forwarding. VPN/RADIUS accounting can be integrated for better analysis. And, as explained earlier in this chapter, integrating Windows Defender ATP will advance the detection capabilities in your organization by providing better context for the algorithms.

You can also specify honey token accounts (dormant accounts used as a trap for hackers) and sensitive accounts under Entity tags. You can additionally mention any exclusions that apply to your organization's clients, IP ranges/subnets, and users/groups.

An Azure ATP service account should be able to enumerate SAM Remote Protocol correctly. Do not forget to add the service account to the group policy discussed earlier.

Email alerts can be configured to be sent about sensor health issues or upon receiving an alert.

Another advantage of Azure ATP over ATA is that you can schedule reports daily, weekly, or monthly, and receive an alert based on your setting, as shown in Figure 4-19.

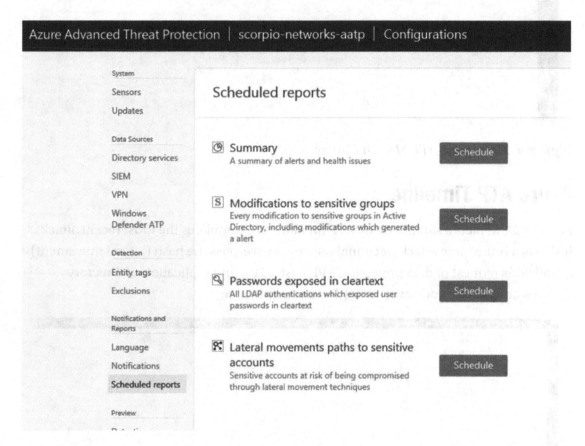

Figure 4-19. *"Scheduled reports" in Azure ATP*

Azure ATP's Health Center, shown in Figure 4-20, reports any issues with regard to the sensor or any misconfigured information.

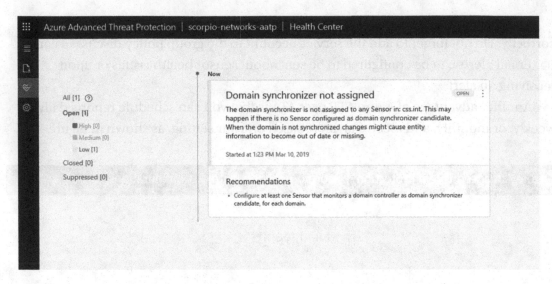

Figure 4-20. *Azure ATP Health Center*

Azure ATP Timeline

Figure 4-21 depicts a sample Azure ATP timeline as it populates the most recent attacks. It shows a brute force attack (reconnaissance), an overpass the hash (lateral movement), a malicious request of data protection API master key, and replication of directory services and remote code execution (domain dominance).

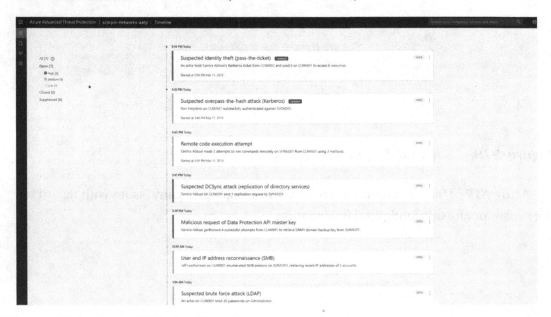

Figure 4-21. *Azure ATP timeline showing attacks*

A more detailed view of an attack/alert is shown in Figure 4-22. It includes information about the time of the attack, where it happened, who conducted it, and so on. You can see a graphical attack view and the evidence as well.

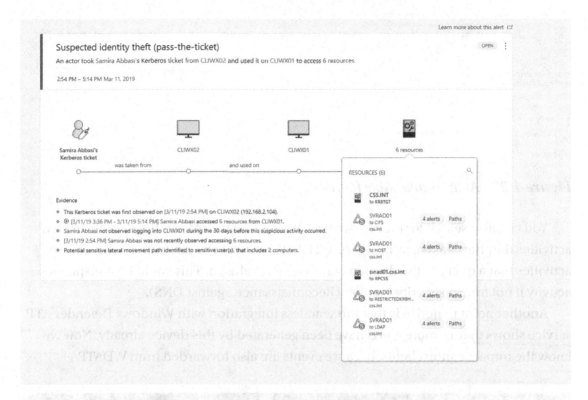

Figure 4-22. *Detailed view of an Azure ATP alert*

Figure 4-23 shows a screen on which you can take further action on these alerts, accessible either from the detailed alert view in the previous screenshot or from the main timeline. You can either close and suppress an alert and be alerted again if the incident happens again within seven days, or close and exclude the alert and it will stop generating alerts from that system in the future. This can be helpful if you use it cautiously to suppress false positives.

5:14 PM Today

Suspected identity theft (pass-the-ticket) Updated   OPEN   ⋮

An actor took Samira Abbasi's Kerberos ticket from CLIWX02 and used it on CLIWX01 to access 6 resources.

Started at 2:54 PM Mar 11, 2019

5:10 PM Today

Suspected overpass-the-hash attack (Kerberos) Updated   OPEN   ⋮

Ron Helpdesk on CLIWX01 successfully authenticated against SVRAD01.

Started at 2:45 PM Mar 11, 2019

☒ Close
  Close now but alert if it recurs

☒ Suppress
  Ignore ongoing activity, but alert if it resumes after 7 days

☒ Close and exclude CLIWX01 ⓘ
  Close and don't generate future alerts for these activities from CLIWX01

⤓ Download Details
⟲ Share

🗑 Delete
  Delete this alert

3:43 PM Today

Remote code execution attempt   OPEN   ⋮

Samira Abbasi made 2 attempts to run commands remotely on SVRAD01 from CLIWX01 using 2 methods.

Started at 3:36 PM Mar 11, 2019

3:41 PM Today

Suspected DCSync attack (replication of directory services)   OPEN   ⋮

Samira Abbasi on CLIWX01 sent 1 replication request to SVRAD01.

Figure 4-23. Actions available for alerts

You can also search for entities such as devices and users from the console to view activities they have taken, as in Figure 4-24. In this case, I can see from the timeline of activities that a query to the domain controller was refused. This could be a suspicious activity if not from a security scanner (Reconnaissance against DNS).

Another point to notice is that the seamless integration with Windows Defender ATP service shows that 15 more alerts have been generated by this device already. Now we know the impact context better because events are also forwarded from WDATP.

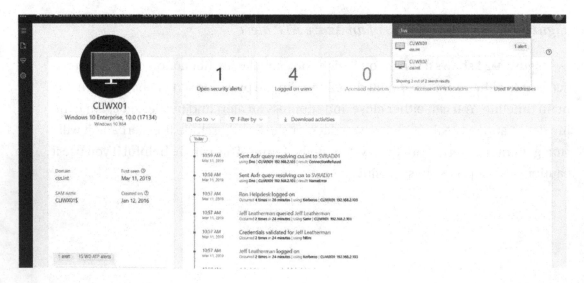

Figure 4-24. Activities of devices and users

Figure 4-25 is a timeline of information and activities executed by users, with Azure ATP marking admin accounts as sensitive. Beyond activities, we can also see directory data and lateral movement paths.

Figure 4-25. *Azure ATP timeline of user-based information and activities*

The directory data shown in Figure 4-26 gives us information about the UAC, or user account control; group memberships the user/device might be part of; and so on.

Figure 4-26. *Azure ATP directory data*

The lateral movements of the accounts are also tracked if there are any. In Figure 4-27, we can see that the LabAdmin account tried to access the domain controller server with an administrator account and that the Jeff Leatherman nonadmin account accessed the device CLIWX01 with admin credentials.

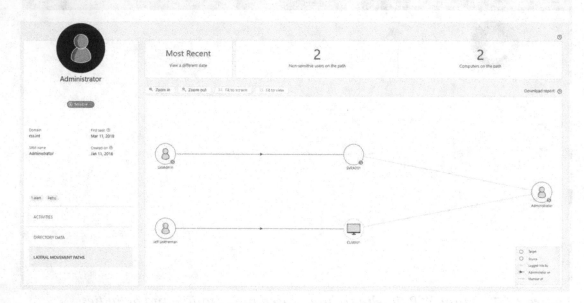

Figure 4-27. *Tracking of lateral movement paths*

Azure Active Directory Identity Protection

Azure AD Identity Protection aids in protecting your cloud/hybrid identities (and we now know how important it is to have your credentials protected). It further helps in limiting an attacker's ability to exploit a compromised identity by looking into suspicious activities or anomalous behavior. An attack such as pass the ticket will initially aim to masquerade as a standard user and proceed to harvest admin credentials. So, the protection should be applied to:

- all identities regardless of their privilege level

- preventing compromised identities from being abused

To do this, Azure AD Identity Protection helps in:

1. identifying vulnerabilities pertaining to identities, providing recommendations for vulnerabilities, calculating user risk and session risk, and other such functions.

2. configuring automated responses for suspicious activities by sending notifications for alerts, tracking investigations, and more.

3. investigating suspicious incidents and taking action around them by creating risk-based policies to mitigate these risky sign-ins (e.g., to block the user/enforce Multi-Factor Authentication, or MFA).

Now let's take a look at the onboarding process for Azure AD Identity Protection:

1. In `https://portal.azure.com`, find "Azure AD Identity Protection" by going to "All Services," "MarketPlace," and then "Identity." Then choose to create the feature (onboarding is only possible for a global administrator).

2. The first view you'll see is that of a dashboard with information about what's happening in your system. I have selected the "Security overview (Preview)" dashboard shown in Figure 4-28, as it lists your organization's identity secure score. Security and global admins can also choose to configure the user risk policy and sign-in risk policy.

Figure 4-28. *Azure AD Identity Protection "Security overview" dashboard*

3. To get started with the configuration, we have to decide the action to be taken upon the detection of a vulnerability or an abuse of credentials. First, we can require that all the users in the organization are registered for MFA and require them to go through MFA upon the observation of a vulnerability or abuse of credentials.

4. Now let's enforce MFA registration for all the users in the organization as shown in Figure 4-29. You can review the status of registration under "Current registration status" and enforce the policy.

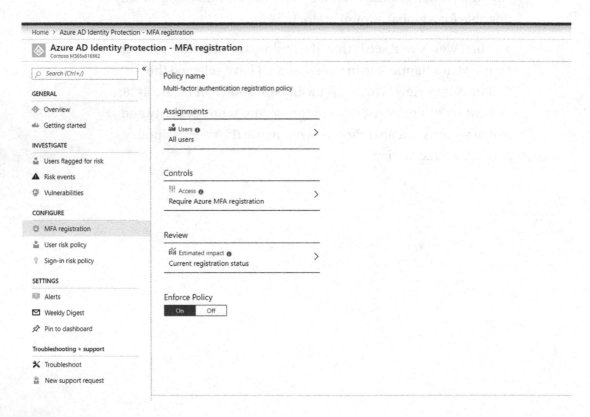

Figure 4-29. *Enforcing MFA registration*

5. If a user sign-in risk is noticed, you can block the user's access or require a password change to gain access to corporate resources. As shown in Figure 4-30, I've applied the policy to all users; however, you can choose to apply the policy to only a specific group of users as well.

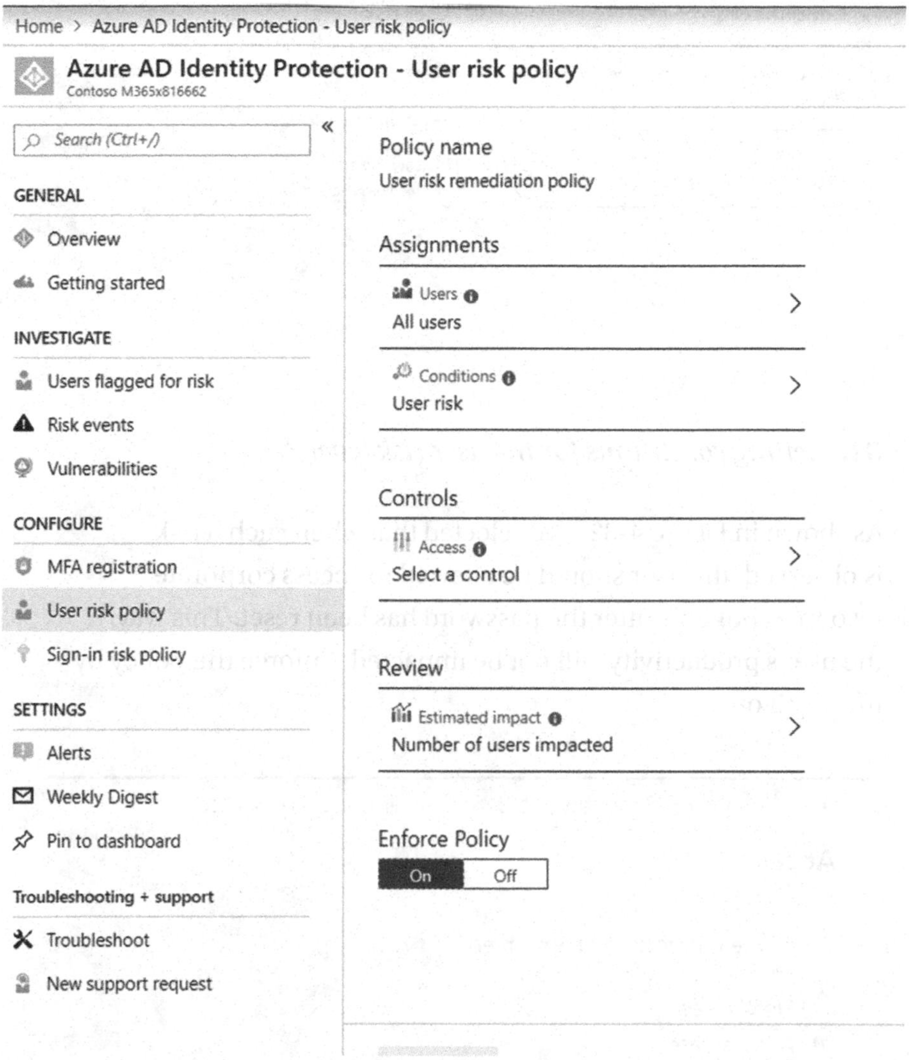

Figure 4-30. *Setting up a user risk policy*

6. The user's risk level is now analyzed by machine-learning algorithms and given a rating—low, medium, or high—based on the severity of the risk. In Figure 4-31, I've chosen the "Medium and above" risk level.

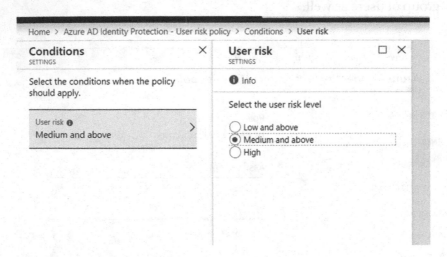

Figure 4-31. *Setting conditions for the user risk level*

7. As shown in Figure 4-32, I've selected that when such a risk is observed, the user should be allowed to access corporate resources but only after the password has been reset. This way, the user's productivity will not be impacted. Enforce the policy by turning it on.

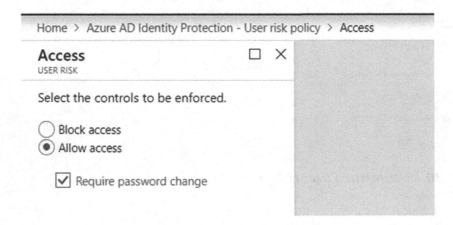

Figure 4-32. *Granting access based on the user risk policy*

8. We also have to configure the sign-in risk as shown in Figure 4-33.
    Here, machine learning is again leveraged to understand and rate
    the risk as low, medium, or high. However, the condition used will
    now enforce or require MFA if a risky sign-in is observed.

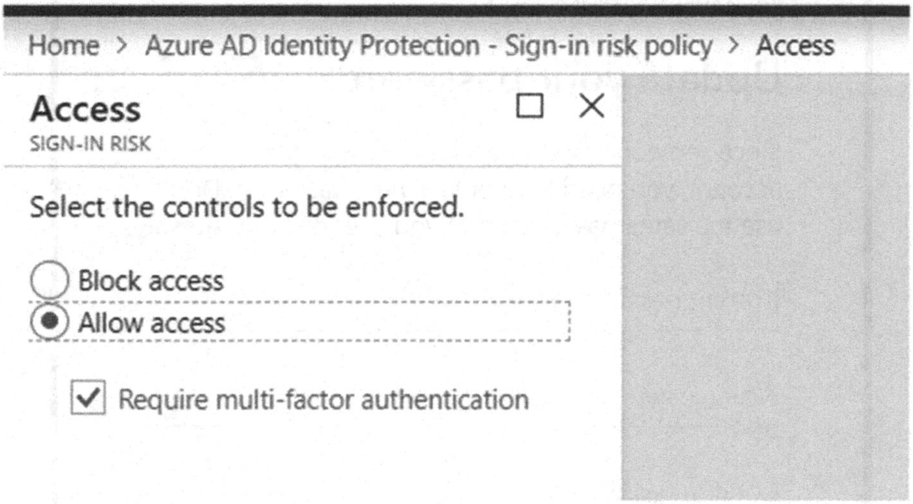

Figure 4-33. *Granting access based on sign-in risk policy*

9. Figure 4-34 shows the message users will get if risky behavior is
    detected, prompting them to change their password.

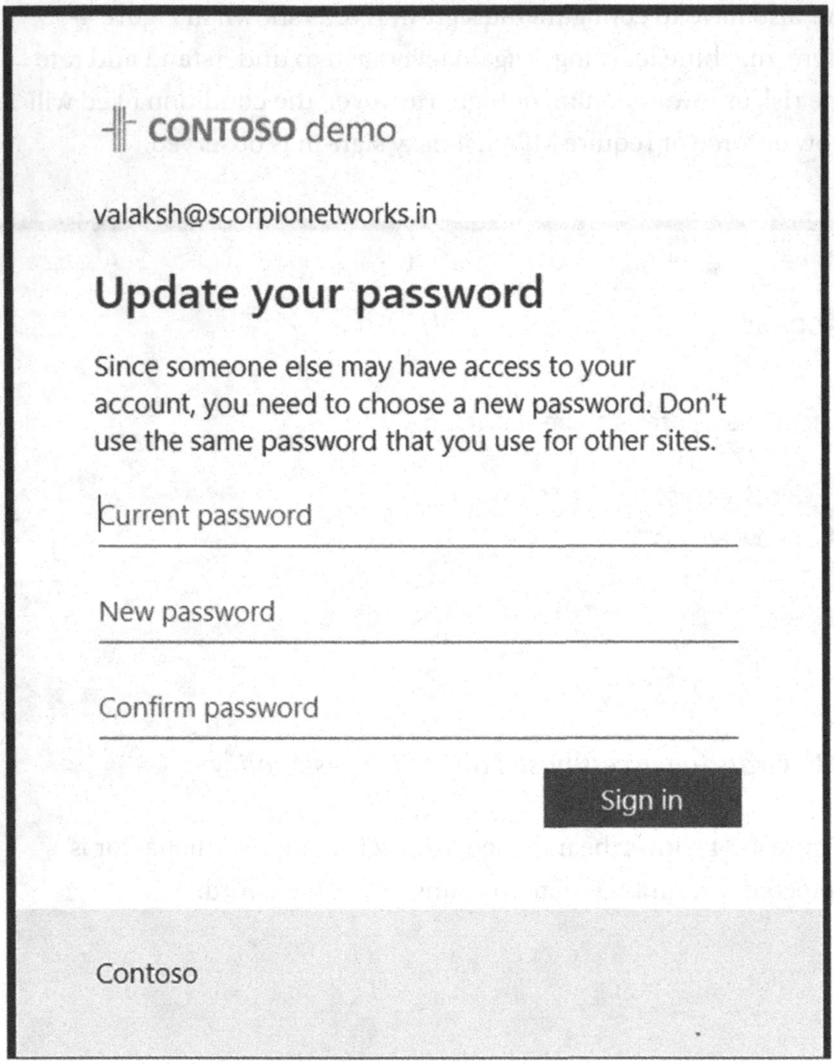

CHAPTER 4   IDENTITY PROTECTION

Figure 4-34. "Update your password" message

10. If a high-risk event is observed during the user's sign-in, it will generally be required that an admin is immediately notified. We can set up this notification in the "Settings" section as shown in Figure 4-35.

156

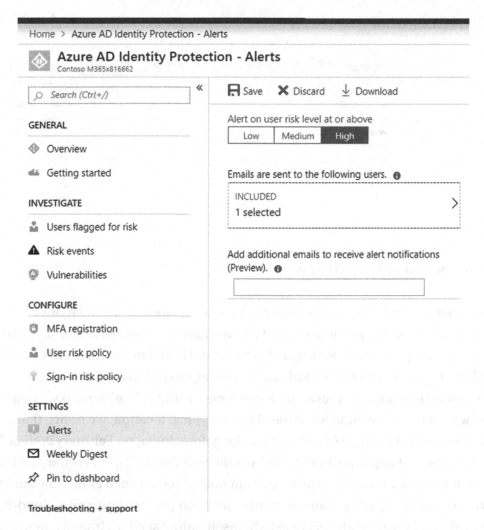

Figure 4-35. Setting up a notification for a high-risk event

Risky User Accounts and Vulnerabilities

Let's now get to investigating user accounts that are designated as risky, other risk events, and vulnerabilities. In Figure 4-36, we can see various levels of risky events across an organization's users. The global admin account has a high-risk level with two events observed. The screen even gives us a glimpse of the policy applied. If the user does not change the password per the policy, the account is still marked "at risk." A few accounts are being remediated as well.

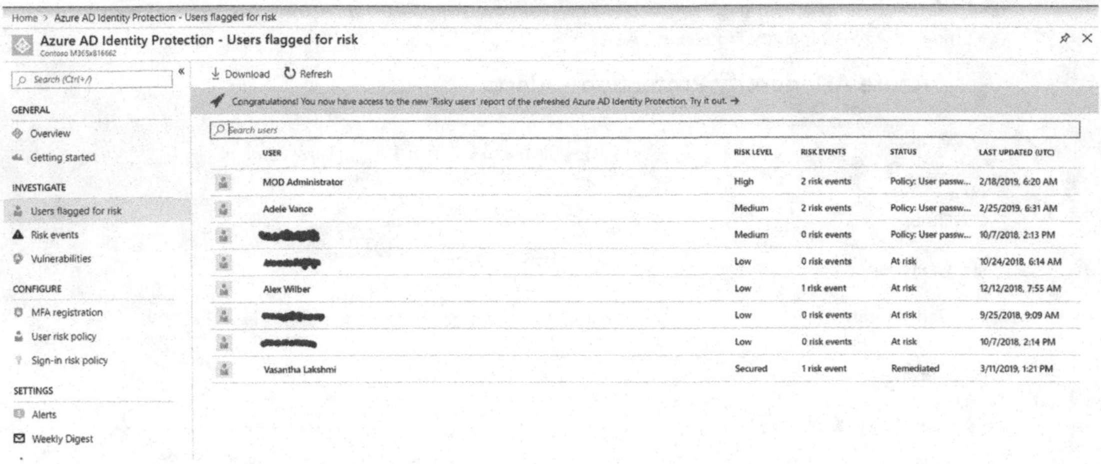

Figure 4-36. Risks identified by user

Let's take a deeper look into one of these events. As we can see in Figure 4-37, an atypical location for the user was noticed and the fact that there were sign-ins from geographically separate locations was also noticed. These findings are really cool if you think about it—the large IT overhead and nearly impossible task of identifying login risks are now easily solved by leveraging machine-learning algorithms. If we look into the further details of the impossible travel to an atypical location, we notice that the first location the user logged in from was in Bangalore, India, on February 25th at 5:18 AM and the second login was from California the same morning of February 25th at 6:22 AM. It would be impossible to log in from both places at such close times unless your VPN connectivity server were in another location (or you deployed a cloud-based server in another location and accessed Microsoft online services from it). In the case that you know the incident to be a false positive, you can choose to mark it as a false positive or just ignore it.

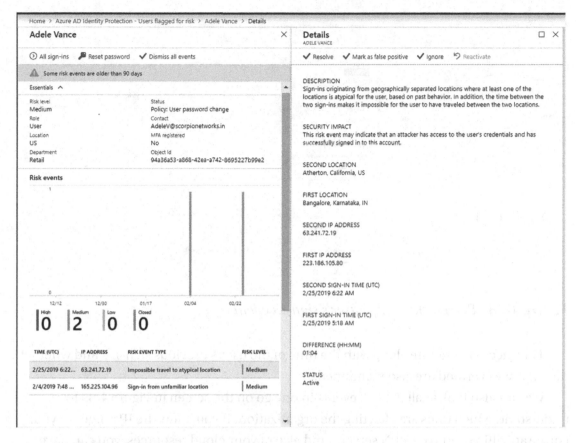

Figure 4-37. Detailed view of risks for a user

If you would like to investigate this user further and check all her sign-ins or manually reset her password, you can do so from the screen showing a list of her sign-in events in Figure 4-38.

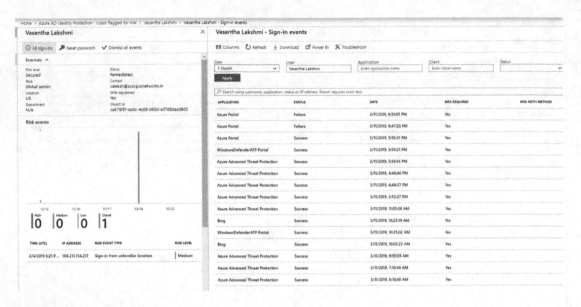

Figure 4-38. *Screen showing a user's sign-in events*

The success or failure along with the time of the user's previous sign-ins and whether the MFA was verified are also mentioned.

We can also look at all the risk events in one go on the screen in Figure 4-39 to understand which ones are affecting the organization. If you know the IP ranges of your corporate office and your VPN servers, and also of your cloud resources, you can have them all mentioned under "Add known IP address ranges."

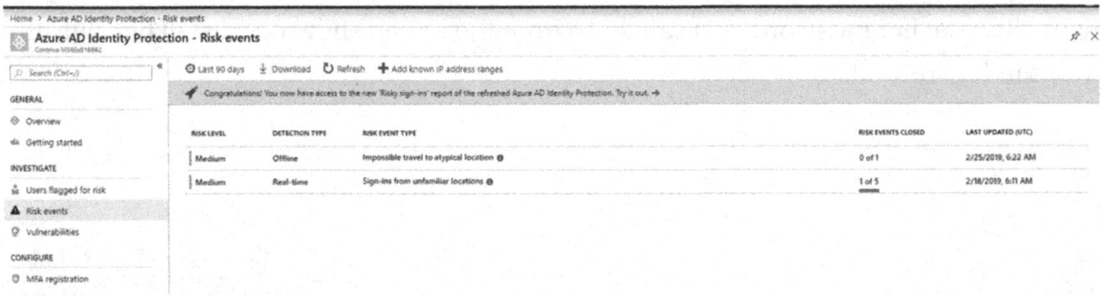

Figure 4-39. *"Risk events" screen in Azure AD ID Protection*

Once all the users listed in Figure 4-40 go through MFA, all these alerts will be autoremediated. The last account is an example of closed/autoremediated account.

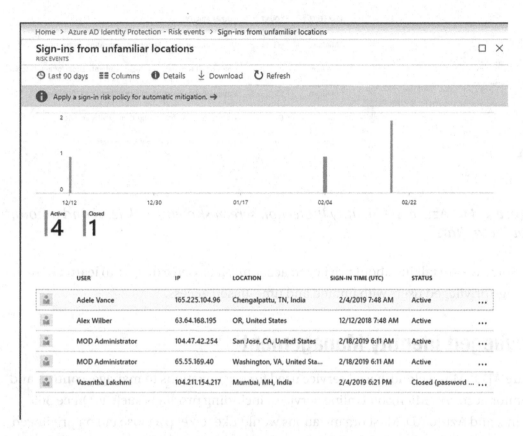

Figure 4-40. Autoremediation process for sign-ins from unfamiliar locations

In Figure 4-41, all the vulnerabilities are detected. This can also be viewed as an implementation of best practices. Enforcing MFA for your user accounts helps to autoremediate user/sign-in risks and keeps your credentials safe. Privileged roles should be granted very carefully and assigned in a timely manner and removed when not required. Stale accounts ideally should not have privileged roles. Having too many admin accounts with privileged roles and a lot of global admins can create more surface area for an attacker, since there are more accounts to tamper with or abuse.

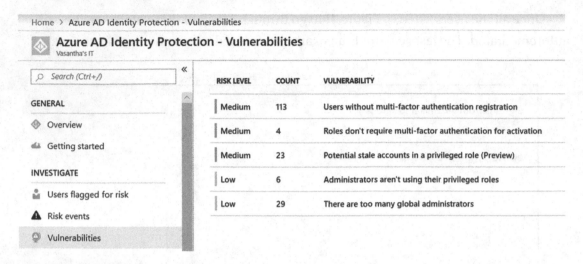

Figure 4-41. *Azure AD Identity Protection screen showing risk level and amount of vulnerabilities*

Since we are talking about privileged accounts, let's delve deeper to learn about and manage privileged users with limited and time-based access.

Privileged Identity Management

Azure AD PIM is a cloud-based service used for organizations to manage, control, and monitor access to Microsoft Online Services, including products such as Office 365, Intune, and Azure AD. Most organizations would like to keep a close tab on privileged accounts and enable access to them only when it is required. The idea is to reduce the chance of a malicious actor gaining access to a user credential that could be a stale privileged account or a sparsely used account.

PIM helps by providing information about who accessed a resource, which resource was accessed, when and where it was done, and why it was it used.

To solve the problem of having multiple admin accounts, most of them unused; to ensure that Azure resources are accessed only after account verification (with just-in-time access); to ensure that an interim approver manages access to these resources (with approval required); to enforce the requirement of MFA to activate a privileged role; to enforce time-bound access to resources (with a set date and time); to require justification to access a privileged role and receive alerts, and send notifications when a privileged role is used; to conduct access reviews; and to keep tabs on audit history are all reasons why PIM should be leveraged by every organization.

The current security perimeter is defined by the authentication and authorization controls in an organization. The old network security perimeter approach is obsolete in today's mobile/BYOD world, which ranges from using on-premise apps to using SaaS-based apps.

Let's jump into getting started with the PIM service (both PIM and Azure AD Identity Protection are Azure AD Premium P2, EMS E5, and Microsoft 365 Enterprise E5 features).

In `https://portal.azure.com`, search for "Privileged Identity Managed" in "All Services." To begin, you will have to consent to use PIM, as shown in Figure 4-42. The user/global admin's identity will be verified through MFA, which will be required if not already set up for the user account.

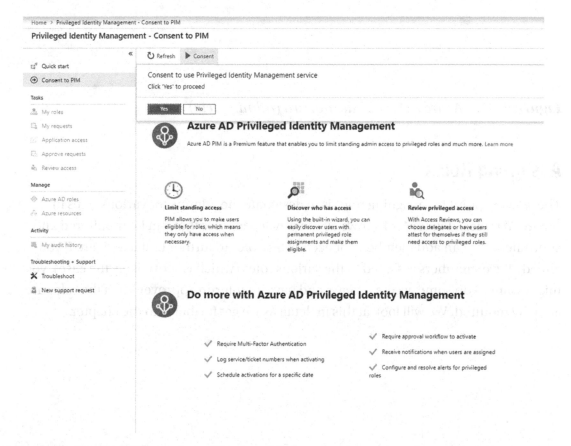

Figure 4-42. *Providing consent to use PIM*

In the "Manage" section, we can define Azure AD roles and Azure resources. A look at PIM's intuitive "Azure AD roles" dashboard in Figure 4-43 gives us information about the PIM roles activated over the past seven days; notifications that require our attention; a distribution of eligible, permanent, and active privileged IDs; and information about directory roles and how many of them are MFA enabled, active, and eligible.

Figure 4-43. *"Azure AD roles" dashboard (admin view)*

Assigning Roles

The starting point for assigning roles is to designate the admins for various roles in "Azure AD roles." Figure 4-44 shows all the privileged roles that can be monitored and controlled. We can add members for each of the roles to further manage them. If you already have members assigned to the various roles (which is most likely the case), you might want to do some access reviews and have an interim approver see if the roles are actually required. We will look at this in detail as we get further into the chapter.

Figure 4-44. *Assigning roles in PIM*

As shown in Figure 4-45, upon adding a new member to a role, you can choose to keep the person eligible, make him or her permanent, or remove the user. (Users that are marked as eligible will be given just-in-time access, where they are required to activate their role when they perform privileged actions. Their access will be time bound, ranging from hours to days, with the time starting upon the activation.)

Figure 4-45. *Defining members' roles*

Activating Roles

We will next require users to activate their roles. All users with assigned eligibility have access to the PIM portal. They can navigate to "My roles" under "Tasks" on the "Azure AD roles" page, as shown in Figure 4-46. Here they will be given the option to activate their roles.

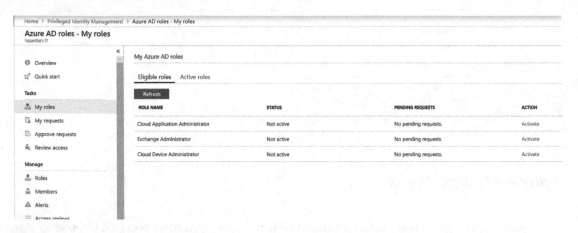

Figure 4-46. *PIM page for users to activate their roles*

Then, as shown in Figure 4-47, users/temporary admins need to verify their identity with MFA if they are already registered to do so. If not, they can register for MFA here.

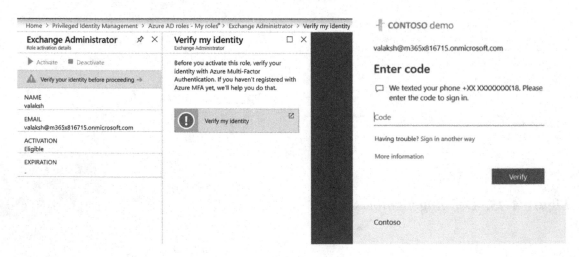

Figure 4-47. *Verification of identity with MFA*

The exchange administrator will then need to activate the users' roles as shown in Figure 4-48. The administrator can provide custom activation time, too, which will require him or her to prove and document that the reason is mandatory. He or she will then be provided with an hour-long access to the exchange console after which it will be deactivated.

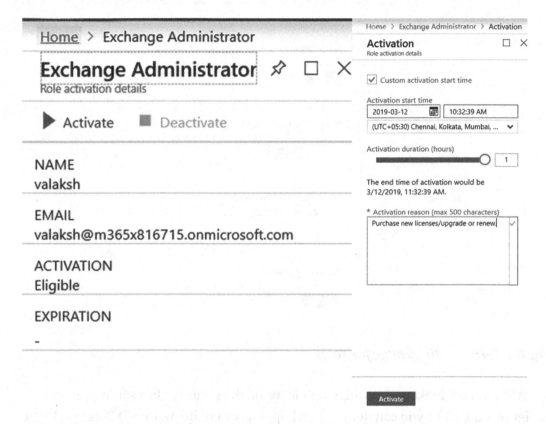

Figure 4-48. *Activating Exchange Administrator role from PIM console*

To set the time frame for the activation, go to "Azure AD roles," "Roles," and, as shown in Figure 4-49, choose either "Default for all roles" to set a standard time frame or define individual timelines for each role. Notice that I have enabled "Require approval" to let the security admin or global admin decide if the role should be activated.

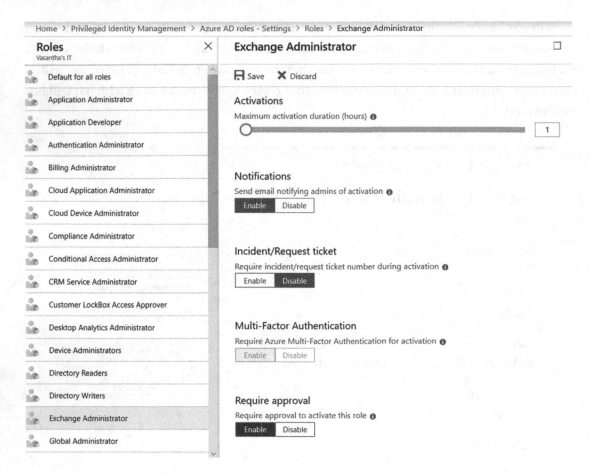

Figure 4-49. *Settings page for roles*

While we are looking at settings, let's focus on the security alert settings, shown in Figure 4-50. Here, you can define what happens when the Azure AD Roles (in PIM) activation does not happen within a few days (in this case, the admin will revoke the privilege after 30 days), what happens to stale accounts, what happens when roles are assigned outside of PIM, and so on. You will be sent a notification for these alerts.

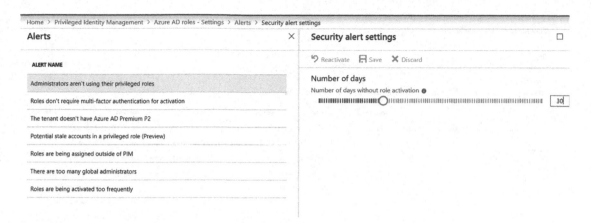

Figure 4-50. "Security alert settings" page

Approving Requests

If you have enabled approvals to be required for admin roles, those requests will show up under "Tasks"/"Approve requests." The approver for each role can also be defined under the settings for the roles.

Auditing

The last important step in the process is to be able to audit. On the "My audit history" page shown in Figure 4-51, we can see the role setting changes and other actions taken with PIM and the corresponding details. Every change made from the PIM console and the activation of roles is captured here.

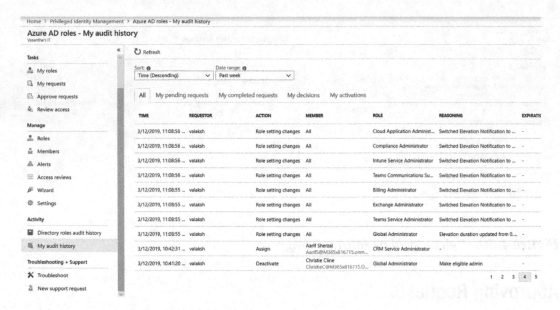

Figure 4-51. *"My audit history" page*

Figure 4-52 shows an alert email sent to notify you that a global administrator was assigned outside of PIM. You can see this alert not only in this email but also as part of all organization-wide alerts, available under "Manage alerts."

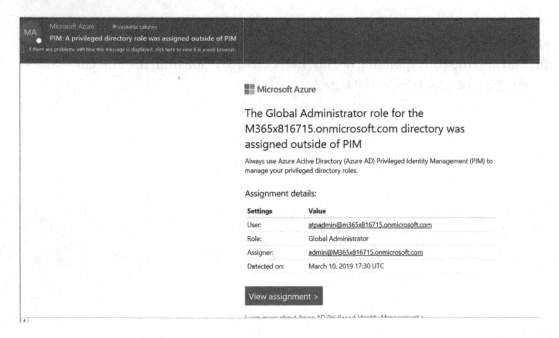

Figure 4-52. *Alert about a global administrator being assigned outside of PIM*

Access Reviews

Last but not the least, we need to identify all the members in order to help an
organization ascertain if all its global admins are even necessary. Doing so will be
useful because an administrator might find it challenging to cover all the groups and
users. You could also identify a team manager to do so if you choose. This can be done
as a one-time activity or frequently conducted to ensure that all the privileged roles are
kept in check.

You can create access reviews for Azure AD roles or Azure Resources. In Figure 4-53,
I have selected to do an access review on "Device Administrators."

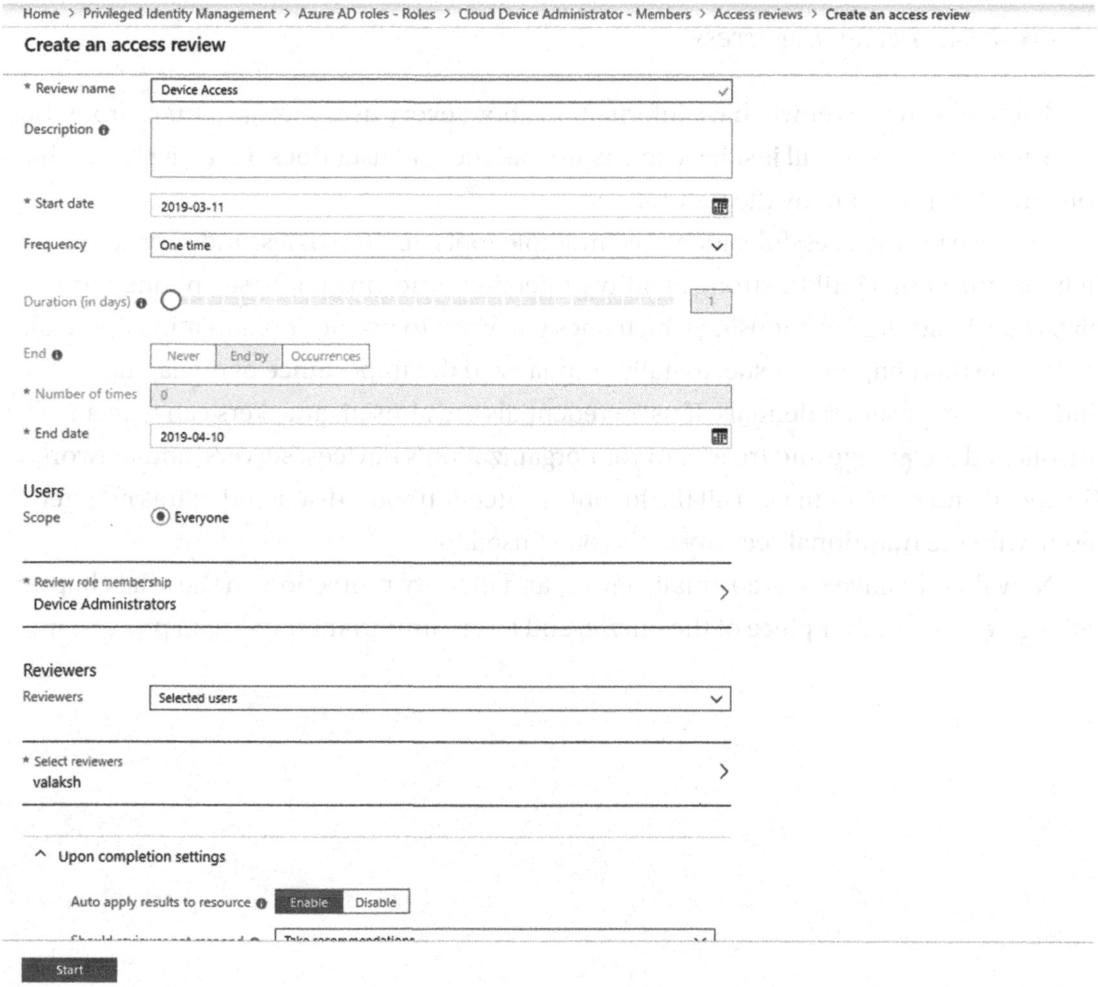

Figure 4-53. *Creating access reviews*

You can review the access in the PIM console under "Review access" as shown in Figure 4-54. Here I've selected to do an access review on just one role, but it can also be leveraged for multiple role reviews.

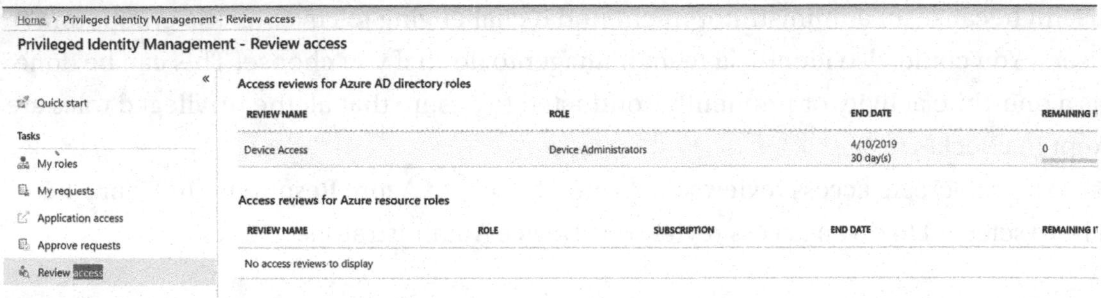

Figure 4-54. *Reviewing access*

The access reviewer will have information about every user's usage pattern from the algorithms. He or she will just have to ensure that the end user does not actively use the roles and approve or deny the request.

We have now successfully identified multiple tools, technologies, and services to help organizations build a strong identity protection. Knowing all these options should give you a head start in choosing which ones you want to use or implementing them all.

I hope this chapter has successfully emphasized the importance of managing and protecting user credentials. If user credentials are abused, attackers can gain an unsolicited advantage and tread into your organization's devices, servers, and network. Go ahead and stop them with all the identity protection tools discussed in this chapter along with the traditional security tools you're used to.

Now that we have covered email, device, and identity protection, in the final chapter let's delve into another piece of the puzzle, and a very important one—data protection.

CHAPTER 5

Data Protection

Collaboration and data sharing by employees are necessities in today's world, as they increase productivity among users. With these tools, data protection in the mobile-first, cloud-first world is a little more challenging and requires a slight shift in mindset. No longer is the data just stored on the premises; the data can be on both corporate and BYOD devices such as desktops, laptops, Androids, and iOS mobiles. The data can also be stored in SharePoint, Exchange and other Office 365 apps, third-party SaaS-based apps, and thumb drives, and can be sent to multiple organizations' email addresses.

So, the onus is on everybody to ensure that the data is safe. Along with educating users about the importance of securing corporate data and setting policies, it is also vital to ensure we have the right set of controls in place for protecting the data wherever it might reside.

In this chapter, we will look at the different ways to protect your data—at the document and document library levels and in OneDrive, Windows, mobile apps, and SaaS-based/cloud apps.

Azure Information Protection

Figure 5-1 shows some of the options for securing enterprise data with various solutions offered by AIP.

© Vasantha Lakshmi 2019
V. Lakshmi, *Beginning Security with Microsoft Technologies*, https://doi.org/10.1007/978-1-4842-4853-9_5

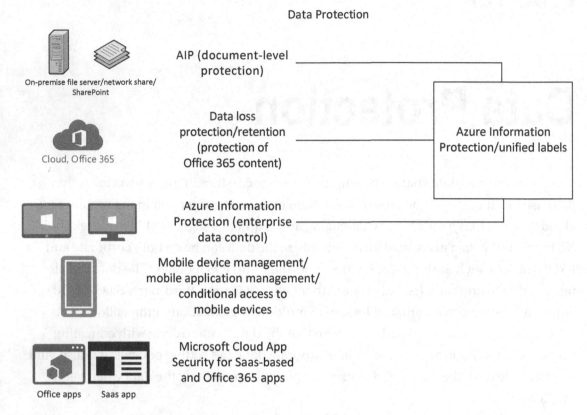

Figure 5-1. *Azure Information Protection solutions for securing enterprise data*

To put it simply, AIP embeds protection into documents and labels them, too. The applied protection/encryption gets carried along with the document wherever it travels. The protection itself comes from the underlying technology Rights Management Service (RMS).

AIP can help manually apply the label or apply the label automatically as well. Users can also be given recommendations about the security label requirement of a document based on the conditions or policies set up the organization.

Here's a look at how the RMS protection technology works, as shown in Figure 5-2:

- The document gets encrypted using AES (Advanced Encryption Standard) with a symmetric key that is unique for each document.

- The defined policy is used for the document, specifying if the content, when shared, will give the receiver usage rights, such as to view, coauthor, print, save, and so on. The header of the file contains a content key that is protected by a tenant root key. The key uses an RSA (Rivest, Shamir, Adleman) protection algorithm.

- The policy also defines which users are allowed to access the documents.

- At no point does Azure see the content of the document but only the policies that are defined through the Azure RMS service/AIP blade in Azure. In case your organization requires additional security, you can plan to use bring your own key (BYOK) or hold your own key (HYOK).

- When the document is shared with a user, that person will have to authenticate with a Azure RMS service. The usage rights get applied, and the AES content key gets extracted, when the document gets decrypted (it is reencrypted using the public RSA key) and embedded into the RMS client.

- The RMS client on the user's system will start operating the user's private key for decrypting the body of documents as needed.

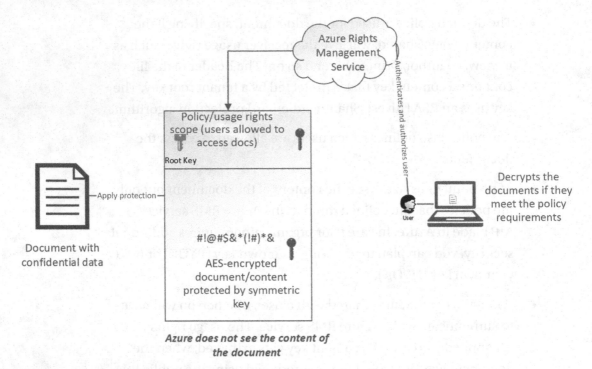

Figure 5-2. *RMS protection technology process*

AIP Policies

Now that we understand the concept of AIP, let's delve into setting the policies. To do so:

1. Go to `https://portal.azure.com` and click "All Services," then select "Azure Information Protection." You will see some default labels and protection templates, as shown in Figure 5-3. You can edit one of the default labels or create a new label by clicking "+ Add a new label."

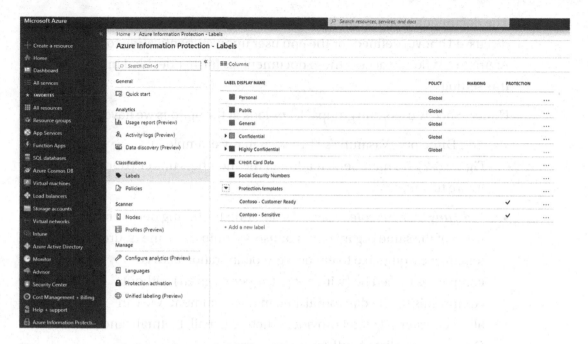

Figure 5-3. *Labels and templates available on the AIP site*

2. Start by giving a name and description to your new label in the "Label display name" box on the right side of the screen shown in Figure 5-4.

3. Then, under "Set permissions for documents and emails containing this label," choose "Protection," then "Azure (Cloud Key)." Select the set of users to whom you would like to target this label and the set of permissions, as specified in the following list, that should be granted to the selective list of users.

    - *Coowner*: has the same rights as the creator of the document.

    - *Coauthor*: has all rights except change, save as, export, and full control.

    - *Reviewer*: has full control; can print, copy, change, save as, and export rights.

    - *Viewer*: only has the right to view, open, read, and allow macros.

    - *Custom*: permissions can be defined and customized for this user.

The document, when shared, will have the usage rights (as discussed above) defined for the end user upon authenticating to Azure AD. Who can access these documents is further decided in this setting.

Under "Specify users and groups", let us look at the options we have:

- Add Directory (Vasantha's IT as seen in my example in Figure 5-2): All members: It adds all the members under your Azure tenant.

- *"Add any authenticated users"*: In addition to sharing between users of the same organization or users within the same Azure tenant, we would like to encourage collaboration across companies if need be (with apt permissions given) without compromising the data published in the document. We can also add external email providers such as Gmail, Hotmail, and Outlook to the list of authenticated users.

- *"Browse directory"*: adds all the members under your Azure tenant.

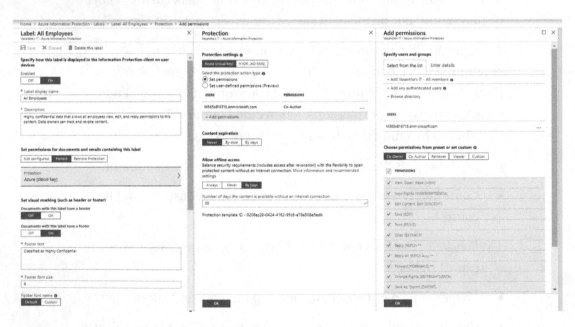

Figure 5-4. *AIP label and its protection*

Note   In Azure Key, the Azure tenant key is automatically generated by Microsoft. In Azure, the HYOK, the RMS key that we discussed earlier, is held by the enterprises. You should plan to use this key especially for opaque data and top-secret data. Keep in mind that it works with AD and Active Directory Rights Management Services (ADRMS) only and requires you maintain your on-premise server along with less external collaboration features.

---

4. We can also set the content expiration. If you want to allow some or all the users to access the documents you share for only a certain number of days, select how long they can access the content either by date or by days. Likewise, you can permit your audience to view documents offline without authentication for only certain number of days or never or always.

5. There is one more important setting and that is the one where you set the conditions for the label, as shown in Figure 5-5. To set a condition, click "+ Add a new condition" in the left panel. If your documents match any condition already set up and you would like to automatically apply these labels to the documents in your organization, you can arrange to do that here.

    Generally speaking, it is a good idea to set a policy for any document with sensitive information, such as your financial, medical, and private documents that contain information such as your bank account number, insurance number, and passport number. These documents will then be automatically labeled and protected, or can even be set to pop up as a recommendation.

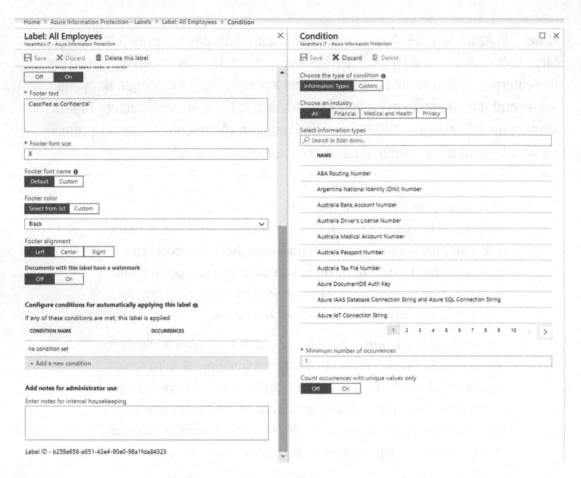

Figure 5-5. *Setting conditions for your label in AIP*

6. As shown in Figure 5-6, if you choose to select a custom word that should be automatically applied to your labels, or even to recommend one, it is a good idea to use what is known as a regular expression, or regex, which refers to a specific set of characters that can be used to search within a text. Here I have chosen to use a custom condition and in the "Match exact phrase or pattern" search field, I have searched for key terms such as "Credit Card," "Bank," and "Contract." If there is a match, the label and protection will be applied.

7. If you would like to have the number of occurrences of these words (multiple credit card numbers or SSN, or multiple custom words) increased in the document, you can increase the number in "Minimum number of occurrences."

Figure 5-6. *Setting custom words and conditions for your label*

8. Once the conditions are set, you can decide how the label should
    be created by choosing "Auto"/"Default" or "Custom" for the
    options in Figure 5-7. If you want to set the label automatically, it
    is important that you have an Azure Information Protection P2,
    EMS E5, or Microsoft 365 Enterprise E5 license. If your policy does
    not work, this is the first thing you will want to look into.

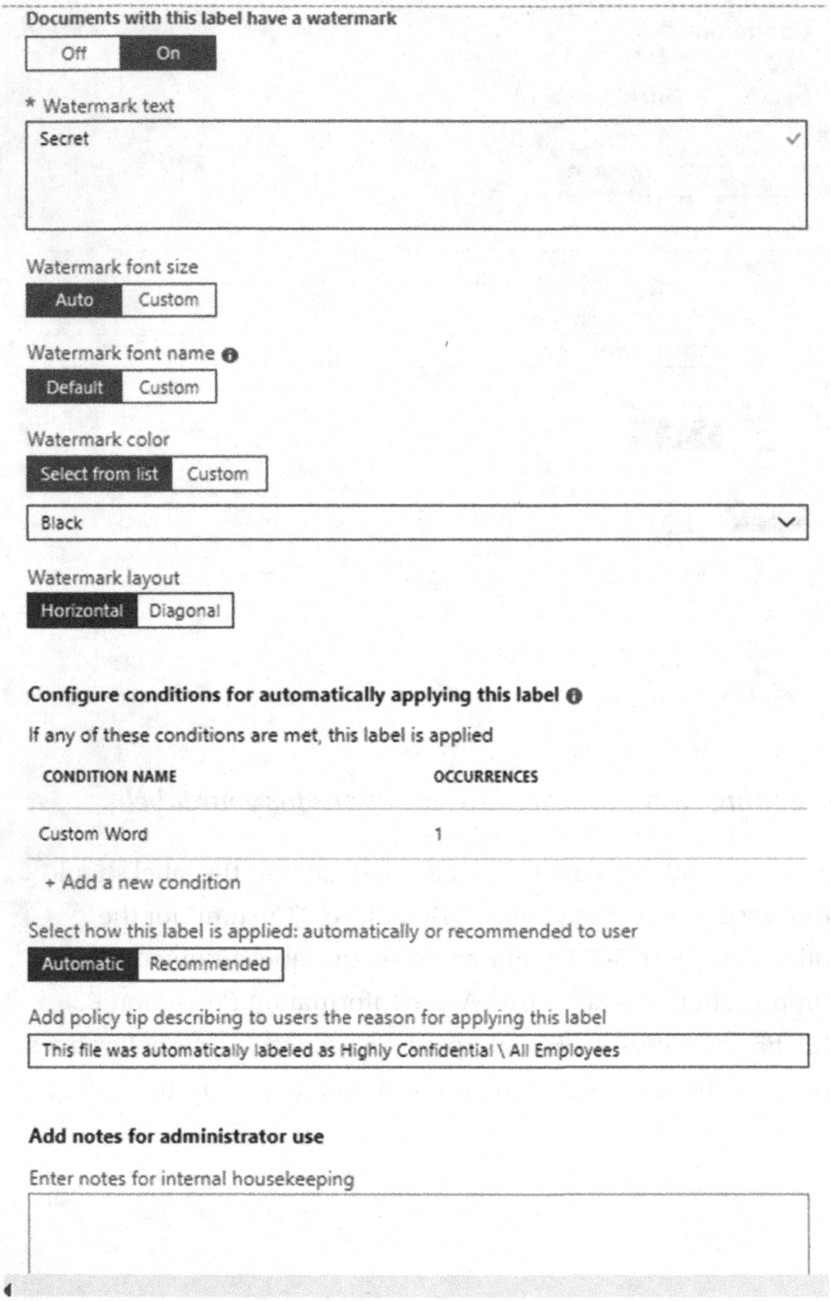

Documents with this label have a watermark

| Off | On |

* Watermark text

Secret ✓

Watermark font size

| Auto | Custom |

Watermark font name ❶

| Default | Custom |

Watermark color

| Select from list | Custom |

Black ⌄

Watermark layout

| Horizontal | Diagonal |

Configure conditions for automatically applying this label ❶

If any of these conditions are met, this label is applied

CONDITION NAME	OCCURRENCES
Custom Word	1

+ Add a new condition

Select how this label is applied: automatically or recommended to user

| Automatic | Recommended |

Add policy tip describing to users the reason for applying this label

This file was automatically labeled as Highly Confidential \ All Employees

Add notes for administrator use

Enter notes for internal housekeeping

Figure 5-7. AIP Label Automatic Application

9. We then want to choose the global policy settings to ensure the labels are visible, as shown in Figure 5-8. I have enabled a few other settings as well, such as to have a label applied by users for all documents and emails and to automatically have a label applied matching the highest classification for emails with attachments.

Home > Azure Information Protection - Policies > Policy: Global

Policy: Global
Vasantha's IT - Azure Information Protection

≡≡ Columns   🖫 Save   ✕ Discard   🗑 Delete   ↓ Export

▶ ■ Highly Confidential   Global

Add or remove labels

Configure settings to display and apply on Information Protection end users

* Title

| Sensitivity |

Tooltip

| The current label for this content. This setting identifies the risk to the business if this content is shared with unauthorized people inside or outside the organization. |

Select the default label

| None ⌄ |

Send audit data to Azure Information Protection analytics ❶

| Off | Not configured |

All documents and emails must have a label (applied automatically or by users)

| Off | On |

Users must provide justification to set a lower classification label, remove a label, or remove protection

| Off | On |

For email messages with attachments, apply a label that matches the highest classification of those attachments

| Off | Automatic | Recommended |

Add policy tip describing to users the reasons for applying this label

| This email was automatically labeled as ${Attachment.Label} ✓ |

Display the Information Protection bar in Office apps

| Off | On |

Add the Do Not Forward button to the Outlook ribbon

| Off | On |

Make the custom permissions option available for users

| Off | On |

Provide a custom URL for the Azure Information Protection client "Tell me more" web page (optional; otherwise keep blank)

| *Enter a custom URL or keep blank* |

◀

Figure 5-8. *Choosing settings for your labels*

It's time to check for user experience.

Checking the Protection

Now let's look at how to install the AIP client on a user's desktop/laptop by going to `www.microsoft.com/en-us/download/details.aspx?id=53018`. This agent will connect the user to the AIP service and create the labels for that particular user after the authentication is done.

Close all the documents and reopen them to see that the AIP plug-in is loading correctly. We have chosen that the label be set as "Highly Confidential," as shown in Figure 5-9, to detect terms such as "contract," "credit card," and the like. The document will then recognize such terms when you save or send emails.

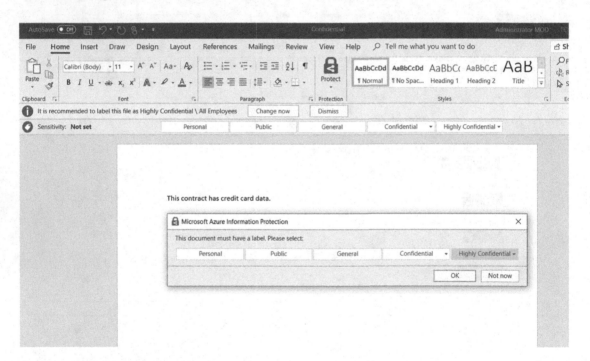

Figure 5-9. *AIP Label: User Experience*

Once you protect the document when saving, wherever it then travels it will take the encryption along with it, and only the users/groups added in the permissions will be given access based on the usage rights defined.

Protecting the document can be done automatically from the Azure portal as shown in the previous screenshot, or as an author you can decide to apply the protection yourself on the system. If you right-click the document and select "Classify and protect,"

it will let you define customized policies for new users or groups. In Figure 5-10, I have
decided to give view-only rights to a user (audience of the document). You can also
choose to have the content expire by a certain date.

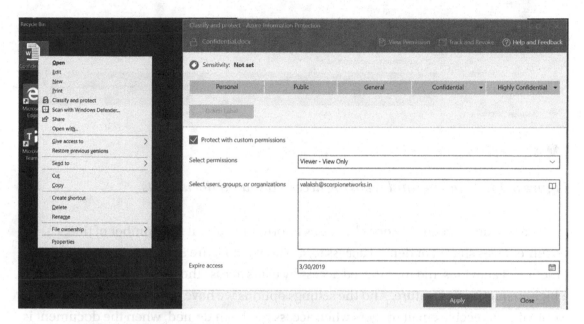

Figure 5-10. *Applying AIP labels using File Explorer*

Document Tracking for Document Authors

The user/author can keep track of or even revoke access to his or her shared documents,
as shown in Figure 5-11, by going to the "protect" add-in under O365 Documents,
Outlook and clicking "Track and Revoke."

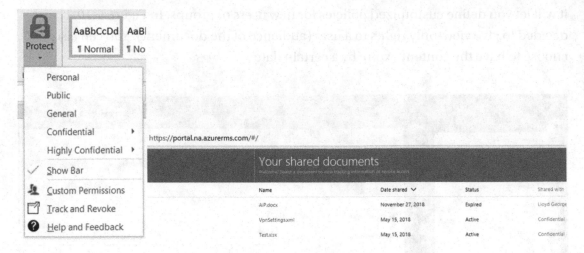

Figure 5-11. *Tracking and revoking access to shared documents*

The tracking screen "AIP.docx" gives us information about the number of times a document was shared or denied access to, as shown in Figure 5-12. You can also see a timeline of activities and map-based access by users across the globe, which has been a highly sought-after feature. And the settings options we have here let us decide if we would like to receive email triggers when access has been denied, when the document is opened, and so forth.

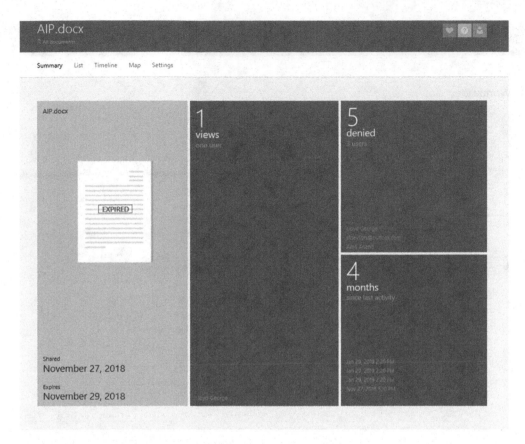

Figure 5-12. *"AIP.docx" tracking screen*

Figure 5-13 gives us another look at the global document distribution for all cases in which the document has been opened and authenticated with Azure AD. At any point in time, you, as the author of the document, can also revoke access to the shared documents.

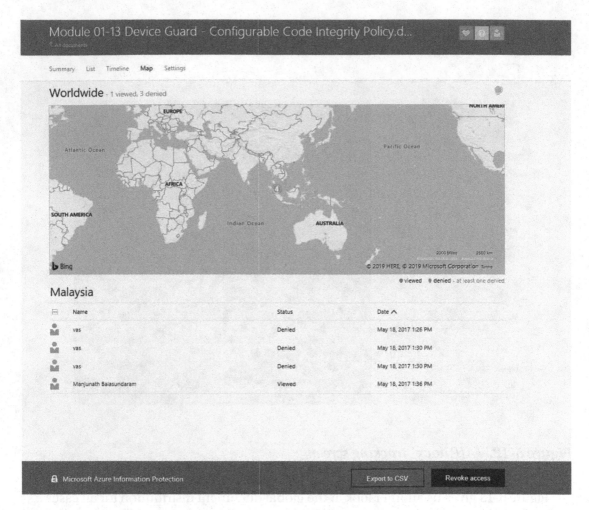

Figure 5-13. Global document distribution for a document

The advantages of creating these policies in AIP are that doing so ensures that the author has the control and reduces the IT overhead in the time spent identifying the critical documents.

At the same time, the documents can also be enforced to apply labels and protection automatically if they are company-confidential documents.

I would recommend setting it up to enable both of these scenarios.

Applying Settings in the SharePoint Document Library and Exchange Online

To cater to a scenario in which we would like to apply IRM (Information Rights Management) settings in SharePoint or Exchange Online, we can get started by enabling protection activation under the AIP blade. It is important to remember that IRM helps to encrypt and protect documents in SharePoint and Exchange but not to label them. This activation can also be enabled from the Microsoft 365 or Office 365 admin center under the "Rights Management" setting (Office 365 or Microsoft 365 Enterprise E3 are required to do so, or Azure Rights Management can be added as add-on feature).

Applying IRM Settings in SharePoint

We then go to the SharePoint settings in the SharePoint list/library that we would like to edit and select "Information Rights Management."

Figure 5-14 shows the IRM settings that apply to a library. Here, I've chosen to restrict permissions to the library upon download, which prevents documents from being opened in the browser itself. These documents will only be allowed to print, and I've set the document expiration date for 20 days after the download. It is required that users verify their credentials every once in a while, and I've enabled group protection so that users will be able to share with members of the same group.

In this way, all the documents in the RMS demo library will be encrypted/protected.

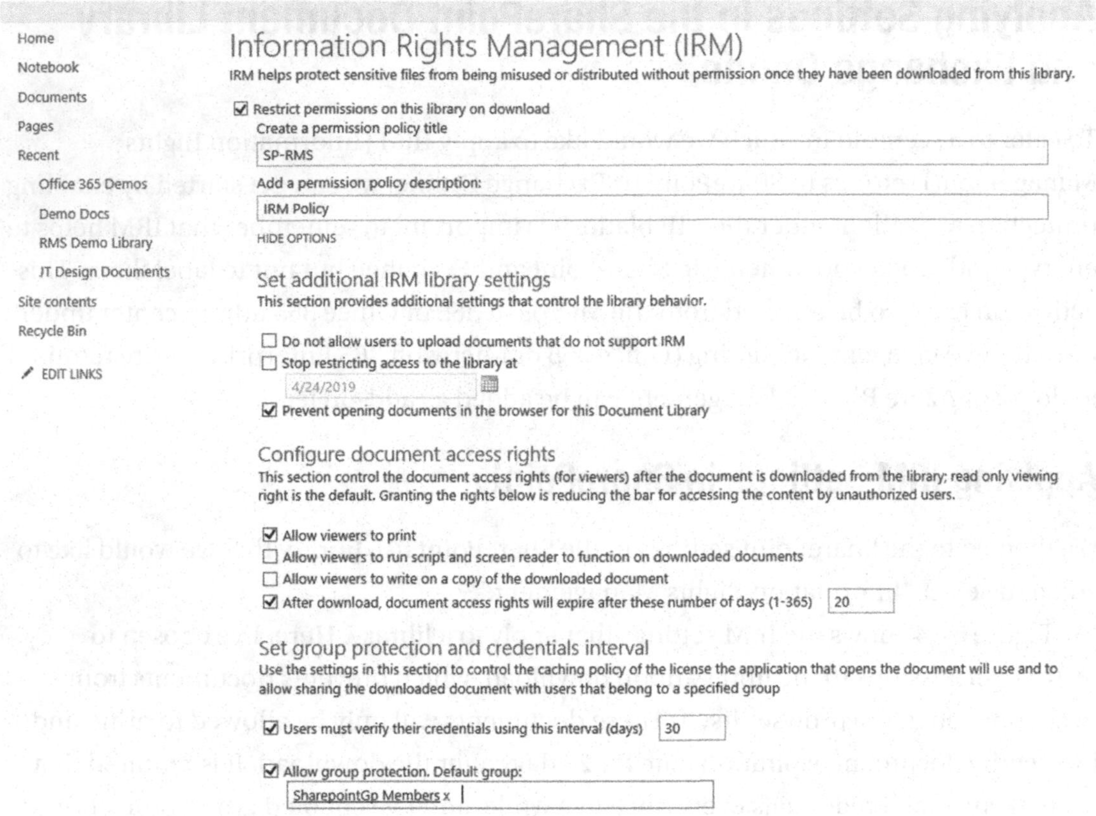

Home
Notebook
Documents
Pages
Recent
    Office 365 Demos
    Demo Docs
    RMS Demo Library
    JT Design Documents
Site contents
Recycle Bin

✎ EDIT LINKS

Information Rights Management (IRM)

IRM helps protect sensitive files from being misused or distributed without permission once they have been downloaded from this library.

☑ Restrict permissions on this library on download
Create a permission policy title

| SP-RMS |

Add a permission policy description:

| IRM Policy |

HIDE OPTIONS

Set additional IRM library settings

This section provides additional settings that control the library behavior.

☐ Do not allow users to upload documents that do not support IRM
☐ Stop restricting access to the library at
    | 4/24/2019 | 🗓 |
☑ Prevent opening documents in the browser for this Document Library

Configure document access rights

This section control the document access rights (for viewers) after the document is downloaded from the library; read only viewing right is the default. Granting the rights below is reducing the bar for accessing the content by unauthorized users.

☑ Allow viewers to print
☐ Allow viewers to run script and screen reader to function on downloaded documents
☐ Allow viewers to write on a copy of the downloaded document
☑ After download, document access rights will expire after these number of days (1-365) | 20 |

Set group protection and credentials interval

Use the settings in this section to control the caching policy of the license the application that opens the document will use and to allow sharing the downloaded document with users that belong to a specified group

☑ Users must verify their credentials using this interval (days) | 30 |

☑ Allow group protection. Default group:
    | SharepointGp Members x |

Figure 5-14. *IRM library settings in SharePoint*

Figure 5-15 shows the document the end user sees after downloading or opening a document from the SharePoint library. The yellow ribbon indicates that the document is restricted. When the user clicks "Change Permissions," he or she will see the same set of settings as applied before.

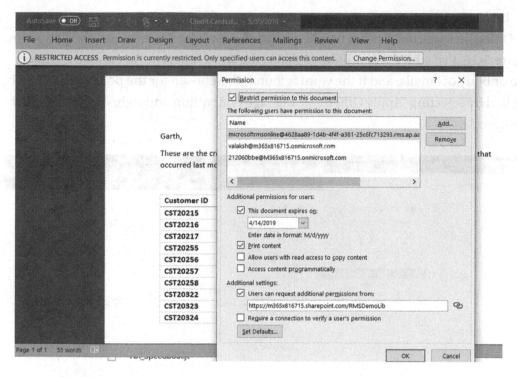

Figure 5-15. *SharePoint IRM: User Experience*

That's how data protection with IRM is managed for SharePoint. Let's next look into the options we have for Exchange Online.

Applying IRM Setting in Exchange Online

IRM has been integrated with Office Message Encryption (OME). We can get started by testing the IRM connection. Ensure that the testing pulls up the RMS templates available in your tenant and that it successfully verifies the connection.

```
$UserCredential = Get-Credential
$Session = New-PSSession -ConfigurationName Microsoft.Exchange
-ConnectionUri https://outlook.office365.com/powershell-liveid/ -Credential
$UserCredential -Authentication Basic –AllowRedirection
Import-PSSession $Session -DisableNameChecking
Test-IRMConfiguration -Sender <user email address>
```

In the Exchange Admin Center, go to "mail flow." We can either create a policy for Office message encryption or edit one we already have for message encryption. In Figure 5-16, I've added a condition to detect the word "encrypt" in either the subject line or body of emails, and if the word is found, I've chosen for the policy or OME to be applied by selecting "Apply Office 365 Message Encryption and rights protection to the message . . . ."

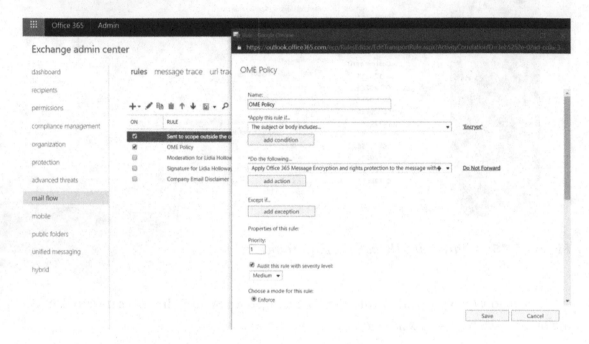

Figure 5-16. *Setting the OME policy*

The detection of the word "encrypt" in the subject line or body of the message will apply the IRM policies. Figure 5-17 shows the message that the recipient of the email will see, "Do not forward: Recipients can't forward, print, or copy content."

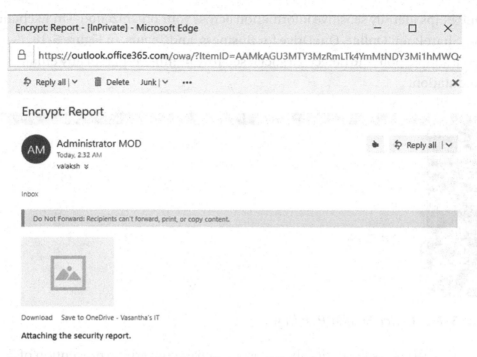

Figure 5-17. Message received when "encrypt" is in the original email

This has the advantages of allowing us to apply IRM policies to an entire SharePoint Library and protecting all the files and folders in it.

IRM/OME policies for Exchange Online will ensure that appropriate emails with customized key terms (such as "encrypt" in the body or subject line) are applied with RMS protection.

It is also recommended that you set this up in organizations to protect data.

Labels and Data Loss Prevention in Office 365

Labels and DLP policies have been available in Office 365 for a while. We can set them up by going to the Office 365 Security & Compliance center. Labels can be used to create categories for different levels of sensitive content, such as personal, public, general, confidential, and highly confidential, and can also be applied to the metadata of the email or document. Labels can also encrypt emails or documents; mark the content; and prevent data loss.

DLP helps identify sensitive information across your organization—in Exchange Online, SharePoint Online, OneDrive for Business, and Teams. In Figure 5-18, I've created a simple policy to detect if a social security number is part of any email/documentation.

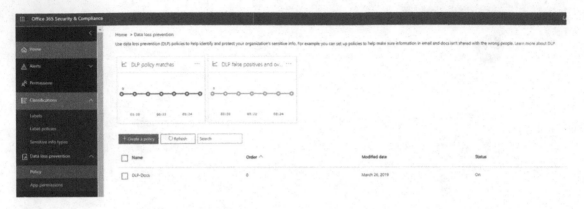

Figure 5-18.   *Office 365 DLP policy*

Figure 5-19 shows the notification a user receives concerning prevention of accidental sharing of sensitive information and how to help in staying compliant.

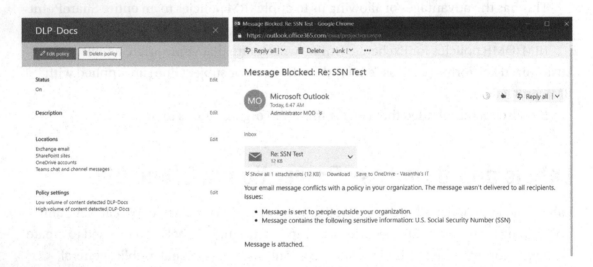

Figure 5-19.   *Message about the prevention of accidental sharing of sensitive information*

Alright, now you have seen that the labels in Office 365 are very similar to those in AIP. But they aren't the same and that often leads to confusion and repetitive tasks, as

AIP labels do not apply to Office DLP. However, that has now been changed with the introduction of Microsoft Information Protection and Unified Labeling, as detailed in Figure 5-20.

Figure 5-20. *Microsoft Information Protection and Unified Labeling process*

The whole concept of unified labeling comes into the picture when we want to create and implement labels from a single place. In this case, if you are just getting started with implementing information protection or even if you are already managing labels, you can choose to migrate labels from AIP to the Microsoft 365 admin center and manage the labels centrally.

There are some considerations, as the management of these labels might not entirely be entirely the same as in Azure, with the color coding and the prompt for custom permission settings not being visible here.

And the AIP client installed on the systems might need to be updated. You can download the update here: `https://www.microsoft.com/en-us/download/details.aspx?id=53018`.

But before you attempt to use unified labeling, you should note that it is still in preview at the time of the writing of this book. So, you can instead get started by migrating your labels and unifying them at Microsoft 365 admin center:

1. Go to AIP blade under `https://portal.azure.com` and activate the "Unified Labeling (preview)," as done in Figure 5-21. You can see whether labels were activated and migrated in the next step.

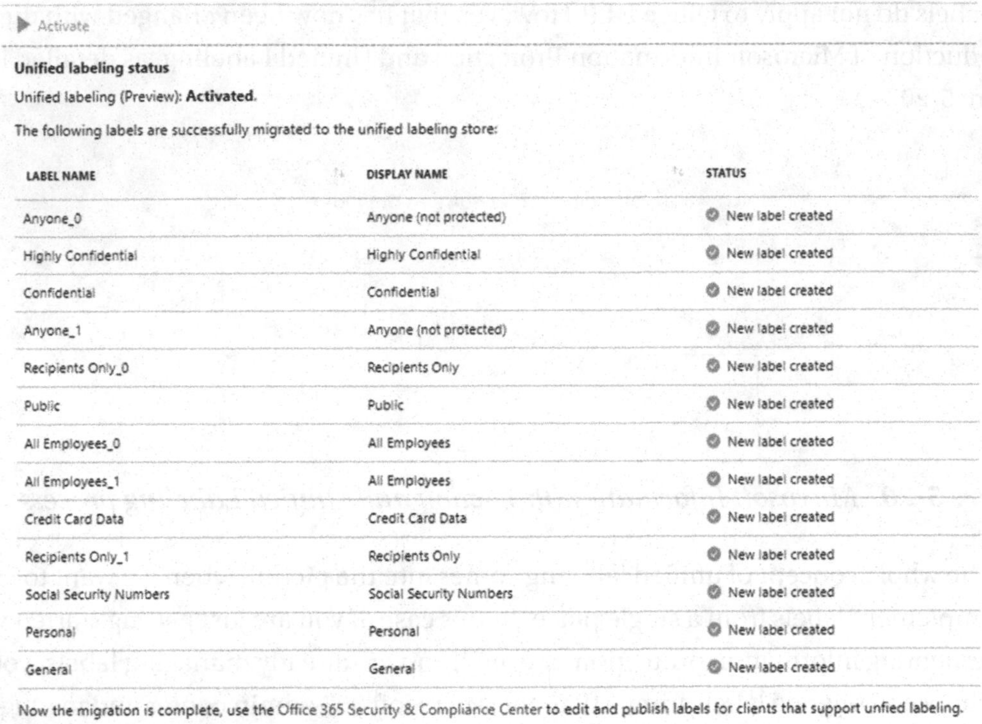

▶ Activate

Unified labeling status

Unified labeling (Preview): **Activated**.

The following labels are successfully migrated to the unified labeling store:

LABEL NAME	DISPLAY NAME	STATUS
Anyone_0	Anyone (not protected)	⊘ New label created
Highly Confidential	Highly Confidential	⊘ New label created
Confidential	Confidential	⊘ New label created
Anyone_1	Anyone (not protected)	⊘ New label created
Recipients Only_0	Recipients Only	⊘ New label created
Public	Public	⊘ New label created
All Employees_0	All Employees	⊘ New label created
All Employees_1	All Employees	⊘ New label created
Credit Card Data	Credit Card Data	⊘ New label created
Recipients Only_1	Recipients Only	⊘ New label created
Social Security Numbers	Social Security Numbers	⊘ New label created
Personal	Personal	⊘ New label created
General	General	⊘ New label created

Now the migration is complete, use the Office 365 Security & Compliance Center to edit and publish labels for clients that support unfied labeling.

Figure 5-21. *"Unified labeling status" screen showing activation success*

2. Now in Microsoft 365 admin center shown in Figure 5-22 we can
    see that the labels have all been unified and are easy to manage.

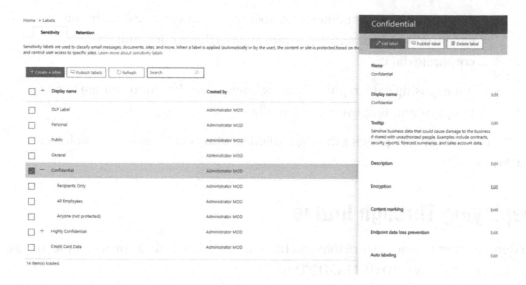

Figure 5-22. *Migrated labels in the Microsoft 365 admin center*

Windows Information Protection

With the advent of BYOD devices combined with the use of company data, the risk of accidental data leaks is increased. Employees might try to save corporate data on their personal OneDrive, on personal thumb drives, or in other such places. To prevent scenarios like these from happening, deleting the data if an employee leaves the company or even if he or she loses a device becomes very essential.

WIP helps with:

- encrypting corporate data on users' devices when downloaded from such places as SharePoint, a network share, or an enterprise web location.

- protecting corporate apps so that any enterprise data on them will not come into contact with nonenterprise or personal apps. (You can leverage WIP policies to block your employees from copying and pasting the data.)

- selecting a list of managed or corporate apps and defining restrictions for them.

- encryption at rest for enterprise documents. Enterprise documents can be edited by enterprise-aware apps as these docs contain corporate data.

- not exposing data to public spaces, such as public cloud storage like Dropbox and Box, even accidentally.

We can deploy WIP policies through MDM solutions such as Microsoft Intune and SCCM.

Deploying Through Intune

To deploy using Intune, ensure that you have the MAM and MDM providers set in Azure AD under "Mobility (MDM&MAM)." Then:

1. Go to Azure Intune and select "Client Apps—App protection policies" to create a new policy, as shown in Figure 5-23.

2. Once you have entered a name and description, since WIP is specifically for Windows 10 devices, select "Windows 10" for the platform.

3. We have two options under "Enrollment state." They are: With Enrollment (devices enrolled in Intune) and Without Enrollment (MAM policies can also be applied to devices that are not enrolled in Intune but still use applications such as Outlook and Word to access corporate data). MAM policies can also be applied to devices that are not enrolled in devices but still use applications (enterprise aware) such as Outlook and Word to access corporate data.

4. Next we have to select the apps on which we want to apply WIP. I have selected a whole list of Microsoft store apps, some desktop apps, and an AppLocker file. You can also create a custom AppLocker file with all the apps on which you plan to apply WIP. I am not excluding any apps from the WIP policy.

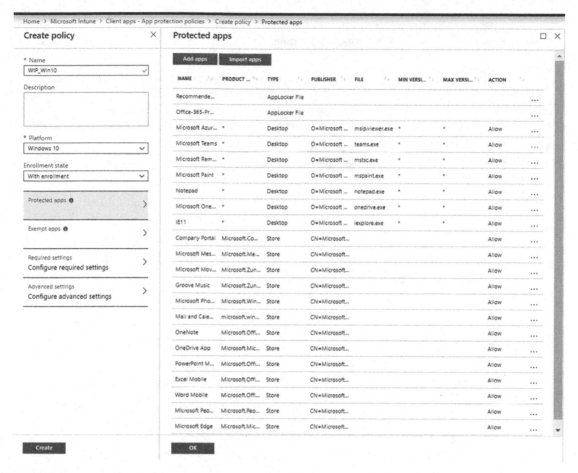

Figure 5-23. *Creating a new policy in Intne*

5. In "Required settings," shown in Figure 5-24, it is important to select the right option to provide your end users. I've chosen to block users from decrypting the data or to save as personal documents, as I absolutely do not want accidental leakage of data to personal apps or public cloud storage or even personal USBs.

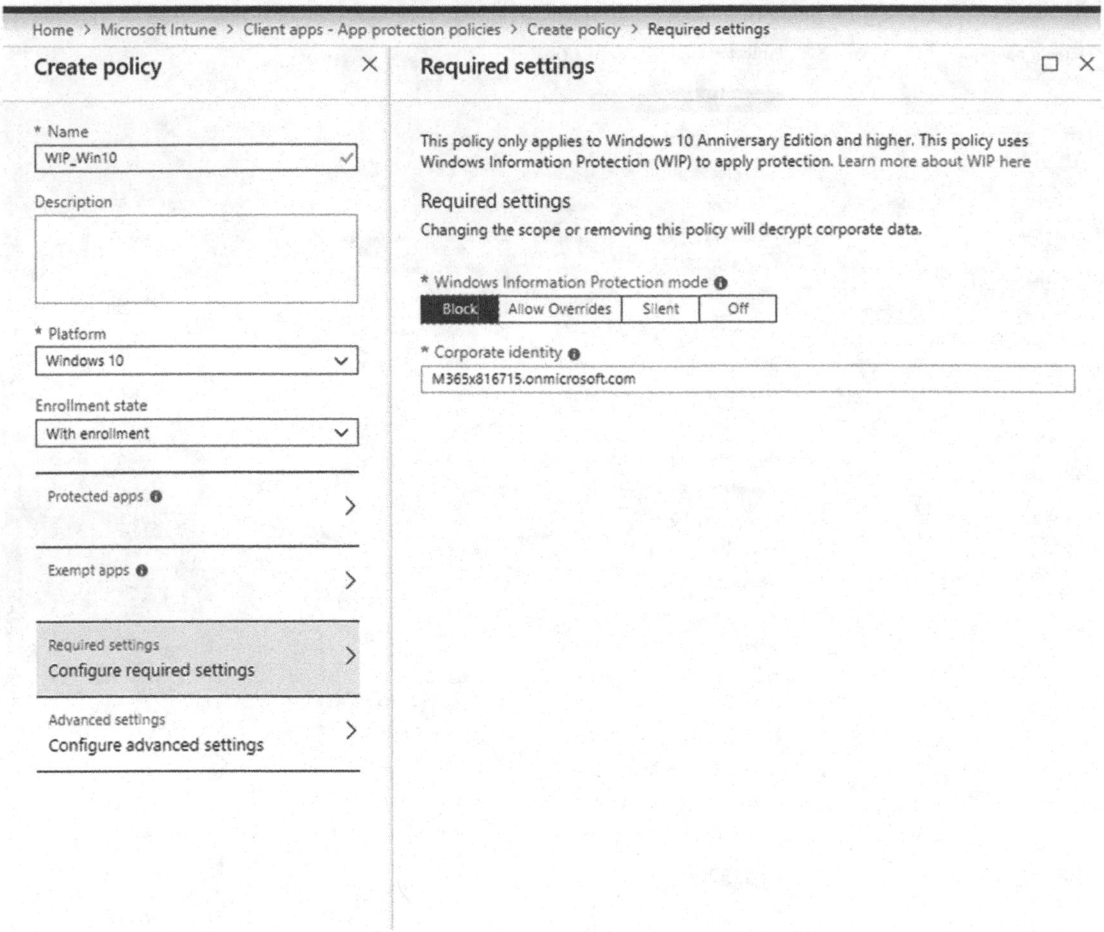

Figure 5-24. *Blocking data decryption of corporate documents from users*

However, you can also choose to let the users be the judge of what to do with the data. When they move or copy corporate data, these actions will be logged (and can be viewed through Azure Monitor). The silent option does not prompt the user to do anything but simply logs any action in which they move data from managed apps. Turning off the policy can decrypt the data if it is already encrypted.

And, as we can infer, the corporate identity is currently set to my tenant. We will add any additional domains under "Advanced settings."

Next, let's ensure that the WIP policy is aware of your network, domain(s), proxies, and IP ranges, so that it applies the policy thoroughly. To do so:

6. Under "Advanced settings," add a network boundary for your organization to apply for cloud resources (SharePoint site URLs, Visual Studio URLs, etc.), as shown in Figure 5-25, and for
•   protected domains to mention domains, subdomains, and so on. You can also specify the DNS suffixes under network domains as well as IPv4 and IPv6 ranges.

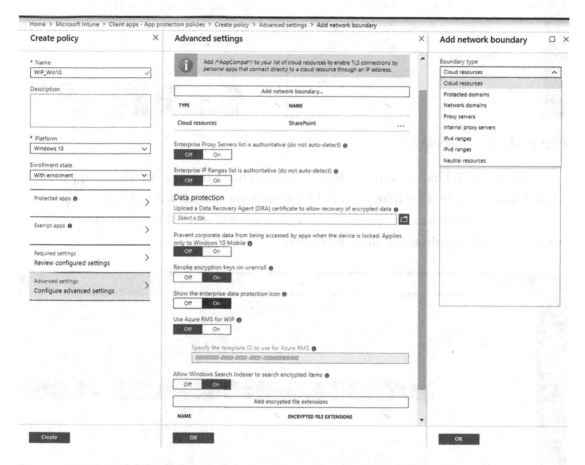

Figure 5-25. *Adding a network boundary to be applied for cloud resources*

7. It is very important to have a data recovery agent certificate (you can manually create one using a cipher) to allow the encrypted data to be recovered in case of an accident or lockout that results from the loss of local encryption keys. Once the policy is created, do not forget to add groups in assignments to test/apply the policy.

Figure 5-26 shows what the user will see. All the applications listed for the WIP policy will have a protected icon that shows that the app/website is managed by your organization.

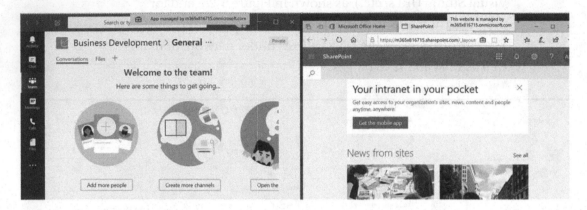

Figure 5-26. *User view*

In Figure 5-27, I have attempted to copy the text from Teams (a managed app) into a Word document (not yet managed, as I have not signed in). It will not let me copy the text but instead pastes the message "Your organization doesn't allow you to use work content with this application" onto my screen.

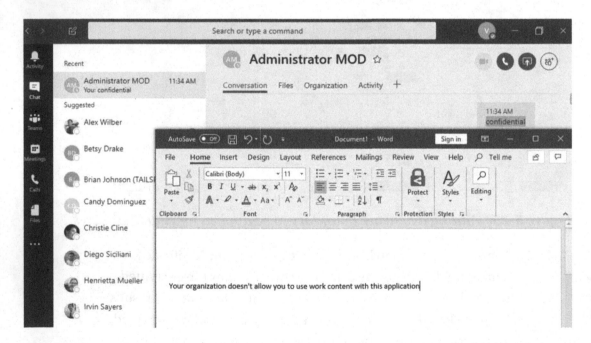

Figure 5-27. *The message the user sees in Microsoft Word when using data protection*

Users can have a similar experience when they download an Excel document from SharePoint (a managed app) and try to save the file. As you can see in Figure 5-28, I am allowed to save the file only as an Enterprise document. Since in the previous setting, I did not choose the option of overriding, I am not given the option to save the document as a personal one.

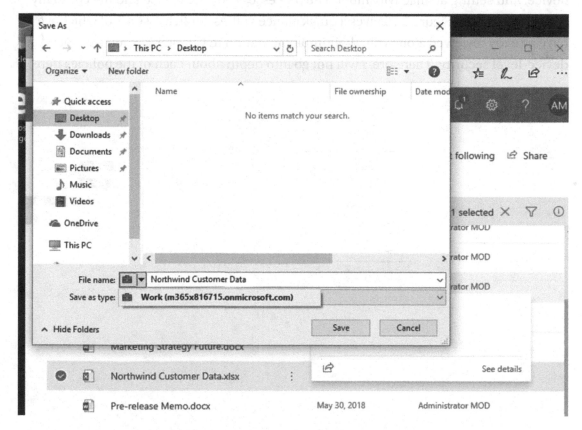

Figure 5-28. *Documents downloaded from SharePoint (WIP protected cloud resource) are saved as corporate documents*

The advantage of WIP is that you can ensure that enterprise data in a Windows 10 device will be saved with corporate protection through WIP.

The protection applied will ensure that copying and pasting corporate data is prohibited for other unmanaged or personal applications on the device.

These are also my recommendations for the setup.

Intune Policies for Device and Data Protection

Intune MDM and configuration policies, as well as compliance policies in conjunction with conditional access, help devices such as Windows 10, Android, iOS with device-level procedures such as enforcing a pass code, enabling BitLocker, encrypting the device, and setting an inactivity timer. The processes keep the device and the company data inside it safe. Figure 5-29 gives a quick glance at these policies, some of which we have already reviewed along with their implementation in Chapter 3 when we looked at device-level security. Therefore, I will not go into depth about each of the policies here.

Figure 5-29. *Intune compliance policies*

Figure 5-30 shows a screen with Intune configuration policies for iOS devices. Again we are just taking a peak, as going into detail about Intune would make up another book! Here I've chosen to block data/diagnostic sharing and use screen capture to protect enterprise data. We can also enable kiosk if we only require that half the apps are running. This way, all the important data will stay within the bounds of the device.

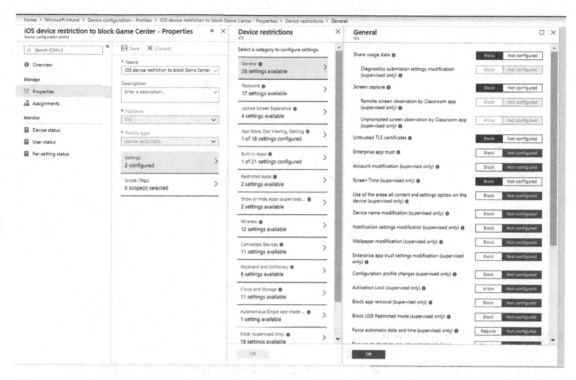

Figure 5-30. *Intune configuration policies for iOS*

Figure 5-31 shows the various profile types available for Android (there are similar options available for iOS and Windows systems as well). Device restrictions can help you block factory reset, camera, and other apps. Deploying certificates (trusted certificates, SCEP [Simple Certificate Enrollment Protocol] certificates, etc.) is the recommended way to access company data or services, as password sign-ins can be compromised by an attacker in some circumstances.

Figure 5-31. *Creating an iOS profile*

There are MAM policies for Android and iOS devices that ensure that the data transfer between Intune policy-managed applications is seamless, while the data transfer to any personal applications are blocked. We can also restrict cutting, copying, and pasting so that they are only available for corporately managed apps. Additionally, you can ensure that the organization's data is encrypted by these policies, as shown in Figure 5-32.

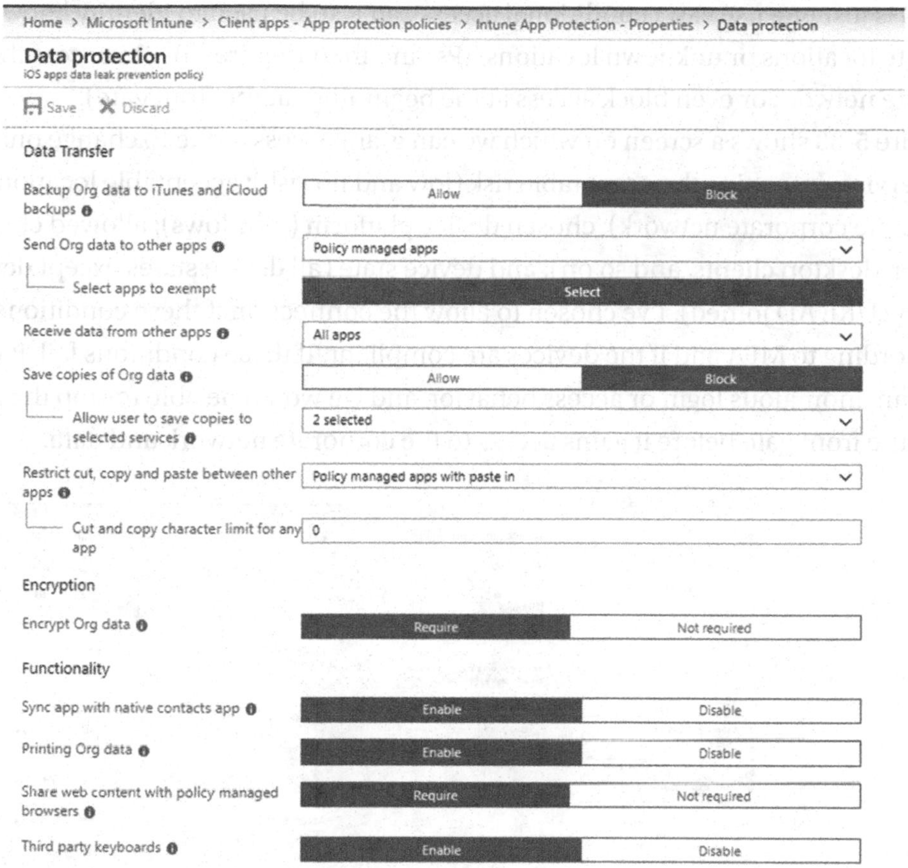

Figure 5-32. *Data protection for mobile applications through Intune MAM policy*

Protecting Data at the Front Gate Using Intune/Azure AD Conditional Access

There are some common parameters that we can identify as usual modes of attack. For instance, an attacker will look for weak, default, or stolen credentials to access the corporate network and data. Most of these actions will result in an anomalous activity and we need to have the right algorithms in place to recognize such activities.

Conditional access to corporate resources/services and applications is allowed or denied by checking if any login is anomalous due to a brute force attempt or impossible travel, and then associating a risk value with the login, such as high, medium, and low.

This is just one use case; conditional access can also be used to identify known corporate locations or unknown locations/IPs, and then require MFA to access the corporate network or even block access at the beginning (at the front gate).

Figure 5-33 shows a screen on which we can grant access to the Exchange online cloud service, by setting the acceptable risk (low and no risk); acceptable location (outside the corporate network); chosen device platform (Windows); allowed client apps (browser, desktop clients, and so on); and device state (all device states except device hybrid AZURE AD joined). I've chosen to allow the connection if these conditions are met according to MFA and if the devices are compliant. If these conditions fail, it could well be an anomalous login or access behavior, and we would be able to stop the attacker right at the front gate before it gains access to the corporate network and data.

Figure 5-33. *Setting a conditional access policy in Intune*

Microsoft Cloud App Security

There are no boundaries when it comes to data in the modern world. Corporate data can be moved across companies, multiple devices, and cloud/SaaS-based applications. We have already seen that AIP can protect data that moves across users and companies and can also be revoked at any point in time. Device data can also protected from policies in Intune and other management tools. However, if we need granular-level visibility into cloud apps and any associated activity to ensure that corporate data is not abused, it is highly recommended to leverage MCAS.

Over the last couple of years, MCAS has significantly grown and can now be integrated with other threat management tools such as Windows Defender ATP, SIEM, Azure AD, Intune, and AIP for better threat analysis and context building, and can be applied for any incident that occurs in your organization.

MCAS is Microsoft's CASB solution.

Framework

MCAS's framework includes:

- *Cloud discovery*: How many organizations can be sure about the number of cloud apps users are running in their company and the data traversing multiple platforms? How do we know if these apps are even secure? MCAS can discover cloud apps through shadow IT and control and risk assessment.

- *Data protection*: MCAS can monitor and control our data and prohibit the misuse of it, too. It does so by gaining visibility about the data in the cloud app enforcing DLP policies to ensure the data complies with the compliance policies of organizations, alerts, and investigations.

- *Threat protection*: MCAS can also automatically remediate anomalous activities reducing the risk to the organization.

- *Cloud app-compliance assessment*: Assess to check if cloud apps meet compliance requirements, regulatory compliance, and industry standards.

Architecture

When a user connects to or makes any request to access cloud apps, including Office 365 and other third-party, SaaS-based apps such as Dropbox, G Suite, Box, and Salesforce, they can be monitored to the extent that their access and session control is also established by MCAS using Azure AD (conditional access), as seen in Figure 5-34.

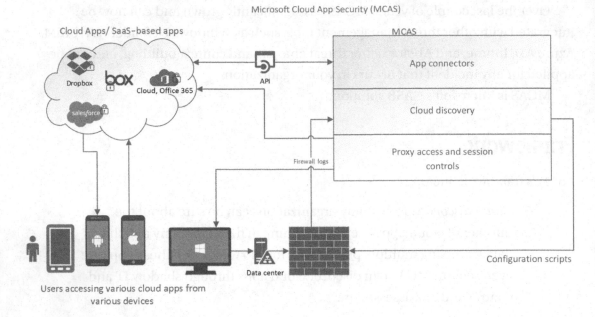

Figure 5-34. MCAS architecture

All the cloud apps accessed in the organization can be analyzed further by uploading the firewall/proxy logs for discovery.

Individual SaaS-based apps can be connected in MCAS through app connectors, which use APIs from the cloud app providers themselves. They help in scanning all the files, and the time it takes might depend on the API limits set by the provider.

Let's see these features come to life as we take a further look at these steps and the MCAS site.

Dashboard

MCAS has a very intuitive dashboard and just by looking at it, you will be able to get information about the types of activities happening in your organization. You will see a list of open alerts categorized by time, severity, and alert type. At first glance, you will also get to see the total activities, files, accounts monitored, discovered apps, actions taken, user notifications sent, and a lot of other information.

You will also see information about the activity matches and content matches (appears if a policy matches). In addition, you will see graphs and a world map of activity and user trends.

The screen has "Discover," "Investigate," and "Control" sections. Any new discovery of the MCAS service is found in the "Discover" section. To further analyze and find out more information about any logs, accounts, and files, we can look at the "Investigate" section. To create policies and policy templates (some predefined and some customized with filters) and to create alerts for DLP, threat detection, and compliance, we use the control section of the MCAS portal.

The first step in getting started with MCAS is to better understand your organization's cloud app usage. It is vital to know where your corporate data is going and that it is protected or encrypted and capable of recognizing any anomalous behavior. To do this, we will get started by doing cloud app discovery and uploading your company's firewall logs. It is recommended that you upload the logs manually the first time you use them before you set them to upload automatically. Also set your information for firewall logs to the highest level to get more visibility at a granular level. To create a Cloud Discovery snapshot report:

1. Under "Discover," select "Create snapshot report," as shown in Figure 5-35. After you have entered the report name and description, you will be asked to select the data source. The firewalls log can come from a wide range of devices, such as Barracuda, Sophos, and Websense, and be in a range of custom formats as well. You can then upload the log and create the snapshot. The log file will be parsed, the data analyzed, and a report generated, which can take up to 24 hours.

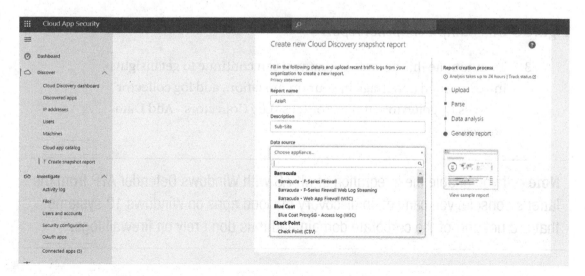

Figure 5-35. *Creating a Cloud Discovery snapshot report in MCAS*

2. Figure 5-36 is a sample of a report that will be generated. You can see sanctioned apps in green, unsanctioned ones in red, and some others in other colors. You will also get insight into the risk score of these applications. And you will see which regions of the world your users are accessing them from.

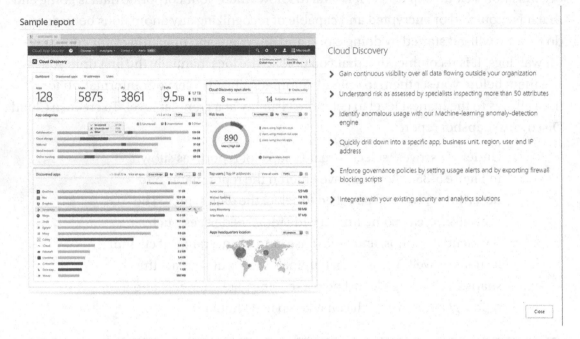

Figure 5-36. *Sample snapshot report*

3. To automate this process so that you can continue to get insights into the cloud app usage in your organization, add log collector sources by going to settings, Sources- Log Collectors - Add Data Source.

Note   If you enable the integration of MCAS with Windows Defender ATP from the latter's console, you can set up discovery of cloud apps on Windows 10 systems that are not part of the corporate domain and thus don't rely on firewall logs.

---

4. Along with these steps, you'll have to add a log collector source by selecting an on-premise server, as shown in Figure 5-37. You'll also need to configure the on-premise server with the deployment steps shown on the screen.

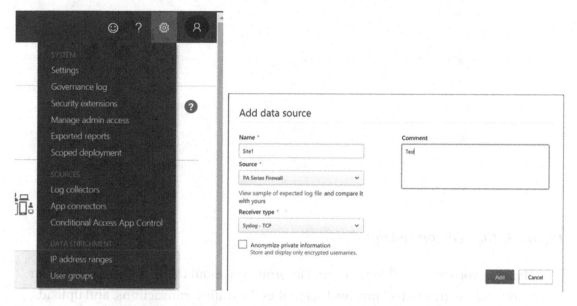

Figure 5-37. *Adding a data source in MCAS*

Still under discovery blade, when we open the "Discovered apps" tab shown in Figure 5-38, we will get a list of all the apps that were parsed and analyzed. As you can see, we can categorize the list of apps and search for them and there will be a risk score associated with each of them. We will look at and understand this score more in the next screenshot. Discovered apps also show traffic, data uploaded, and transactions, which can be filtered to get a better understanding of the apps used in your organization.

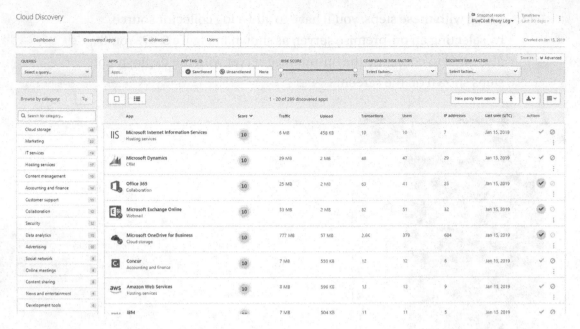

Figure 5-38. "Discovered apps" tab

Likewise, you can see all the captured information about the IP addresses and user accounts (and the machines) involved, as well as the traffic, transactions, and uploads for each IP address or user account.

Risk Score

Every cloud app that can be recognized or whose API information is part of MCAS is given a risk score based on multiple parameters.

The cloud app catalog section on the web site rates the risk for your cloud apps based on regulatory certification, industry standards, and best practices. These parameters are constantly updated using four complementary processes:

- *Automated data extraction*: used for attributes such as SOC 2 compliance, terms of service, sign-in URLs, privacy policy, and HQ location.

- *Automated advanced data extraction*: applied to attributes such as HTTP security headers by CAS (cloud app security) algorithms.

214

- *Continuous analysis*: covers attributes such as encryption at rest and is done by an analyst team.

- *Customer-based revision requests*: accepted after they are reviewed by the analyst team.

Figure 5-39 shows how to request a score update.

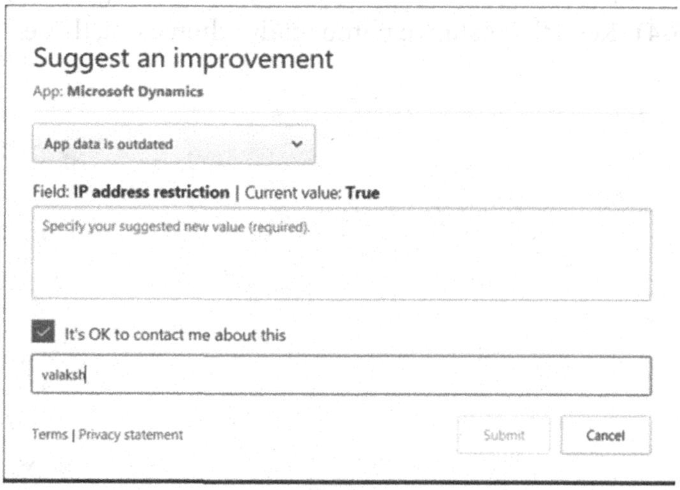

Suggest an improvement

App: **Microsoft Dynamics**

| App data is outdated ⌄ |

Field: **IP address restriction** | Current value: **True**

Specify your suggested new value (required).

☑ It's OK to contact me about this

valaksh

Terms | Privacy statement   Submit   Cancel

Figure 5-39. *Requesting a risk score update*

We are all set now to receive log uploads. We know the cloud app usage pattern in our company and would like to sanction apps with good risk scores and manage them with policies as we get further into increasing visibility and control. But first, we need to get connected to these apps from the MCAS site. To do so, select "Connect apps" as shown in Figure 5-40.

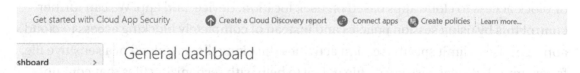

Get started with Cloud App Security   Create a Cloud Discovery report   Connect apps   Create policies   Learn more...

shboard   > | General dashboard

Figure 5-40. *Connecting apps for cloud app security*

App providers' APIs are used to get greater visibility and control with MCAS. Each app provider/service has its own framework and service, and MCAS worked with the services to optimize API usage and to deliver best performance.

App Connector Flow

MCAS scans and saves authentication permissions and requests the user list. Scans for first-time users take time, after which MCAS moves on to scanning activities and files and then makes some activities visible on its site. After the completion of the scans, MCAS continues to periodically scan users, activities, and files.

There are eight apps that are available for connection through the app connectors as shown in Figure 5-41. Keep the instance name ready when using these.

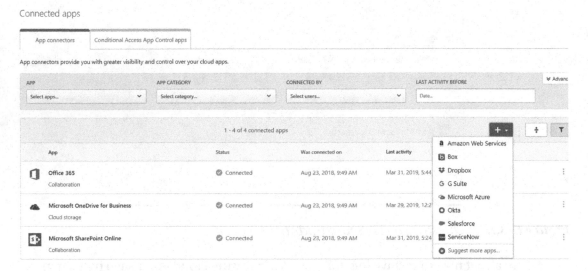

Figure 5-41. *App connectors available in MCAS*

Let's now get started with creating policies for these applications. As we can see in Figure 5-42, there are multiple types of policies and a wide range of scenarios MCAS can be applied to. We can create access policies to enable real-time monitoring or to allow or block access to cloud apps based on user, location, device, and app. We can further control this by using session policies and instead of completely blocking access to cloud apps, choose to limit specific session activities (blocking the download of a sensitive file, for example). We can also create file policy to help with recognizing files that contain source code, PII, or PHI (protected health information).

Policy templates

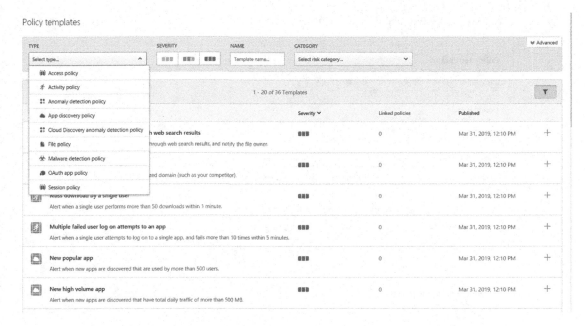

Figure 5-42. *MCAS policy templates*

Let's start creating a policy. I will set up a policy using the template for "Multiple failed user logon attempts to a service" located under "Policy name," as shown in Figure 5-43.

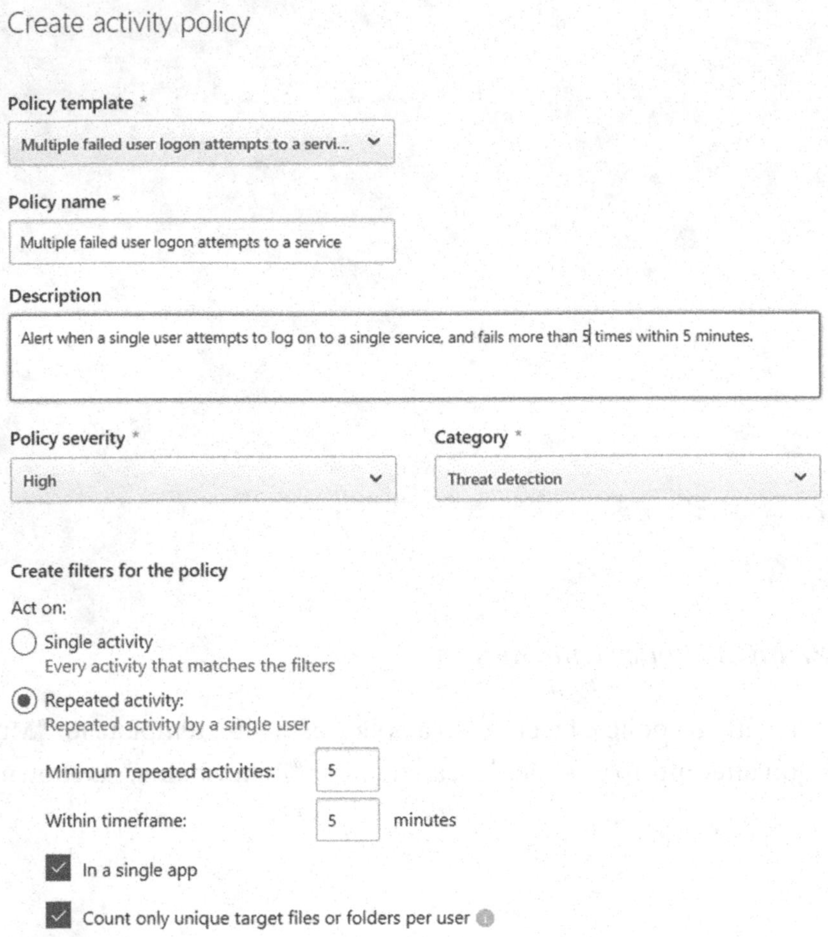

Create activity policy

Policy template *

Multiple failed user logon attempts to a servi...   ⌄

Policy name *

Multiple failed user logon attempts to a service

Description

Alert when a single user attempts to log on to a single service, and fails more than 5 times within 5 minutes.

Policy severity *   Category *

High   ⌄   Threat detection   ⌄

Create filters for the policy

Act on:

◯ Single activity
   Every activity that matches the filters

◉ Repeated activity:
   Repeated activity by a single user

   Minimum repeated activities: 5

   Within timeframe: 5   minutes

   ☑ In a single app

   ☑ Count only unique target files or folders per user ⓘ

Figure 5-43. *Creating an activity policy*

The next step is what makes MCAS unique. There are options for what to do next if MCAS finds a match with an activity/policy, as shown in Figure 5-44. We can define actions for all apps and apply actions to Azure AD users, or specifically choose the connected apps for which we want to take further actions, such as suspending a user's account or forcing a password change.

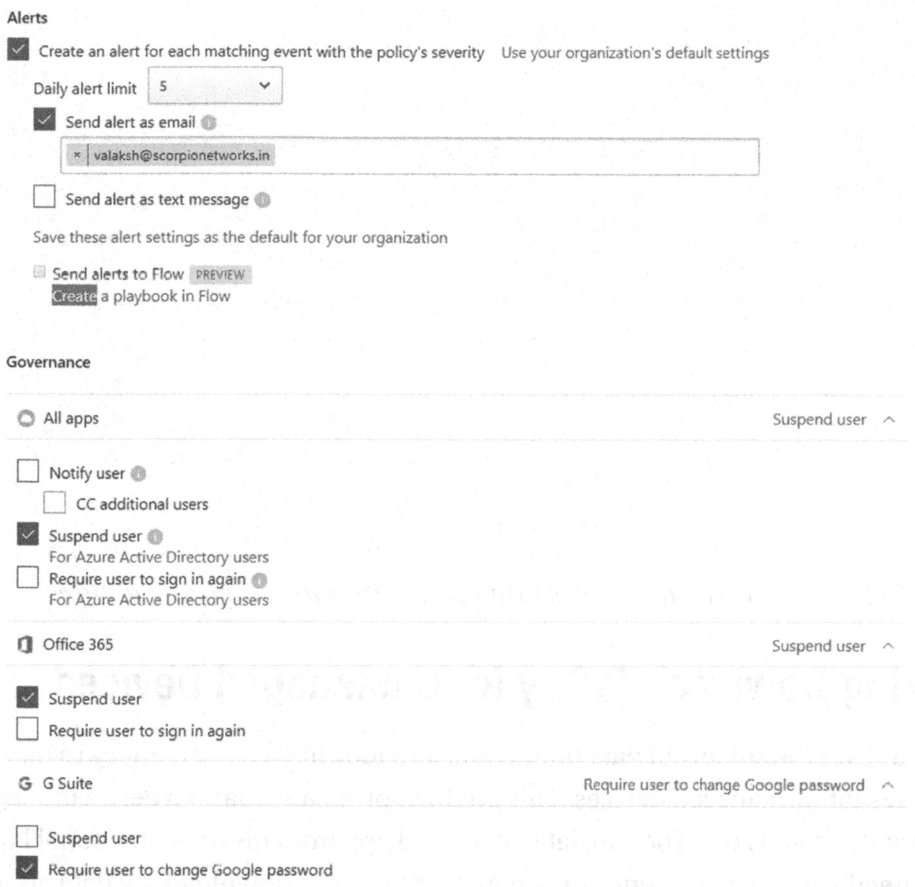

Alerts

☑ Create an alert for each matching event with the policy's severity   Use your organization's default settings

Daily alert limit | 5   ⌄ |

☑ Send alert as email ⓘ

| × | valaksh@scorpionetworks.in |

☐ Send alert as text message ⓘ

Save these alert settings as the default for your organization

☐ Send alerts to Flow PREVIEW
Create a playbook in Flow

Governance

◎ All apps	Suspend user ⌃

☐ Notify user ⓘ
  ☐ CC additional users
☑ Suspend user ⓘ
  For Azure Active Directory users
☐ Require user to sign in again ⓘ
  For Azure Active Directory users

🗋 Office 365	Suspend user ⌃

☑ Suspend user
☐ Require user to sign in again

G G Suite	Require user to change Google password ⌃

☐ Suspend user
☑ Require user to change Google password

Figure 5-44. *Creating an activity policy (continued)*

Figure 5-45 gives a simple example of a policy that uses an available template. Using such a policy does not stop you from creating your own custom policies as well based on your organizational requirements, using the filters from these policies, and changing them accordingly. Here, I've selected to monitor G Suite login activities on all devices except PCs.

Figure 5-45. *Activity creation by setting conditions and defining actions*

Blocking Download Policy for Unmanaged Devices

While we're on the subject of data protection, let's look at creating a policy to block downloads for unmanaged devices. This might apply to a scenario where a manager is looking at the details of corporate data on a cloud app from his or her personal laptop and we need to block any attempts the manager makes to download the data, as it is secure corporate data and should not be downloaded on unmanaged devices.

This will require implementing both an Azure AD conditional access policy, as shown in Figure 5-46, and an MCAS conditional access app control. Ensure that you have the right user/group and the cloud app that you want to test with specified for this policy. (I've selected "Exchange Online" and to have SSO configured for it in Azure AD.).

Microsoft Cloud App Security Conditional Access App Control supports SAML (Security Assertion Markup Language) and OpenID Connect apps with SSO enabled. The figure shows the conditional access policy with the session access control set to "Use Conditional Access App Control" and "Block downloads (preview)."

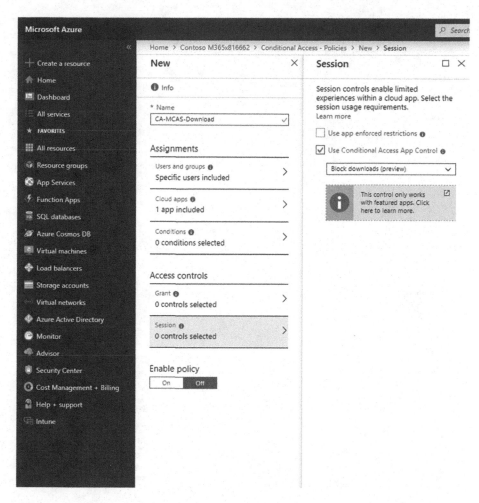

Figure 5-46. *Setting up conditional access for session policies in Azure*

The next step is to create a session policy in MCAS, which, as shown in Figure 5-47, Control - New Policy-Session Policy.

I have defined the session control type as "Control file download (with DLP)." This gives you the ability to monitor all the activities of your users within their sessions and gives you the ability to block and protect.

I've set a condition to check if the device is compliant or domain joined or has a valid client certificate—either one of which would be enough to prove that the device is managed. I've selected the cloud app to be Exchange Online, and for the purpose of testing, I've limited this setting to just one user.

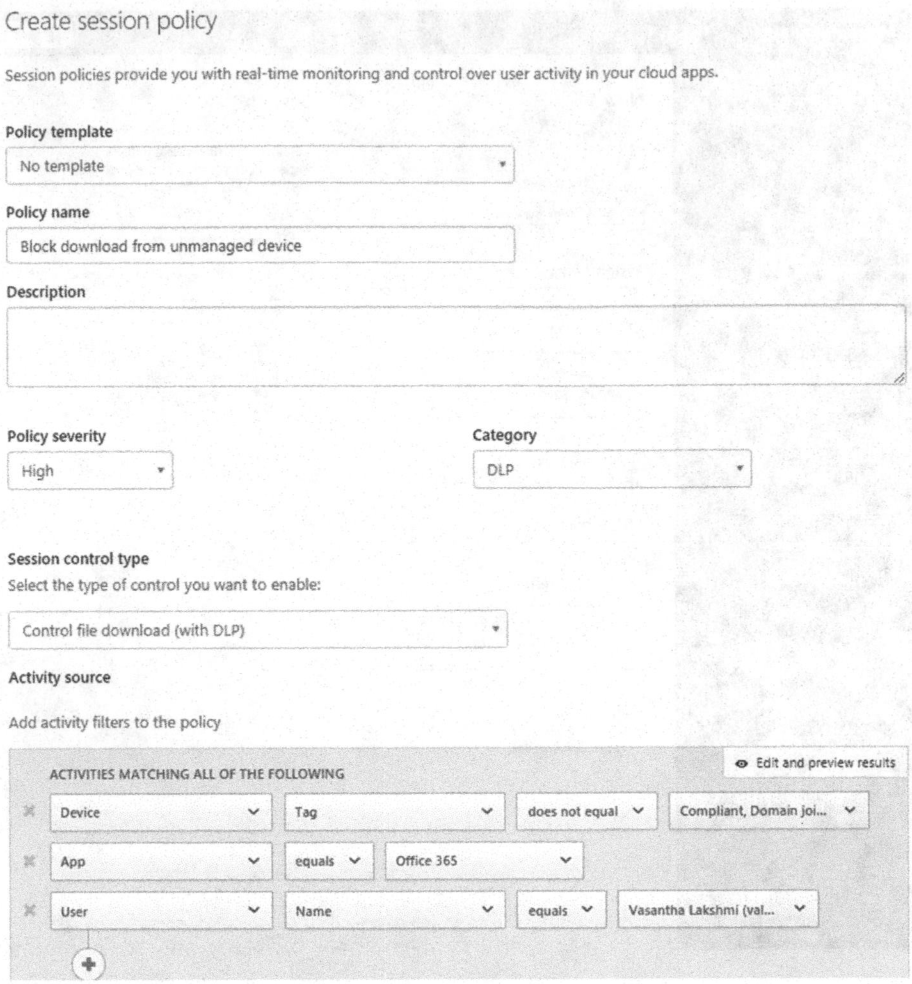

Create session policy

Session policies provide you with real-time monitoring and control over user activity in your cloud apps.

Policy template

| No template | ▾ |

Policy name

| Block download from unmanaged device |

Description

Policy severity

| High | ▾ |

Category

| DLP | ▾ |

Session control type
Select the type of control you want to enable:

| Control file download (with DLP) | ▾ |

Activity source

Add activity filters to the policy

ACTIVITIES MATCHING ALL OF THE FOLLOWING			⊙ Edit and preview results
✖ Device ▾	Tag ▾	does not equal ▾	Compliant, Domain joi... ▾
✖ App ▾	equals ▾	Office 365 ▾	
✖ User ▾	Name ▾	equals ▾	Vasantha Lakshmi (val... ▾

⊕

Figure 5-47. *Creating a session policy in MCAS*

I'm applying these conditions to AIP protection–applied documents with the term "Contract" present in them and designating the documents as "Confidential—All Employees." This requires enabling content inspection. Figure 5-48 shows the screen with all these settings.

Add file filters to the policy

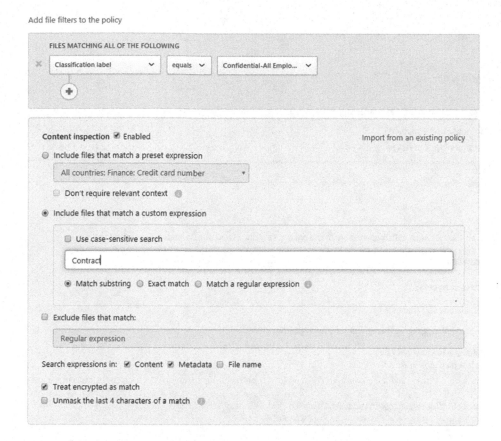

Figure 5-48. *Setting session policy conditions and content inspection*

As I have set up in Figure 5-49, if there is a match for this condition, the action/ download of the data or document will be blocked and the user will be notified with an email.

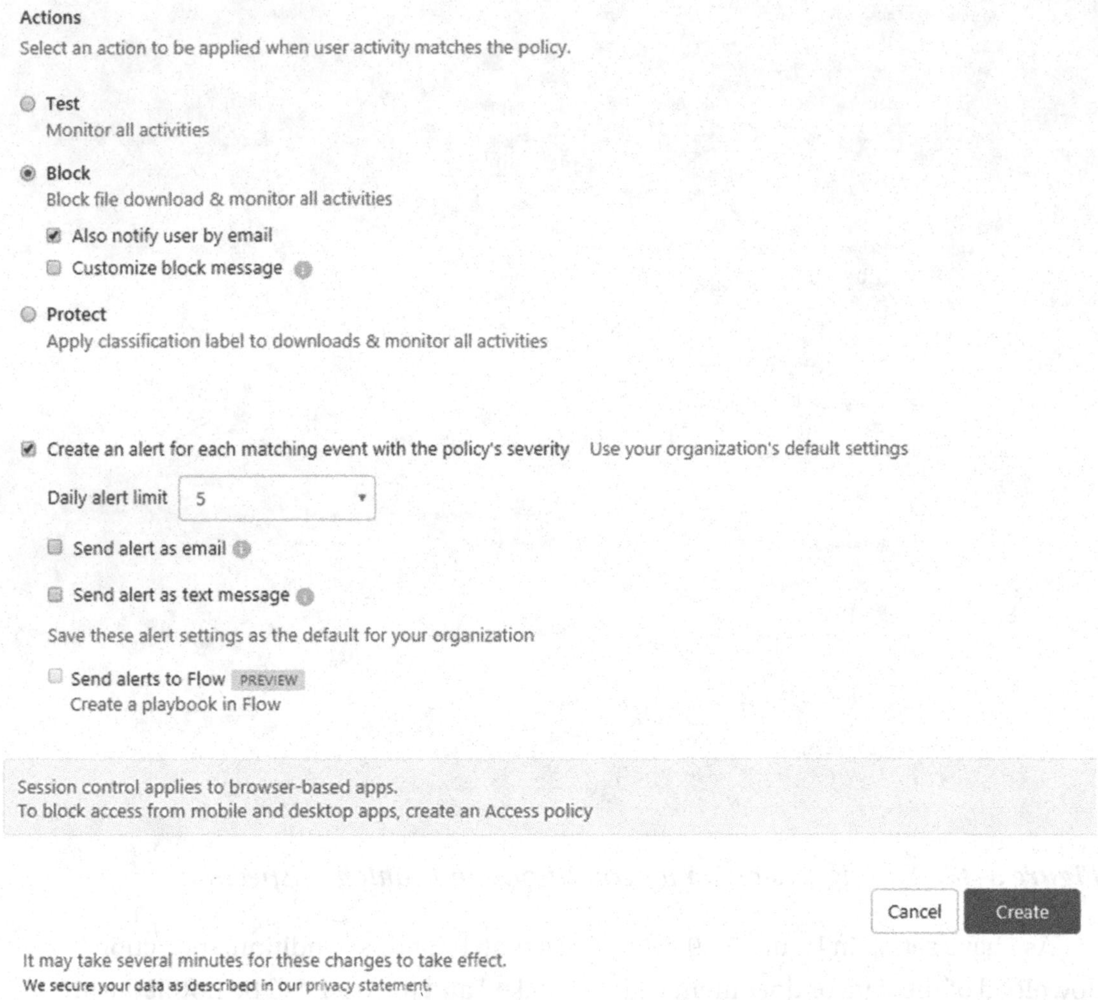

Actions

Select an action to be applied when user activity matches the policy.

○ **Test**
Monitor all activities

⦿ **Block**
Block file download & monitor all activities

    ☑ Also notify user by email
    ☐ Customize block message ⓘ

○ **Protect**
Apply classification label to downloads & monitor all activities

☑ Create an alert for each matching event with the policy's severity   Use your organization's default settings

    Daily alert limit | 5   ▾ |

    ☐ Send alert as email ⓘ

    ☐ Send alert as text message ⓘ

    Save these alert settings as the default for your organization

    ☐ Send alerts to Flow PREVIEW
    Create a playbook in Flow

Session control applies to browser-based apps.
To block access from mobile and desktop apps, create an Access policy

Cancel   Create

It may take several minutes for these changes to take effect.
We secure your data as described in our privacy statement.

Figure 5-49. *Setting session policy actions*

As shown in Figure 5-50, ensure that MCAS is set to read AIP information and, similar to this, that it can receive device-based information and that it is integrated with Windows Defender ATP.

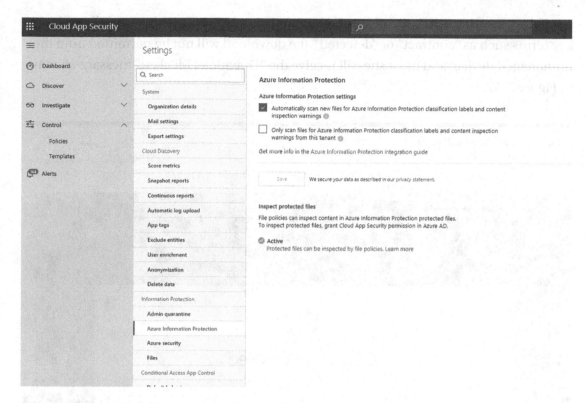

Figure 5-50. *Enabling automatic AIP file scanning in MCAS*

Figure 5-51 shows the message the user gets when he or she tries to access Microsoft Exchange Online from the OWA, or Outlook Web App, or from an unmanaged device (one that is not enrolled in Intune or not marked compliant or not domain joined). As you can see, the session control policy kicks in and indicates that the session is monitored.

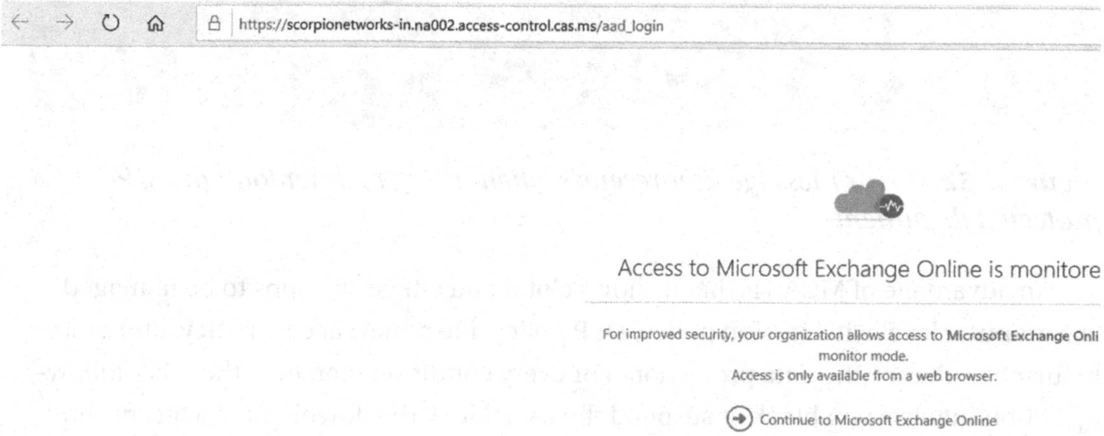

https://scorpionetworks-in.na002.access-control.cas.ms/aad_login

Access to Microsoft Exchange Online is monitore

For improved security, your organization allows access to **Microsoft Exchange Onli**
monitor mode.
Access is only available from a web browser.

⊕ Continue to Microsoft Exchange Online

Figure 5-51. *User message generated by session policy*

If the user tries to download an attachment that is AIP protected, especially with key terms such as "contract" or "detected," the download will not be permitted from the unmanaged device, and he or she will receive the "Download blocked" message shown in Figure 5-52.

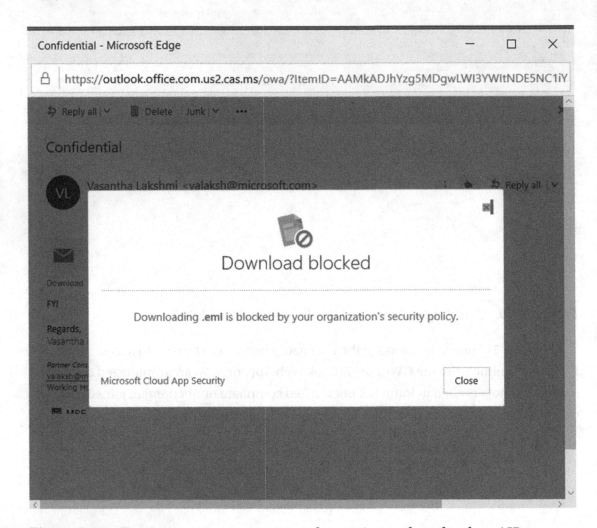

Figure 5-52. *Error message user receives when trying to download an AIP-protected document*

An advantage of MCAS is that it allows cloud and Office 365 apps to be managed at a granular level with session policy, DLP policy, file policy, access policy, and more to further enhance the data protection. For every condition matched, there is a follow-up action that lets you block or suspend the user, block the download of a file, or send notification to the admin.

If users in your organization use a lot of third-party cloud apps, you can further monitor and access them and see a risk score as well.

Compliance Manager

While we're looking at data protection, I should mention that it is also important for organizations to follow privacy and compliance standards, such as the EU General Data Protection Regulation (GDPR); ISO (International Organization for Standardization) 27001 and 27018; NIST (National Institute for Standards and Technology) 800-53 and 800-171; HIPAA (Health Insurance Portability and Accountability Act of 1996); and more. Which standards they follow depends on the country the organization is located in or the sector or vertical (health, finance, etc.) it is be part of.

In Figure 5-53, Compliance Manager has assigned a compliance score to GDPR, NIST ISO, and HIPAA standards for Office 365 and Azure. This is based on both Microsoft-managed and customer-managed actions.

Figure 5-53. *Compliance Scores for various Microsoft Services*

Taking a deeper look at one of these compliance scores, that of Office 365-GDPR, it lists all the in-scope cloud services as well as the general components of Office 365, security enablers, and identity providers. There are quite a few Microsoft-managed and customer-managed controls. We will look into those controls that are under our organization's and the customer's control. Let's pick one of the controls: security.

Under security, I am creating an implementation plan for Control ID 6.6.2. We can proceed to assign these to individuals to test and update the results. Upon successful completion, it will update the compliance score by 3, as shown in Figure 5-54.

We can see that the articles the plan applies to range from GDPR Article (5)(1)(f); to HIPAA; to NIST CSF; to ISO 27018:2014; and so on. The goal here is "User registration and de-registration." This seeks to manage user identity. To help organizations approach these requirements, we need to help them be aware of the best practices and steps to set up the policies. Fret not, the highlighted links in the "Customer Actions" section will guide you in choosing the best policies and setting them to be compliant.

Note that GDPR contains nearly 100 articles pertaining to a variety of services and control tiles. This is just one example of such an article.

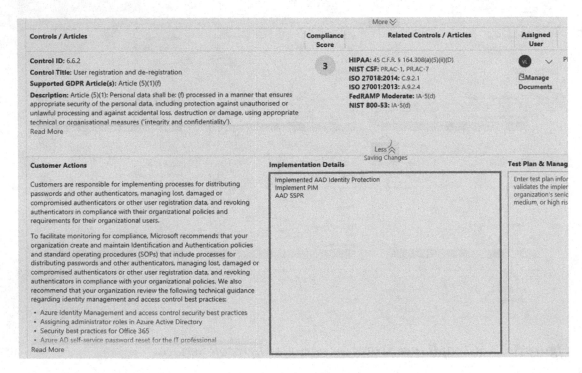

Figure 5-54. *Example of GDPR article for Office 365*

Microsoft Secure Score

We have so far successfully seen the implementation of security for devices and identity, and protection for email and data. If you are happy you've done all this, how do you ensure that your organization is compliant and that there are no gaps? Put simply, Microsoft Secure Score enhances your visibility and control over your organization's security position.

You can go to Microsoft 365 Security Center and click on the Secure Score tab (Figure 5-55).

Figure 5-55. *Microsoft Secure Score for identity, data, device, apps, and infrastructure*

Here you can look at some of the actions you can take to increase the total secure score too. Some of these actions can be to enable MFA or to turn on Self Service Password Reset (SSPR), use limited administrative roles, and so on.

This tab is also a good place to start building your security posture if you are confused about where to start. So, at the end of this chapter and also the book, we can confidently say that we have begun securing enterprises with Microsoft technology by protecting Office 365, devices, data, and apps!

Final Thoughts

In this chapter, we've seen that we're able to protect data with various tools, technologies, and services from Microsoft. All of the features that we've looked at are part of Microsoft 365 Enterprise E5 and some of them are available in Microsoft 365 Enterprise E3 as well. I've tried to give you a holistic view of all the options that Microsoft technologies offer for securing your enterprise and ensuring that attackers are kept at bay and get their playbook broken. This chapter has provided you, as a security administrator or decision maker in your company, all the details pertaining to any particular incident occurring in your organization by leveraging threat insights and the Microsoft Intelligent Security Graph. Along with the details of the incidents, you've gotten insights and context about various security tools.

I hope this book becomes your starting point for learning about security products and how the better-together story comes into the picture. This book is intended for starters, as each security topic is an ocean in itself and could take an entire book or more to cover. As you develop an interest and start exploring security products on your own, you do not have to limit yourself to just the Microsoft 365 security services, but can get into the security services offered for Azure such as Azure Security Center and Azure Sentinel. The Azure security products can be integrated with some of the security services discussed in this book providing you with holistic information or security status.

It would be a great idea to leverage this book to get a bird's-eye view of most of the security services and to start the journey of creating secure enterprises by learning more about them, their integration, and other security services they can work with. Good luck!

Index

A

Access control lists (ACLs), 45
Active Directory Rights Management
    Services (ADRMS), 179
Address space layout randomization
    (ASLR), 64
Advanced threat analytics (ATA), 7, 122,
    128, 139
Advanced threat protection (ATP), 2, 18
AIP scanner, 10
ATP policies, 26, 27
Azure AD identity protection
    autoremediation process, 161
    MFA registration, 152
    PIM, 162
        activate roles, 166–169
        assigning roles, 164, 165
        auditing, 169, 170
    reviewing access, 171, 172
    risk identifier, 158
    risk policy, 153, 155–157
    risks for user, 159, 161
    security overview, 151
    vulnerabilities, 162
Azure ATP
    architecture, 140
    setup
        account credentials, 141
        installing sensor, 142

        scheduled reports, 146
        sensor configuration, 144
        sensor on DC, 143
    timeline
        alert, 147
        attacks, 146
        device activities, 148
        directory data, 149
        tracking paths, 150
        user-based information, 149
    UEBA algorithms, 139
Azure information protection (AIP),
    10, 173

B

Bottom-Up ASLR, 64, 65
Bring your own technology (BYOT), 85

C

Connection filter, 18–20
Control flow guard (CFG), 63
Controlled folder access, 81–84

D

Data execution prevention (DEP), 64
Data loss prevention (DLP), 193

© Vasantha Lakshmi 2019
V. Lakshmi, *Beginning Security with Microsoft Technologies*, https://doi.org/10.1007/978-1-4842-4853-9

Data protection, 9, 10
    AIP policies
        AP site, 177
        checking protection, 184
        choosing settings, 183
        DLP, 193–196
        exchange online, 191–193
        features, 182
        RMS technology, 174–176
        for securing enterprise data, 174
        setting conditions, 180, 181
        SharePoint settings, 189, 191
        track and revoke document,
            185–188
Device guard, 45
Device protection, 5, 6
Distributed denial-of-service (DDOS)
        attacks, 1, 8

E, F

e-mail protection, 3, 4
Endpoint detection and response (EDR),
        5, 99
Endpoint protection (EPP), 5
Enhanced Mitigation Experience Toolkit
        (EMET), 67
Enterprise Mobility and Security
        (EMS), 141
Exchange Online Protection (EOP)
        antimalware protection, 14
        antispam protection, 14
        connection filter, 18–20
        outbound filter, 23, 24
        spam filter
            block lists, 21

        e-mails, 20, 21
        international spam, 21, 22
        options, 22, 23
    thwarting spam, 14–18
    workflow, 11, 12

G

General Data Protection Regulation
        (GDPR), 2, 9, 227
Global unique identifier (GUID), 72

H

HeapValidate function, 66
High-Entropy ASLR, 65
HyperVisor Code Integrity (HVCI), 58

I, J, K

Identity protection, 6–8, 43
    Azure active directory (*see* Azure AD
        identity protection)
    credential guard (*see* Windows
        Defender Credential Guard
        (WDCG))
Information gathering, 43
Input-output memory management units
        (IOMMU), 58
Intelligent Security Graph (ISG), 3, 47

L

Local Security Authority (LSA)
        process, 123
Local Security Subsystem Services
        (LSASSs), 75

M

Malware filter, 14
Mandatory ASLFR, 64
Microsoft 365
    action center, 25
    quarantine, 26
    restricted users, 26
Microsoft Advanced Protection Service
    (MAPS), 94
Microsoft cloud app security (MCAS), 10
    App connectors, 216–219
    architecture, 210
    block downloads for unmanaged
        devices, 220–226
    compliance manager, 228
    dashboard, screen discovery, 211–214
    framework, 209
    risk score, 214, 215
Microsoft Intune, 46
Microsoft Malware Protection Center
    (MMPC), 95
Mobile device management (MDM), 5

N

National Institute of Standards and
    Technology (NIST), 2, 227
Network protection, 76–81
New Technology LAN Manager (NTLM),
    75, 123

O

Office ATP quarantine, 41
    adding domains, 40
    adding users, 39

    antiphishing policy, 38, 39
    infected files, 38
Office 365 ATP
    safe attachments, 31–34
        options, 32
        redirecting, 33
    safe links
        accessing, 29
        policy, 30, 31
        security process, 28, 29
    spoof intelligence, 34–37
Open Mobile Alliance Uniform Resource
    Identifier (OMA-URI), 53, 97
Outbound filter, 23–24
Outlook Web App (OWA), 73, 225

P

Postbreach
    Windows Defender ATP (*see* Windows
        Defender Advanced Threat
        Protection (WDATP))
PowerShell payload fileless attacks, 43
Prebreach
    device guard, 45
    WDAC, 45
    WDAG, 84
    WDAV, 91
    WDEG, 62
    WDSG, 89
Privileged identity management (PIM),
    162–164
Program settings, 66–70

Q

Quarantine, 26

R

Reconnaissance, 43
Remote script execution, 43
Role-based access control (RBAC), 45

S

Second-level address translation
    (SLAT), 58
Security Account Manager (SAM), 135
Spam confidence level (SCL), 20
Spam filter, 20, 22, 23
Spoof intelligence, 34–37
Structured exception handling (SHE)
    technique, 65

T

Threat & Vulnerability Management
    (TVM), 119
Thwarting spam, 14–18
Trusted platform module (TPM), 58, 90

U

Unified Extensible Firmware Interface
    (UEFI), 58, 124
User Mode Code Integrity (UMCI), 46

V

Virtualization-based security, 125

W, X, Y, Z

Windows Defender Advanced Threat
    Protection (WDATP), 70
    alerts queue, 104–107

API, 115–118
automated investigation and
    remediation, 107–109
hunting, 113, 114
incident queue, 101–104
management and APIs, 114, 115
Microsoft threat protection, 118, 119
secure score, 110, 111
threat analytics, 111, 112
TVM, 119
Windows Defender Antivirus (WDAV), 70
cloud-delivered protection, 91
enabling process scanning, 91, 92
Intune, 92, 93
SCCM, 93, 94
windows security baselines
    apply, 98
    managing updates, 94–97
Windows Defender Application Control
    (WDAC)
cloud scenario, 56, 57
group policy, 50–53
hardware requirements, 57, 58, 61, 62
hypothetical scenarios, 47
Intune settings, 53
planning considerations, 46, 47
policy creation, 48–50
SCCM, 54–56
Windows Defender Application Guard
    (WDAG)
BYOT, 85
enterprise managed mode, 85, 88, 89
stand-alone mode, 85–87
Windows Defender Credential Guard
    (WDCG)
ATA
    architecture, 130–132
    entering domain, 132, 133

installing Lightweight Gateway,
133, 134
phases, 129
SAM, 135, 136
timeline, 136–138
enabling Intune, 126
LSA, 123
NTLM password hash, 123
readiness tools, 127, 128
requirements, 124
turning on virtualization-based
security, 125
Windows Defender Exploit Guard (WDEG)
attack surface reduction rules
executable files, 73
GUID, 72
Intune, 71
LSASS, 75
ransomware, 74, 75
SCCM, 72, 73
scripting threats, 73, 74
WDAV, 70
controlled folder access, 81–84
exploit protection
ASLR, 64
bottom-up-ASLR, 64, 65

CFG, 63
DEP, 64
EMET, 67
heap integrity, 66
high-entropy-ASLR, 65
mandatory ASLR, 64
program setting, 66–70
SHE, 65
windows security, 63
XML file, 68
network protection, 76–81
Windows Defender System Guard
(WDSG)
platform integrity, 90, 91
system integrity, 90
TPM, 90
Windows Information Protection
(WIP), 197
Intune, 198–203
compliance policies, 204
conditional access, 207, 208
configuration, 205
iOS profile creation, 206
MAM, 207
Windows Server Update Service
(WSUS), 94

Printed in the United States
By Bookmasters